THE WINE LOVER'S GUIDE
TO THE WINE COUNTRY

THE WINE LOVER'S GUIDE
TO THE WINE COUNTRY

THE BEST OF **napa, sonoma,** AND **mendocino**

by **lori lyn narlock** and **nancy garfinkel**

photographs by **michael carabetta**

CHRONICLE BOOKS

SAN FRANCISCO

Library of Congress Cataloging-in-Publication Data available.

ISBN 0-8118-4242-8

Manufactured in the United States of America.

Designed by Sara Cambridge.

Distributed in Canada by Raincoast Books

9050 Shaughnessy Street

Vancouver, British Columbia V6P 6E5

10 9 8 7 6 5 4 3 2 1

Chronicle Books LLC

85 Second Street

San Francisco, California 94105

www.chroniclebooks.com

For Jack and Harry, our own personal whine lovers.

ACKNOWLEDGMENTS

Writing this book involved interviewing and asking questions of hundreds of people, too numerous to thank and mention individually. So to those who helped us but who remain nameless in these pages, please know we remain thankful for your contributions of fact and lore, and for sharing your deep appreciation of wine and of this part of the world.

For your influential opinions and ideas, we extend special gratitude to Lisa Ekus, Sheila Franks, Tom Fuller, Gwen McGill, Ann Rolke, Monty Sander, Richard Swearinger, Andi Werlin, Laura Werlin, and Matt Wood.

Chronicle Books brought our idea to life. Thank you to Michael Carabetta, Laura Harger, Jan Hughes, Bill LeBlond, and Amy Treadwell.

We also want to express our infinite gratitude to Dan Dawson for generously answering our large and small questions at every turn. Dan truly represents the best of the wine country.

And for never failing to make us laugh, we send our love to Luke, Tony, Vern, and Willits.

CONTENTS

GRAPES to GLASSES

GLASSES to GRAPES

INTRODUCTION

Even without the fruit of its land and labor, the wine country of Northern California would still be intoxicating. Verdant and bucolic, it meanders through three counties—from Napa through Sonoma up to Mendocino.

The subject of countless books and articles, the wine country is a destination for people from all over the world. But "the wine country" is in actuality something of a misnomer in that it describes not just one thing, not just one place, not just one demographic, attitude, or even climate. What all of "the wine country" has in common is obvious: it's the wine. And what makes the wine so eminent is terroir, that place-specific blend of soil, topography, and climate. In this regard, Napa, Sonoma, and Mendocino counties have received an unfair multitude of blessings—all of which go toward creating not only magnificent world-class wines, but a magnificent destination to match.

WHY WE WROTE THIS BOOK

Like a stone thrown into a still lake, the Northern California wine industry is surrounded by ever-expanding circles of commerce and commercialization, from wineries and tasting rooms to hospitality and food service, from schlocky souvenirs to spectacular, artful keepsakes. Navigating the wine country thus becomes a question of making choices—and, one would hope, *good* choices.

In search of the best choices we could find, we've driven, trekked, visited, sipped, tasted, swallowed, spit, revisited, taken notes, and visited again. We've made joint decisions about what to include, and when there was dissent or disagreement we did the whole thing over until a consensus was reached. The result: a wholly subjective, highly personal compilation of what we think is the best there is to do in this part of the world.

HOW WE CHOSE OUR DESTINATIONS

We began our research with one question: "If you had only one day in the wine country, where would you want to spend it?" We made lists of places we knew and loved, we surveyed friends and colleagues, and we combed through every single piece of printed material we could find to be sure we left no stone unturned.

As we toured through the wine country to visit each winery, attend all the events, and sleep, eat, and shop at every establishment we've included, we asked ourselves, "Is this it? Is this where you'd want to come?"

Comparison between places was inevitable, so we tried to put it to good use, allowing each good experience to raise the bar. At all times we strove to find the unique charm and seduction of each destination, and to capture these in its description. Ultimately, the places that made it into the book did so through an unabashedly unscientific screening process, one that factored in an intuitive combination of personality, uniqueness, quality, aesthetic allure, and emotional resonance. If we loved it, we figured, you might, too.

THE ROLE OF WINE IN OUR SELECTIONS

Every person, place, or thing we've included in this book has made the cut for being the wine-centric best in its category. Our goal was to appeal to the hearts, minds, and palates of passionate wine enthusiasts.

But strangely enough, wine itself did not play the only role in selecting the wineries we ultimately recommend. While this may seem odd at first glance, think about how subjective the experience of drinking wine often is. What you might love your best friend may not; what we may lust for may leave you cold. So instead of concentrating only on the wines, we concentrated on the wineries; instead of stomping the grapes, we tried to glide on the gestalt of our experience.

Of course, where there was a wine we already loved, we did seek out its home (like calling a friend when you're in the neighborhood). And there are a few instances when we included a winery that could use some real sprucing up—but where the wines are undeniably fantastic. However, these acts of wine ardor are counterbalanced by the handful of times we were particularly captivated by a winery environment—yet not too fond of its wines. You will find those wonderful wineries also happily included in our book.

WHAT'S IN AND WHAT'S OUT

In the spirit of sharing all the information that *we'd* want to know if we were visiting the wine country, we've provided an insider's perspective on what to pack, what to wear, where to go, and what to expect. We've tried to capture the tone and style of all the places, events, and shops we've chosen to profile, so you can decide what sounds right for your visit.

What we've deliberately omitted is much of the rich history and many of the unique stories that characterize the places we write about. You will have the pleasure of making these discoveries on your own as you travel about from place to place. Nor have we focused on winemaking techniques or the viticultural practices of wineries; you'll learn all about those topics and more during your tours.

Simply stated, our goal is to clearly guide you toward what interests you most—because ultimately, it's what happens when the book is closed that makes travel so alluring. So as you begin your own exploration, enjoy the opportunity to peel back that top layer. Learn about the folks who dug the earth to plant the first vineyards; meet the visionaries who shaped a region; get to know the families that have lived and farmed the same property for generations.

Our hope is that with this book as your trusted guide, your visit to the Northern California wine country will leave you sated, happy—and very excited about coming back soon.

Right: A domesticated grapevine.

MAKING *the* MOST *of* YOUR VISIT

First-time visitors to California's wine country are often surprised by just how far and wide it actually extends. In fact, it stretches from as far south as Riverside County to the northern reaches of Mendocino, and from the Santa Cruz Mountains in the west to Amador County in the eastern part of the state. This means you could conceivably spend weeks, months, or even longer exploring California's wine country—and still not see it all.

In this book we concentrate only on Northern California's three most prominent wine-producing regions: Napa, Sonoma, and Mendocino. This, for us, is "the wine country." Although it's possible to drive between any two points within the three counties in just a few hours, the best plan is to focus on one area, allowing plenty of time between stops. At all times it's best to take into account the winding roads, the out-of-the-way destinations, and the essential ingredient of leisure. To travel slowly is to truly enjoy the journey.

To ensure a slow pace and thorough exploration, we've divided the wine country along its natural borders: first into counties, and then into appellations (defined wine-growing regions). There are several advantages to this. First, by staying within one region you really get a feel for it—for the landscape, the wineries, the people, and the history. Second, you'll spend more time at wineries and other attractions than on the road.

PLANNING YOUR VISIT

Getting the most out of your experience without ever feeling rushed is the goal of a successful wine country visit. The best way to do this is to pick the area that you want to explore, and within it select no more than five wineries to visit in a single day.

Expect to spend between thirty minutes and a couple of hours at a given winery, depending on your level of interest in the wine, the graciousness of a host, or just your general desire to hang out at a special place. In general, it's best to allow yourself an hour and a half at each winery. This may be more than you need, but you can use that extra time to drive to the next spot, especially in areas that aren't familiar.

Good organization is key to making the most of each day. Once you've picked your destination, get a map. You can use a road map or one designed specifically for winery touring. Every county has at least one organization that offers a comprehensive map by mail or online. Try **www.napavalleyvintners.com** for Napa, **www.wineroad.com** for Sonoma, and, in Mendocino, **www.avwines.com** for Anderson Valley and **www.atasteofredwoodvalley.com** for Redwood Valley.

Next, make a list of the wineries you want to visit, and mark each one on your map. This will help you determine the best route—north to south, clockwise or counterclockwise for loops. Then assign each an approximate time of visit (don't forget to allow time for lunch!). Finally, call the wineries and make an appointment, starting with those you most want to see so that you can be flexible if the times you request aren't available.

For reasons known only to vintners, a majority of wineries offer tours at 10:30am and 2pm. If this holds true for the wineries you want to visit, consider making only two appointments a day. Between appointments, you can drop in at two to three other wineries that don't require reservations.

Finally, to receive the most personal service, visit during the week or in the off-seasons (winter and spring). If you must visit on a weekend, schedule tours at wineries that are off the beaten track, and consider exploring smaller wineries that limit the number of visitors they host each day.

WHAT *to* EXPECT *at a* WINERY

There's one thing you can count on: every winery has wine. But beyond that, what wineries offer their visitors can vary dramatically from place to place. Here's a basic guideline for what you can expect.

Tastings Almost all wineries offer wine tasting as part of a visit. Some wineries freely pour everything they make; others offer only one wine. Typically, wineries that offer a tour conclude it with a wine tasting.

Tours Apart from tasting, tours are the primary activity a winery offers, and nearly every winery offers a tour of some sort. Some wineries will let you join a tour on the spot if there is room, but most wineries request, if not require, advance reservations.

Tours can last from a few minutes to an hour and a half. If you're on a tight schedule, be sure to inquire in advance about the length of the tour.

Fees You can expect to pay a fee for wine tasting, whether it's at a tasting bar or included in the price of a tour. With the exception of a handful of wineries, Napa Valley wineries charge between three dollars for a single taste and upward of forty dollars for a tour and tasting (typically, the price of a tasting corresponds to bottle price). Sonoma and Mendocino wineries are evenly split between wineries that do and don't charge a fee. But as the number of visitors increases, expect the number of wineries charging a tasting fee to keep up with growing demand.

Groups If you plan on traveling with more than four people, you'll definitely want to call ahead. Even small groups need to make arrangements for both tours and tastings.

Retail sales Selling wine is the business of wineries, so you can be assured that almost all will offer their wine for sale. Most wineries have a retail area. Sometimes it's a full-fledged gift shop that sells everything from T-shirts, lingerie, and novelty toys to cheese and wine safes. Sometimes it's as minimal as a desk or table where your order form is fulfilled from the inside of a storage closet.

Wine clubs During a visit, wineries also offer the opportunity to join their wine clubs. There are plenty of incentives for doing so, including free tastings, discounts on wine sales, invitations to special events, and regular shipments of wine delivered to your door. But you do have to pay for that wine, and the vast majority of wine clubs dictate the selection of wine you receive. So if you're picky, you may be better off buying only what you like without the constraints of a club.

Picnics The tremendously beautiful surroundings of many wineries beckon you to pack food for an al fresco meal. But many wineries request that you make a reservation to use their picnic areas. So definitely check that it's okay before you load up the wicker basket. And keep in mind that it's bad form to drink anything at a winery picnic besides the wine sold by your host (with the exception of nonalcoholic beverages).

"Sit, Junior, Sit!" It's generally true that wine tasting is neither a child- nor dog-friendly activity. Bringing pets should be avoided at all costs, given that it can be downright dangerous when the temperatures soar and Buddy has to stay locked in the car. But sometimes touring with children can't be helped. Don't despair; your vacation can still be enjoyable for everyone if you follow a few simple guidelines.

First, if you are traveling with kids, avoid tours, because no one—least of all you—wants to be distracted by a bored child. Reduce the number of wineries you'll visit in a day, and make your visits in the morning, when it's less crowded and generally quieter. Then spend the afternoon doing family stuff. **Sonoma Train Town** (20264 Broadway, Sonoma, 707.938.3912) has been a children's favorite for decades; with its train, fair rides, and petting zoo, it can take up the better part of an afternoon. Children also love **Connolly Ranch** (3141 Browns Valley Road, Napa, 707.224.1894), where they can get up close and personal with a wide range of animals, from ponies to lambs. Or spend a warm afternoon at Calistoga's **Indian Springs Spa** (1712 Lincoln Avenue, Calistoga, 707.942.4913), where parents can take turns getting a spa treatment while the other one swims with the kids in the Olympic-size, year-round, naturally heated pool.

DECIPHERING *the* APPOINTMENT CODE

What would seem to be a simple concept—listing the hours of accessibility for wineries and tasting rooms—isn't always that. Instead, many of these establishments set rather unclear rules for visitation. Some allow visitors to drop by unannounced at any time during business hours; most others require an appointment. These differences are due largely to the type of usage permit each winery obtains when it begins operations.

Throughout this book we've listed the accessibility of each winery using the most concise and uniform terms possible. This is what they mean:

Days and hours No appointment or advance reservation is required. Doors are open and visitors are welcome to drop by at any time during listed days and times.

Days and hours with tours and/or tastings by appointment only This means that the winery grounds are available for self-touring during listed days and hours, but all tastings and/or tours must be scheduled by advance reservation.

Retail sales This means the winery is open to the public to conduct sales during the hours listed but is not necessarily open for tastings or tours.

With prior appointment For permit purposes, wineries and tasting rooms that specify this type of reservation for any kind of visit (for retail sales, for tastings, and/or for tours) require an "official" prior appointment. But often a phone call made just a few minutes prior to your arrival may be official enough (in some cases, it could even be from your cell phone as you're sitting parked outside the visitor center).

By appointment only When a winery is listed as accessible by appointment only, you must make prior arrangements to visit. It's best to book as far in advance as possible, especially on weekends and during harvest. Just for the record, the reason these types of wineries have such restrictions is that they don't have the resources to host visitors who don't make an appointment. Given this complicated terminology, we strongly recommend playing it safe by phoning ahead. This way, you can double-check a winery's hours and availability for the day you wish to visit. Remember, the wine country is an ever-changing place due to its seasonality and growing popularity, and hours are subject to change at any time.

BE PREPARED

While wine country weather is relatively nice year-round, it does get cold in the winter, and even the warmest of summer days can start and end with fog and cool temperatures. So always pack a light jacket or sweater before you travel about—and think about carrying it into the wineries you'll tour, since you may need it to ward off the chill of cellars and caves. And always, always pack and wear durable shoes. High heels and vineyards simply do not mix.

If you plan on buying wine, invest in a cooler chest of some sort, and pack your wines into it. Even on a mild day, the sun can beat down on a car trunk, spoiling a wine or making a mess by forcing the cork out so far that the bottle leaks.

One last word that bears repetition: always call ahead to all the wineries you want to visit. It will help you gather incidental information, such as whether picnicking facilities are available, and it will provide more vital information, such as whether they are open the day you want to visit. (Although we include hours and other information about each winery, this is, after all, an agricultural area that falls prey to the seasons, which can influence a winery's ability to receive visitors.)

The Rules of the Road Rule number one: **Don't drink and drive**. Everyone knows it's not safe to drink and drive, yet the central paradox of visiting the wine country is that the activity most people come for—wine tasting—by its very nature seems to promote doing exactly that. While it's true that getting around the wine country requires some kind of wheeled vehicle (from bicycles to RVs), this does not give you license to ignore general common sense.

So think outside of the box: there are several safe ways to get from point A to point B while drinking all you like of the wine country's offerings. The first is to **hire a car or limo—with a professional driver** (see "Transportation," page 303). The second is to **designate a driver**. This is one of the most touted ideas in the industry, so much so that many wineries and most events will go out of their way to demonstrate thoughtful hospitality in the form of lower ticket prices and nonalcoholic beverages for those who take on this role. If a designated driver distinction isn't advertised, ask for it.

The third is to **act like a pro, and spit**. You can still savor the experience of tasting wine by swirling, sniffing, swishing—and then spitting. A small amount of wine may still be absorbed, but it's a lot less than if you were actually drinking. We cannot emphasize enough how important it is to be responsible, because even if the worst doesn't occur, you still risk the chance of an unpleasant run-in with the law. (This goes for riding bicycles as well as driving cars.) Why risk marring an otherwise perfect trip?

Rule number two: **Drive slowly and with extreme caution**. The beauty of the wine country is its rural setting. This translates into a series of two-lane highways that are filled with tourists—nice folks who are unfamiliar with the area. As a result, they may stop suddenly, turn without warning, or become so distracted by the amazing scenery that they stop looking at the road altogether. So take the roads slowly if you don't know them, especially the more rural roads. And remember, this really is the country. You never know what might be around the next turn: a slow tractor pulling a load of grapes, a group of bicyclists, or a loose steer. If you find yourself driving at a comfortable speed that's too slow for the car behind you, simply pull over at the next safe place and let it pass. The driver will be grateful, and you can resume touring at your own pace.

PLANNING *the* BEST EXCURSION

Because there are countless places to visit in the wine country, organizing a one- or two-day itinerary can be a mind-boggling challenge. So we've created five getaway plans that take you through some of the best-of-the-best places we know. These excursion guides will ensure that you cover the most ground in the most efficient way, and have the absolutely best time possible.

THE BEST WEEKEND
in ANDERSON VALLEY

When you arrive in Boonville, DROP YOUR BAGS at the **Boonville Hotel**. It's the perfect place to spend a night or two while touring the Anderson Valley, but it's also a destination in its own right. Hip yet homey, cool but cozy, its ten rooms are all unique and expressive. Behind the main hotel are two perfectly private cottages, complete with porch hammocks and vast lawns, surrounded by gardens. To get to the cottages you must pass through a dreamy lavender-lined walkway, fragrant enough to make you swoon (watch out for bees).

When it's TIME FOR DINNER, head to the hotel's superb restaurant for a meal prepared by Johnny Schmitt, son of Don and Sally Schmitt, the original owners of the French Laundry, Napa Valley's famed restaurant. Johnny obviously inherited the cooking gene: his dishes are simultaneously homey and sophisticated. The restaurant is kind of famous in these parts for its excellent food, pleasant service, and extensive local wine offerings. The "scene" is reputed to be on Thursday nights, when the restaurant fills up with a lively sprinkling of locals, including vintners, chefs, and artists.

Wake up and SMELL THE COFFEE at **Horne of Zeese**, a dinky coffee shop just across the street from the hotel that gets its name from the Boontling term for "cup of coffee" (Boontling being the local dialect). It's not fancy, but it serves up a giant slice of country life. Start your WINE TASTING at **Handley Cellars**, the most distant location, and work back toward **Libby's** for LUNCH. Order the *carnitas* plate—Libby's signature dish of succulent caramelized pork, served with rice and beans. Afterward, continue back toward Boonville, stopping at wineries along the way. TAKE A BREAK and slip into the **Boonville General Store** for a cup of coffee and a snack from the all-organic menu. Or, for a different kind of gourmet experience, go next door to the **Anderson Valley Wine Experience** and head straight for the table with the bowls of olive oil.

Wind down in a hammock on your private porch or in a chair set in the hotel's garden; enjoy a PERFECT APERITIF in the form of a chilled bottle of the area's finest while you relax. When it's SUPPERTIME, walk down the road just a few hundred feet to **Lauren's**, a comfy restaurant in the center of town. After another night of peaceful slumber in the quiet countryside, start with a cup of coffee and a homemade scone from the hotel bar. When you're ready to start the day's touring, head north toward the wineries still on your list, and TAKE A DETOUR to the **Apple Farm**. The Boonville Hotel's Schmitt family also runs this exclusive farm, which is additionally a hideaway B&B, cooking school, and purveyor of excellent apple-based foods such as jams, ciders, and vinegars—all sold on the honor system. Stock up, pay up, and head home with your treats keeping you company.

Boonville Hotel: Highway 128 and Lambert Lane, Boonville, www.boonvillehotel.com, 707.895.2210. **Horne of Zeese:** 14025 Highway 128, Boonville, 707.895.3525. **Handley Cellars:** 3151 Highway 128, Philo, www.handleycellars.com, 707.895.3876. **Libby's:** Highway 128, Philo, 707.895.2646. **Boonville General Store:** 17810B Farrer Lane at Highway 128, Boonville, 707.895.9477. **Boonville Tasting Room:** 17810A Farrer Lane at Highway 128, Boonville, 707.895.3993. **Lauren's:** Highway 128, Boonville, 707.895.3869, dinner only. **Apple Farm:** 18501 Greenwood Road, Philo, 707.895.2461.

Relax in a hammock at the Boonville Hotel.

THE BEST WEEKEND
in HEALDSBURG

A trio of prestigious Sonoma County wine-growing regions converge in Healdsburg, so this is the center of the universe if you want to spend a weekend touring Alexander Valley, Dry Creek Valley, or Russian River Valley. Healdsburg is a town with a pedigree in western-cute. At its heart is a square park bordered on all sides by alluring book, shoe, and house-wares shops; tantalizing tasting rooms and wineshops; and enticing bakeries and cafés.

With so much to see and do, you'll want to make this a long weekend. Start off on Friday with wine tasting in Russian River Valley or even the southern part of Healdsburg itself, where there are a handful of wineries within a stone's throw of Highway 101 (a glass of sparkling at **J Vineyards & Winery** will certainly be a perfect kickoff to your weekend). Then head into town for a **LATE LUNCH** at **Zin**, a restaurant appropriately named for its proximity to Dry Creek Valley, where zinfandel rules. After lunch, **CHECK IN** to **Hotel Healdsburg** (be sure to ask for a room away from the noisy front street). After you're settled into your hip and luxurious room, take to the streets, exploring all the tasting rooms that lie within a few blocks of the hotel. On your way back to your room, stop at the **Sonoma Flower Company** and **BUY YOURSELF A POTTED GRAPEVINE** or olive tree. Then take a dip in the hotel pool or a nap on your mile-high feather bed.

When evening falls, stay close by and **DINE** at the hotel's spectacular restaurant, **Dry Creek Kitchen**, an admirable collaboration between the hotel and Charlie Palmer, of New York's Aureole fame. Dry Creek Kitchen features locally inspired dishes prepared with the area's freshest ingredients, and a wine list that showcases only Sonoma County wine.

Rise and shine early on Saturday. Start your day with breakfast from the hotel's complimentary buffet that's offered in the lobby. Then hit the road. Spend the day in Alexander Valley, starting at the northern end and working your way back toward town, stopping at the **Jimtown Store** to **STOCK UP ON SANDWICHES** for a picnic lunch.

When you've hit every Alexander Valley winery on your list, return to the hotel, give your car to the valet, and MEANDER over to the **Healdsburg Museum** or shop in any of the wonderful stores on the square.

When you're HUNGRY FOR DINNER, walk down the street to **Willi's Seafood and Raw Bar**. Every small dish that emerges from the kitchen (there are plenty of nonfish dishes) is so delicious you'll want to eat like you were raised by wolves—fast and furious—before anyone can grab a bite from your plate. The good news is that you'll be feeling no shame, since all inhibitions will have been melted away by the wine you've selected from Willi's exceptional list.

After a good night's sleep, take your time getting up. Read the paper, bring coffee up to your room, make a splash in the pool, or saunter over to the bakery across the park.

After you feel thoroughly rested and are packed up and ready to go, treat yourself to one final indulgence: BRUNCH at **Chateau Souverain**. The winery's restaurant is in a spacious dining room decorated only with portraits of fruit painted in velvety, warm colors and lots of windows that fill the room with natural light. The menu consists of classic brunch dishes and innovative California cuisine, all executed with fresh local foods. Each includes a wine recommendation. There's a fantastic cheese list that showcases the area's best artisanal producers, and the wine list is all Chateau Souverain wines offered by the glass, by the flight, and by the bottle. While you enjoy the last morsels on your plate, don't feel guilty if you don't want to leave; you can always come back.

J Vineyards & Winery: 1147 Old Redwood Highway, Healdsburg, www.jwine.com, 707.431.3646. **Zin**: 344 Center Street, Healdsburg, www.zinrestaurant.com, 707.473.0946. **Hotel Healdsburg** and **Dry Creek Kitchen**: 25 Matheson Street, Healdsburg, www.hotelhealdsburg.com, 707.431.2800. **Sonoma Flower Company**: 315 Healdsburg Avenue, Healdsburg, www.sonomaflowercompany.com, 707.431.9049. **Jimtown Store**: 6706 Highway 128, Healdsburg, www.jimtownstore.com, 707.433.1212. **Healdsburg Museum**: 221 Matheson Street, Healdsburg, www.healdsburgmuseum.org, 707.431.3325. **Willi's Seafood and Raw Bar**: 403 Healdsburg Avenue, Healdsburg, 707.433.9191. **Chateau Souverain**: 400 Souverain Road, Geyserville, www.chateausouverain.com, 888.80.WINES.

THE BEST WEEKEND
in HOPLAND

EATING LUNCH ON THE RUN will give you a jump-start when you're set-ting out for a day of wine tasting in nearby Ukiah or Redwood Valley. Go straight to **Phoenix Bread Company** in Hopland. A slice of its *fougasse*—a plain-but-fancy rustic bread stuffed with anything from olives, mush-rooms, or roasted peppers to cheese, steak, crab, or spinach—will sate you. (Just one pricey slice can easily feed two people.) Share a raspberry tart for dessert. Get it all to go, and enjoy it al fresco at a winery you like or sim-ply at the side of the road; the area is filled with pastoral settings.

After a few hours of touring, head back to see the gorgeous gardens at **Fetzer Vineyards**. You'll want to linger for hours, and do: check into **Fetzer Valley Oaks Ranch**, where you can SLEEP AMONG THE VINES. It's widely known that many wineries include a guestroom on their property for entertaining sales accounts, visiting chefs, or just good friends. Ranging from large, well-appointed homes to pleasant rooms above the garage, these guest accommodations are the most exclusive lodging facili-ties in the wine country. Fetzer has practically performed a public service by turning its guestrooms into lodging for the public. Now anyone with a reservation, a car, and a credit card can experience the splendor of sleep-ing, strolling, drinking, and swimming among the vines (it's a small pool, but it's wet and does the trick on a hot day). Several room and suite styles are available. Some are in a former carriage house, each with a private porch set right in the vineyards. A wonderful one-room cottage comes complete with two small porches for sitting, reading, and communing with wine and nature. If you want to splurge, reserve Haas House for a little less than a thousand dollars a night; it offers more than you can imagine.

When hunger sets in, head over to the **Hopland Inn** for a MEMORABLE DINNER. Housed in what it calls "the oldest remaining building in Hopland," the inn has stood at the gateway to the Mendocino County wine country since 1890. Today it's a historic twenty-one-room inn with quaintly fussy rooms (wingback chairs abound). The inn also boasts an excellent restaurant with an elegant and understated dining room that is worlds away from the Wild West look of the town. The high-ceilinged dining room has soothing beige walls lined with attractive art and soft pastel drapes. The menu is small, seasonal, and expertly prepared, and it relies largely on regional ingredients; even the coffee, Thanksgiving brand, is from a local roaster. Similarly, the vast majority of the wine list is devoted to local wines, further enhancing the strong regional experience. Start or end your dinner with a drink at the inn's beautiful historic bar, or fireside in the library.

Wake up early the next morning to watch the sun rise over the vineyards from your cozy place in bed. After another walk through the fragrant gardens, go back to town for a great **DINER BREAKFAST** at the **Bluebird Café**. Delicious homemade pastries take the place of toast, and you'll be glad they do. Egg dishes are big and hearty—the perfect way to fuel up for a drive to your next destination.

Phoenix Bread Company: 13325 South Highway 101, Hopland, www.phoenixbreadcompany.com, 707.744.1944. **Fetzer Vineyards** and **Valley Oaks Ranch**: 13601 Eastside Road, Hopland, www.fetzer.com, 800.846.8637. **Hopland Inn**: 13401 Highway 101, Hopland, www.hoplandinn.com, 707.744.1890 or 800.266.1891. **Bluebird Café**: 13340 South Highway 101, Hopland, 707.744.1633.

THE BEST WEEKEND
in NAPA

For all its polish, Napa Valley is still a farming region at heart, and it always has been. Physical reminders of its history—like stone bridges, antique carriages, and ghost wineries—are hidden here and there, and everywhere you look, turn-of-the-century homes and buildings catch your attention. So go native and **REST YOUR HEAD** on a pillow at the historic **Napa River Inn**. Well located in downtown Napa, this boutique hotel offers attractive upscale lodgings. The reception area and lobby (as well as some rooms) are in the original Hatt Building; built in 1884, it's listed on the National Registry of Historic Landmarks. The hotel's remaining rooms are housed in the Embarcadero and Plaza buildings, about half a block's distance away. (If you sleep in either of these buildings, ask for a river view, and note that rooms facing the street and adjacent restaurant can be noisy.)

But don't get too comfortable—there's plenty to do! Walk over to **Back Room Wines** for its **WEEKLY WINE-TASTING EVENT**. It's where the locals go to sample owner Dan Dawson's line-up of new and exciting wines. When you've teased your palate long enough, **HEAD TO DINNER** at **Pilar**. This white-tablecloth restaurant is owned by chefs Pilar Sanchez and her husband,

Didier Lenders—the dynamic team who headed the restaurants at Meadowood for years—and is dedicated to seasonal dishes with California flair. If you aren't ready for lights out just yet, try an AFTER-DINNER WINE at **Bounty Hunter**, a wineshop–cum–tasting bar that stays open late.

BREAKFAST IS INCLUDED at the Napa River Inn. Go downstairs to **Sweetie Pies**, where the selections range from a few egg dishes to lots of scrumptious pastries. You'll be a little fatter but really, really happy. Grab an extra cup of coffee and hit the road. From the town of Napa you can reach any Napa Valley appellation within an hour, so take off for a fantastic day of wine tasting.

If you'd rather spend the day without ever having to get behind the wheel, don't. Instead, put on your walking shoes and TAKE A WALKING TOUR OF NAPA'S WINE-TASTING BARS. Start at **Robert Craig Wine Cellars** and taste your way through its current releases. Then start back toward the Hatt Building. Stop at **Vintner's Collective**, where a selection of high-end wines is poured every day. From there, make your way to **Napa Wine Merchants**. When your wine curiosity is sated, it's time for lunch. The patio at **Angéle** is the perfect locale for indulging in a long, leisurely wine country lunch. The menu is pure French bistro fare. The wine list is evenly balanced between local, hard-to-find wine, like *Larkin* cab franc, and French bottles, such as Kermit Lynch's private Rhône blend (even the carafes of house wine are superb).

Not quite ready to go home? Spend the rest of the day at **Copia**. Or venture out to **Farella-Park** if you haven't been there before. A nice little drive in the country will put you in a good mood for the trip home.

Napa River Inn: 500 Main Street, Napa, www.napariverinn.com, 707.251.8500. **Back Room Wines**: 974 Franklin Street, Napa, www.backroomwines.com, 707.226.1378 or 877.322.2576. **Pilar**: 807 Main Street, Napa, 707.252.4474. **Bounty Hunter**: 975 First Street, Napa, www.bountyhunterwine.com, 800.943.9463. **Sweetie Pies**: 520 Main Street, Napa, www.sweetiepies.com, 707.257.7280. **Robert Craig Wine Cellars**: 800 Vallejo Street, Napa, www.robertcraigwine.com, 707.252.2250. **Vintner's Collective**: 1245 Main Street, Napa, www.vintnerscollective.com, 707.255.7150. **Napa Wine Merchants**: 1146 First Street, Napa, www.napawinemerchants.com, 707.257.6796. **Angéle**: 540 Main Street, Napa, 707.252.8115. **Copia**: 500 First Street, Napa, www.copia.org, 707.259.1600 or 888.51.COPIA. **Farella-Park**: 2222 North Third Avenue, Napa, 707.254.9489.

THE BEST WEEKEND
in SONOMA

Drive up to Sonoma early Saturday morning, stopping in Carneros at one or two wineries along the way. This should whet your appetite for what's to come. By the time you pull into town you'll be READY FOR LUNCH. Find a table at **Sonoma Saveurs**, where you may be torn between the rotisserie chicken sandwich and the charcuterie plate. Have both! And marry each with the wine suggested, using the color-coded menu and wine list.

Walk off your meal with a promenade around the town plaza, or cap off your meal with an espresso and pick up the pace, heading east to any of the great wineries mere minutes away: **Ravenswood, Gundlach Bundschu, Bartholomew Park**, or **Buena Vista**. When palate fatigue sets in, CHECK IN to the very quaint **MacArthur Place and Garden Spa** and indulge in a spa treatment. Consider the Red Red Wine signature treatment, a combination grapeseed bath, body polish, and essential-oil massage. If you can move afterward, take a swim in the pool or HEAD STRAIGHT TO DINNER at **Café La Haye**, a modest-size restaurant with great art and even better food. The menu is California cuisine with hints of comfort food, while the wine list is pure Sonoma. There's not a lot of NIGHTLIFE IN TOWN, so choices are slim. But you can't go wrong with **Murphy's Pub** for a taste of local color and a beer before lights out.

FOR BREAKFAST, **Basque Boulangerie** is the most bustling place in town. Commandeer a table or sit at the bar. The croissants are the best you'll get this side of the Atlantic. Have the toasted baguette and a café au lait, or quiche and a glass of freshly squeezed orange juice. Take something chocolatey for later!

Finish your excursion by going north for wine tasting in Glen Ellen or Kenwood, but first be sure to visit **Hanzell Vineyards**, on the western side of town. It's the perfect ending to a perfect Sonoma weekend.

Sonoma Saveurs: 487 First Street West, Sonoma, www.sonomasaveurs.com, 707.996.7007. **Ravenswood**: 18701 Gehricke Road, Sonoma, www.ravenswood-wine.com, 707.933.2332. **Gundlach Bundschu Winery**: 2000 Denmark Street, Vineburg, www.gunbun.com, 707.938.5277. **Bartholomew Park Winery**: 1000 Vineyard Lane, Sonoma, www.bartholomewparkwinery.com, 707.935.9511. **Buena Vista Winery**: 18000 Old Winery Road, Sonoma, www.buenavistawinery.com,

707.938.1266. **MacArthur Place and Garden Spa**: 29 East MacArthur Street, Sonoma, www.macarthurplace.com, 800.722.1866. **Café La Haye**: 140 East Napa Street, Sonoma, 707.935.5994. **Murphy's Pub**: 464 First Street, Sonoma, 707.935.0660. **Basque Boulangerie**: 460 First Street East, Sonoma, 707.935.7687. **Hanzell Vineyards**: 1859 Lomita Avenue, Sonoma, www.hanzell.com, 707.996.3860.

THE BEST BUDGET WEEKEND in NAPA VALLEY

Even if funds are short, there's plenty to do in this neck of the woods that will be entertaining and memorable but won't break the bank. START OUT on a Saturday morning, making the **Napa Valley Museum** your first stop; its interactive wine exhibit will provide a good low-cost start to a weekend of wine country frolicking. When you've had your fill, head north to **Heitz Wine Cellars** for a TASTE OF OUTSTANDING WINE—not only is its wine one of the best made in Napa Valley, it's one of only a few wineries that doesn't charge a tasting fee. LUNCH at the **Martini House** will be your next stop and your biggest splurge, but the twenty-dollar, three-course lunch is the best bargain in Napa Valley. After finishing every last bite, CHECK INTO **El Bonita Motel**, built in 1941. With its iconic sign and single-story structure that curves around the kidney-shaped pool, the El Bonita still evokes the Art Deco era. If it's warm, indulge in a dip; during winter, snuggle up under a blanket and take a nap (they're always free).

Feeling refreshed and energized, HEAD BACK TO TOWN on foot for some window-shopping. Stop in at **Merryvale Vineyards** to check out its historic cask room and taste wine, or just look around the winery. HAVE AN EARLY DINNER at **Taylor's Automatic Refresher**, across the street, where Robert Parker bestowed a 92-point rating upon the burgers, and then continue into town to the **Cameo Cinema** for a movie in a theater that's as charming as the town around it.

MAKE PASTRIES AND COFFEE YOUR BREAKFAST at the **Model Bakery**, where the selection of treats—from green onion–cheddar cheese scones to morning buns, English muffins to sour-cream muffins, and bear claws to chocolate croissants—is phenomenal. Eat every crumb as a prelude to the SUNDAY-MORNING WINE-TASTING CLASS at **Tasting on Main**, just across the street; at fifteen dollars per person, it's a deal. **WORK UP AN APPETITE** for lunch by traveling to Calistoga and visiting **Vincent Arroyo**, another wonderful no-fee winery. Then take the Silverado Trail south to Rutherford and **EAT LUNCH LIKE A LOCAL** at **La Luna**, where the burritos are so filling they'll stay with you on your return trip all the way back home.

Napa Valley Museum: 55 Presidents Circle, Yountville, www.napavalleymuseum.org, 707.944.0500. **Heitz Wine Cellars**: 436 St. Helena Highway South, St. Helena, www.heitzcellar.com, 707.963.3542. **Martini House**: 1140 Oak Avenue, St. Helena, 707.963.2233. **El Bonita Motel**: 195 Main Street, St. Helena, www.elbonita.com, 707.963.3216. **Merryvale Vineyards**: 1000 Main Street, St. Helena, www.merryvale.com, 707.963.3018. **Taylor's Automatic Refresher**: 933 Main Street, St. Helena, 707.963.3486. **Cameo Cinema**: 1340 Main Street, St. Helena, www.cameocinema.com, 707.963.9779. **Model Bakery**: 1357 Main Street, St. Helena, 707.963.8192. **Tasting on Main**: 1142 Main Street, St. Helena, www.tastingonmain.com, 707.967.1042. **Vincent Arroyo**: 2361 Greenwood Avenue, Calistoga, www.vincentarroyowinery.com, 707.942.6995. **La Luna**: 1153 Rutherford Road (Highway 128), Rutherford, 707.967.3497.

The BEST of the BEST

All-Around Best Wineries

Beringer Rich history, stunning setting, great tour selection, compelling culinary program, and fantastic website with information about wine, food, and entertaining (page 144).

Domaine Chandon Gorgeous grounds, elegant restaurant, great staff, and comprehensive website with excellent glossary (page 173).

Schramsberg Comprehensive tour of caves, compelling exploration of historical significance, and a thorough sparkling-wine education (page 75).

Best Winery Art

Clos Pegase Captivating outdoor sculptures and building design (page 94).

Hess Collection Permanent exhibit of museum-worthy art in a museum-like winery setting (page 90).

Imagery Estate Compelling themed art (commissioned for use on bottle labels) interpreted by world-renowned artists (page 217).

Bottle sculpture at Schramsberg.

Best Winery Architecture

Artesa Unusual hillside design (page 84).

O'Shaughnessy Eye-catching mix of aesthetics and craftsmanship (page 79).

Quintessa Inspirational blend of natural setting and sharp design (page 137).

Roshambo Innovative contemporary building design of both interiors and exteriors (page 210).

Best Historic Wineries

Buena Vista California's oldest winery (page 225).

Chateau Montelena Historic structure housing a winery at the center of contemporary winemaking history (page 94).

Simi One of Sonoma's most historic buildings, and the first Sonoma County winery to open a tasting room (page 183).

Spring Mountain Historic estate with gardens (page 163).

Best Winery Gardens

Ferrari-Carano Over-the-top formal gardens (page 190).

Fetzer Enviable and accessible, with a sensuous edible and floral garden (page 250).

Frog's Leap Stunning bounty of flowers, fruits, and vegetables, with a clever and whimsical website to match (page 129).

Matanzas Creek Peerless lavender and indigenous plant collection (page 186).

Newton Entire winery camouflaged as a garden (page 157).

Best Winery Tours

Benziger Superior self-guided and wine-educator-led tours through grounds and Discovery Center (page 213).

Jordan Engaging, in-depth exploration of estate (page 180).

Best Overall Winery Experiences

Barlow Unbeatable hospitality by the Smith family, in their home (page 93).

Frey Remote and unusual, with a strong family feeling (page 247).

Preston Laid-back country site that makes you want to hang out all day (page 192).

Tres Sabores A generous, friendly tour by owner Julie Johnson of the vineyards, property, and winery (page 140).

Best Winery Picnic Sites

Bartholomew Park Pure California landscape that begs for a picnic lunch (page 224).

Chateau St. Jean Flawless formal gardens surrounded by casual picnic areas (page 219).

Diamond Oaks An oak grove with great views of Oakville and Yountville; shaded tables and bocce court (page 115).

Husch Private tables in a dreamy setting (page 243).

Lambert Bridge Private picnic benches within a beautifully landscaped front yard (page 192).

Pride Mountain Sits on top of the world, with staggering views (page 158).

Best Wine-Tasting Bars

Back Room Wines Thoughtful and educational themed wine-tasting events (page 59).

Bounty Hunter Unique, meticulously restored, and hyperdesigned (page 60).

Gallo of Sonoma Tasteful, urbane, and perfectly located (page 51).

Wine Exchange of Sonoma Unpretentious and comfortable (page 68).

Best Winery Visitor Centers

Clos Du Val Sets the bar for tasteful merchandise branding (page 168).

Domaine Carneros Magnificent building and terrific wines served by exceptional staff (page 88).

Louis M. Martini Striking interior and pleasant outdoor area; big-city slick in the middle of the country; a great date place (page 150).

Niebaum-Coppola Best gift shop anywhere, on stunning grounds (page 134).

St. Francis Tranquil and picturesque deck for sit-down food and wine pairings (page 219).

Best Winery Dog

JJ at Vincent Arroyo Talented, friendly, agreeable—everything a winery dog should be (page 98).

Best Events

Anderson Valley Pinot Noir Festival Gorgeous location, superior wines, and delicious lunch (page 282).

Home Winemakers Classic Most laid-back event; fun and funny, with great wines and even better wine names (page 273).

Napa Valley Wine Auction A fairytale event—your dream of a wine country gala (page 274).

Schramsberg Sparkling Wine Symposium A comprehensive exploration of all things bubbly (page 276).

Valley of the Moon Vintage Festival Wacky, wholesome fun for the whole family (page 281).

Winesong Location unequalled; wines exemplary; all three wine country counties well represented (page 284).

GRAPES to GLASSES

COLLECTIVE *and* SINGLE-WINERY TASTING ROOMS

The hands-down best way for a vintner to build a relationship with wine enthusiasts is to pour wine. But some wineries don't have a tasting room, and others are too far off the beaten track to host guests. And some winemakers don't even have their own winery!

The solution for all these dilemmas is simple: open a tasting room in a convenient location. Many labels do this on their own, while others create a collaborative effort, teaming up with other winemakers in similar circumstances. Some rooms are in lovely locations and are beautifully decorated inside and out; some, purely practical, are in unexpected places, like industrial parks. When the wine is good enough, it's worth turning a blind eye to an otherwise less than ideal setting. (Just be grateful that losing one sense sharpens the others.)

NAPA COUNTY

NAPA

Napa Wine Merchants

www.napawinemerchants.com

1146 First Street, Napa

707.257.6796

Daily 10am–6pm

> At Napa Wine Merchants, twelve wineries are showcased on a daily basis. Owner Thrace Bromberger also offers a wine club, private labels, and occasional classes and events designed to enlighten wine enthusiasts on a broad range of subjects, including how to navigate a wine list, throw a wine-tasting party, and identify the *terroir* of Napa's appellations.

Robert Craig Wine Cellars Tasting Room

www.robertcraigwine.com

800 Vallejo Street, Napa

707.252.2250

Tues–Sat 11am–4pm

> Among the charms of Napa Valley is its mix of cultures: high intersects with low; aggie earthiness gets down with city slicking. Anywhere you go, wine is the common thread, so hamburger joints sell it by the glass and the most humble home dinner party buzzes about which vintage is being poured. So it's not too surprising to find a completely awesome vintner pouring wine in an area known more for auto repair shops than for wineshops—and this is where Robert Craig set up shop.
>
> This small storefront tasting room offers the chance to taste its chardonnay; the proprietary blend, Affinity; and at least one of its mountain cabs (some days it's a bottle of the Howell Mountain; other days it's Mount Veeder). With advance notice, you can also try a barrel sample directly from one of its barrels, stored on the other side of the wall from the tasting room. The location may be surprising, but you can always count on the reliably outstanding taste of Robert Craig wines.

Vintner's Collective

www.vintnerscollective.com
1245 Main Street, Napa
707.255.7150
Wed–Mon 10am–6pm

Vintner's Collective has the distinct advantage of being the only bonded winery in downtown Napa that is used solely as a tasting room. No wine is made on the premises, but ten outstanding wineries use the space as their tasting room, including *Patz & Hall*, *Judd's Hill*, *Clark Claudon*, *Melka*, *Elan*, and *Mason*. Four wines are opened every day. The wines of all cooperating wineries are for sale daily, and a wine club that has several options delivers wines to your door four times a year.

The setting of Vintner's Collective is at once historic and contemporary. The structure—Napa's oldest—is also its first stone commercial building, built as a brewery in 1875. In the ensuing years it has served as a saloon and the Sam Kee Laundry (not surprising, given that its location was once the boundary of Napa's Chinatown). Inside there's a rotating collection of artwork, including pieces on loan from the di Rosa Preserve, an art museum that features the works of Bay Area artists.

OAKVILLE

Napa Wine Company's Cellar Door

www.napawineco.com
7830–40 St. Helena Highway, Oakville
707.944.1710 or 800.848.9630
Daily 10am–4pm, tastings with prior appointment

The Napa Wine Company is a four-pronged entity composed of vineyards, a custom-crush facility, a proprietary winery, and a retail space. The Cellar Door sells wines made by Napa Wine Company and by the various other labels produced in its custom-crush facility; these include some of the Valley's most sought-after labels. On any given day you can expect to choose among three or four flights of wine in the dark-wood-accented, clubby room. The selection varies from visit to visit but might include such wines as *Pavi Dolcetto*, *Showket Sangiovese*, *Ottimino Zinfandel*, and *Michael Pozzan Sauvignon Blanc*. The staff is one of the most enthusiastic in the Valley and helpful beyond the tasting bar. Want a lunch recommendation? They'll send you to a great place. Need advice about which winery to visit next? They've got suggestions. Like the business that owns it, the Cellar Door is a magnificent multitasker.

ST. HELENA

Heitz Wine Cellars

www.heitzcellar.com
436 St. Helena Highway South, St. Helena
707.963.3542
Daily 11am–4:30pm

It's easy to draw the conclusion that the stone building used for the Heitz Wine Cellars tasting room symbolizes the indestructible legend of the late Joe Heitz and the solid wines he created. A small vineyard in front of the building reminds you that wine is the focus here, although the wines are actually made a few miles away on Taplin Road. Inside, the light-filled tasting room feels spacious, with ceilings twice as high as the room is wide. A large fireplace balances the pragmatic bar, which is made of a simple slab of mahogany resting on giant concrete drums; these are mirrored by the oversized lampshades above.

Four wines are offered for eleven months of the year. Then, in February, the venerable Martha's Vineyard Cabernet is poured. Stay inside and recline in a leather chair in front of the fire, or step out back, where a large courtyard is bordered by redwood benches. There you can sit and enjoy the view of the vineyards and fig trees, listen to the sounds of the fountain (shaped like an olive oil press), and give thanks to the mighty giants like Joe Heitz who helped build the Napa Valley into the wonderland that it is.

Tasting on Main

www.tastingonmain.com
1142 Main Street, St. Helena
707.967.1042
Sun–Thur 10:30am–6pm, Fri–Sat 10:30am–8pm

Tucked as it is between a Thai restaurant and a lingerie shop, you'd hardly know Tasting on Main was there. But boy, will you be glad you found it. Inside the austere room, with its light-wood bar and fixtures, colorful paintings, and inviting leather chairs, are some amazing wines. *Broman, Richard Partridge, Elhers Estate, Saddleback Ranch,* and *Robert Keenan* make up half the small list of wines sold through this collective tasting room. Different combinations of wine flights are offered daily. Every label carried is a small-production wine made in Napa Valley by a family-owned winery. Owner Rob Piziali worked his way through the ranks of Valley wineries, as did his employees, resulting in a staff who know the wines as well as the winemakers, and can provide you with the kind of insight you'll appreciate.

SONOMA COUNTY

GEYSERVILLE

Locals

www.tastelocalwine.com
Corner of Geyserville Avenue and Highway 128, Geyserville
707.857.4900
Wed–Mon 11am–6pm

Locals is the most exciting thing to hit the tiny town of Geyserville since the geysers were discovered at the height of the resort era. Owned by Carolyn Lewis, a self-proclaimed "nouveau hick" who moved from New York City to the rural back roads of Northern California, Locals is way more nouveau than hick. In fact, this wine-tasting bar is hip, stylish, and sleek. Five or six wines from nearby appellations are poured at the corrugated tin and wood bar, including such small producers as *Crane Canyon*, *Peterson*, and *Hawley Wines*. Stop in at Locals for a sip of wine, some smart talk, and a great reprieve from the ordinary.

HEALDSBURG

Gallo of Sonoma

www.gallosonoma.com
320 Center Street, Healdsburg
707.433.2458
Sun–Wed 11am–5pm, Thur–Sat 11am–7pm

Over the past several years, the Gallo family has been remaking its image with a vengeance. The company's infinitely appealing tasting room, on Healdsburg's darling main square, is living proof that even well-established brands can mature, change identity, and shift public perception in terrifically positive ways.

Simultaneously sophisticated, urbane, and casual, the Gallo of Sonoma tasting room is all cool blue and green, light-colored wood, and well-filtered natural light, reflected in one perfectly tilted mirror. Hospitable wine educators greet you and offer to pour—but the real invitation is to sit and linger in a bistro-like setting and explore, in depth, the winery's various offerings.

All tastings—served in Riedel stemware, which is also for sale—are accompanied by printed wine notes, fresh bread, filtered water, chocolate truffles, and sometimes cheese (generally served only with the estate flights). There is a large handful of functional and decorative wine accessories for sale, from the expected stoppers and corkscrews to more unusual books and copper-dipped grape-leaf bottle ornaments. Private parties are welcome, but even if you are a party of one, this is a tasting-room experience you will not want to miss.

Rosenblum Cellars

www.rosenblumcellars.com
250 Center Street, Healdsburg
707.431.1169
Sun–Thur 10am–5pm, Fri–Sat 10am–6pm

One of the three Rs to have proverbially invented zinfandel (*Ridge* and *Ravenswood* are the other two), Rosenblum makes its juice from a variety of vineyards located as far away as the foothills of the Sierras and as near as the other side of town. At the Rosenblum tasting room, just off the Healdsburg square, two wine flights are offered: each is a good cross-section of the label's almighty zin. This is clearly a must-go-to destination for zin lovers who want to explore how different vineyards and regions treat their favorite grape. In fact, tasting the same grape made by the same hand but grown in a different area certainly gives new meaning to "location, location, location."

Toad Hollow Vineyards

www.toadhollow.com
409A Healdsburg Avenue, Healdsburg
707.431.8667
Daily 10:30am–5:30pm

Toad Hollow Vineyards is playful. The winery's history reads like a children's story. Its annual newsletter is peppered with the language of frogs. The wine names are whimsical. The logo and labels have tongue-in-cheek illustrations of frogs drinking wine or indulging in various other unexpected activites, and the tasting room is one giant frog pond.

When you first enter the room, you'll be drawn to the neat vertical rows of wine bottles hanging on long racks behind the counter. The bar is polished to such a high sheen the wood grain looks like ripples on water. It might take another beat to notice that it's set atop river stones and that the giant vase on the corner is filled with tule reeds.

Founded by Todd Williams and Rodney Strong (this is their idea of retirement!), Toad Hollow has always had a good reputation. All the wines on its list are available to try every day in the tasting room, from its sparkling crémant brut to its Russian River merlot. The staff is engaging and easy to chat with. Check out the really cute framed posters of Toad Hollow's label art; they're for sale, as are small collections of the labels themselves.

KENWOOD

VJB Vineyards and Cellar

www.vjbcellars.com
9077 Sonoma Highway, Kenwood
707.833.2300
Mon–Fri 6am–4:30pm, Sat–Sun 7am–4:30pm

For the Belmonte family, starting a winery was a dream come true, and VJB, their tasting room, showcases their achievements. The family's former life as restaurateurs is evident in every detail of VJB, from the warm, inviting dark-wood interior and neighborly atmosphere to the espresso bar and the jarred sauces, marinades, and tapenades created and sold by Maria, the family matriarch. Whether you're tasting in the area or just driving through, this is a comfortable spot to stop in for a glass of wine or a cup of coffee.

The Wine Room

www.the-wine-room.com
9575 Sonoma Highway, Kenwood
707.833.6131
Daily 11am–5pm

As with Francis Ford Coppola, on the other side of the hill, Hollywood fame preceded Tommy and Dickie Smothers's foray into the wine world. They were a daring counterculture act when they first appeared on television in the late 1960s and were nearly as revolutionary when they began farming grapes in the Sonoma Valley. Today their *Smothers/Remick Ridge* wines are available for tasting at the Wine Room in Kenwood. The small tasting room plays host to a few local wineries, including *Alder Fels, Moondance Cellars,* and *Sonoma Valley Portworks.* While sipping through the bevy of wines, take a minute to peruse Tommy Smothers's book on yo-yoing before picking one up and Walking the Dog. You'll experience the best of all worlds: nurturing your inner child while indulging your inner adult.

MENDOCINO COUNTY

BOONVILLE

Anderson Valley Wine Experience

17810A Farrer Lane at Highway 128, Boonville
707.895.3993
Daily 11am–5pm

Across the street from the fantastic Boonville Hotel (and within walking distance of just about everything else in this pint-size town), you'll find the spacious, light, airy tasting room and art gallery, dedicated to three family wineries: *Claudia Springs, Eaglepoint Ranch* (John Scharffenberger of Scharffen Berger Chocolate is a partner), and *Raye's Hill.* Feel free to look around. Rounding out the store's selections is a Stella Cadente tasting bar that sells the locally produced olive oil in bulk and in bottles, alongside olive oil soaps and dishes. In the back of the store you'll find tchotchkes and books, including a Boontling dictionary—Boontling is the regional dialect. After you thumb through the dictionary, you'll probably want to *horn some frattey* and hang out a while—the staff is genuinely nice.

Right: The signature fencing of Mendocino.

HOPLAND

Domaine Saint Gregory/Graziano Tasting Room

www.domainesaintgregory.com
13251 Highway 101, Suite 3, Hopland
707.744.VINO
Daily 10am–5pm

Part office, part tasting room, this no-nonsense destination is all about good wines. John Graziano built his reputation producing fine Cal-Italia wines made from grapes grown in the Hopland area, and today offers one of the largest selections of Italian varietals in Northern California. Try the nebbiolo, the dolcetto, or the Tanaro, a proprietary blend; all are available for tasting. Graziano offers four labels: Domaine Saint Gregory (a brand featuring Burgundian varietals), Monte Volpe, Enotria, and Graziano. The latter eponymous brand consists of notable zinfandels made from the area's old vines.

WINESHOPS
and
TASTING BARS

A visit to the wine country almost demands a wine purchase. Therefore, the question posed to every visitor isn't "Will you buy wine?" but "What wine will you buy, and where?" Of course, you can always buy wine at a winery. But if you want to choose from a selection of vintners in one stop, Napa, Sonoma, and Mendocino all offer a bevy of top-notch wineshops with distinguished inventories.

All these fine wine merchants benefit immeasurably from their proximity to the wineries themselves. By virtue of nearness, local wine merchants are able to stock highly sought-after boutique wines from small facilities that don't offer visits to the public; wines with very limited distribution; and wines you've probably never even heard of yet. Like the fine wines they sell, every shop—as you'll discover—has its own distinctive personality.

NAPA COUNTY

CALISTOGA

Enoteca Wine Shop

1348-B Lincoln Avenue, Calistoga
707.942.1117
Daily 12–5pm

For several years, Enoteca Wine Shop was hidden up a flight of stairs in a shop that shared space with an antique dealer. Owner Margaux Singleton must be pretty pleased with her new ground-level storefront. With its fancy trompe l'oeil walls, this shop is more worthy of the labels she carries.

Familiar details—like the way Margaux exhaustively documents the bottles with tags that give the history of the maker, facts regarding the vintage, and more—remind us that in another life Margaux was an academic, working at the University of Virginia. There she belonged to a wine-tasting group, which introduced her to two wines that changed her path: a Bordeaux and a Rhône. These discoveries inspired her to change careers and ultimately led her to Napa Valley. In 1997 she opened the doors of Enoteca (Italian for wineshop) and began selling wines from small artisanal producers across the country. She has a startling collection of local vintners, like Napa's *Behrens and Hitchcock*, mixed in with more esoteric wines, like cabernet sauvignon from Virginia. Her hands-on approach is similar to that of the *négociants* of France: she develops a relationship with the vintner, tastes each wine before she buys it, and ensures that each customer enjoys the benefit of her motto, "The right wine for the right home."

Wine Garage

www.winegarage.com
1020 Foothill Boulevard, Calistoga
707.942.5332
Tues–Sat 11am–6:30pm, Sun 11am–4:30pm

The Wine Garage is a stylish store devoted to selling hundreds of wines, all under twenty-five dollars a bottle. Case stacks are lined up in neat rows to form aisles, the better to showcase this well-priced abundance. There are more than two hundred wine labels, a good mix of local and international producers, and a broad selection of varietals. This is the place to search for your next house wine or experiment without breaking the bank.

NAPA

Back Room Wines

www.backroomwines.com
974 Franklin Street, Napa
707.226.1378 or 877.322.2576
Mon–Thur 10am–6pm, Fri–Sat 10am–9pm

When Dan Dawson opened his shop a few blocks away from the hub of downtown, he filled his shelves with the best selection of imported wines that you will find in Napa Valley. He did this while also showcasing a tremendous assortment of local wines that will please even the most jaded wine enthusiast.

What really sets Back Room Wines apart from the rest is its owner. A confirmed wine connoisseur, Dan has vast knowledge and fine-tuned tastes. This makes him a great resource for customers because he can direct you to new labels you'll love, based on what you know you already like.

A former sommelier at the French Laundry, Dan has created an exciting curriculum of tastings that range from formal blind tastings of some of the world's finest wines to casual tastings focused on a particular area, vintage, or varietal. Every Friday night, he hosts a themed tasting that might focus on Alsatian whites, Napa cabs, or anything in between. Once a month he hosts a "Back Room Blowout," featuring half a dozen wines. Guests grab a glass and then "travel from winery to winery"; practically speaking, this means you get to sample great wines while chatting and tasting with the principal or winemaker of a prestigious winery—usually one not open to the public. It's as close as you can get to shaking the hand that nurtured the grape.

Saturdays are also themed, usually leaning more toward Dan's gastronomic interests. A fine cook, he either whips up something himself or imports a favorite chef pal to create the perfect food partner for a notable wine. Anyone for ribs and zin? Niçoise and rosé? Cassoulet and Châteauneuf-du-Pape?

Be sure to ask to be put on the Back Room Wines email list. Dan Dawson's amusing weekly missives are as much fun to read as the wines he sells are to drink.

Gateway to the Napa Valley The downtown area of Napa was once a bustle of commercial activity, which faded and wasn't revived until the beginning of this century, when the riverfront was redeveloped and many of the historic buildings were restored. As downtown Napa began to show new signs of life, several wineshops and bars opened—and those that were already doing business enjoyed renewed vigor. Today these businesses make touring the downtown area as richly rewarding for wine lovers as traveling from winery to winery—with the added luxury of being able to do it all on foot.

Bounty Hunter Rare Wine & Provisions

www.bountyhunterwine.com
975 First Street, Napa
800.943.9463
Mon–Fri 7am–6pm, Sat 10am–4pm

If Ralph Lauren opened a wine-tasting bar, it would look a lot like the Bounty Hunter, gorgeously housed in downtown Napa's 1888 Semorile building. Proprietor Mark Pope had been lusting for the building since first spotting it a century after it was built, when it housed an old grocery store on the ground floor and a home upstairs. In 2003—sparing neither style nor money—Pope's dream of a western-themed retail wine showroom was finally realized.

Not a single design detail has been left to chance. With the original brick walls, oversized doors, oak and redwood floors and trim, and hand-pounded Mexican tin ceiling tiles restored to their original luster, Pope moved on to oversee the rest. The wine bar in the back is of highly polished mahogany, with a foot rest crafted of old railroad track; opposite is a small selection of beautifully displayed large-format bottles.

Here and there are cushy leather stools, bronze and alabaster light fixtures, cowboy paraphernalia, and precious display cases sheltering high-end artifacts for sale. Tables made from barrel components and stand-alone wine racks are all on wheels, allowing the room to be reconfigured to accommodate up to fifty people for a large tasting or private event. The whole effect is western chic: sparse yet luxe, masculine and rugged, and altogether fabulous.

When you sit down to taste, you'll find wines by the glass, several beers on tap, and a very tempting menu of bar food. It is without question one of the handsomest places around in which to sip or purchase wine.

JV Wine and Spirits

www.jvwarehouse.com
426 First Street, Napa
707.253.2624 or 877.4MY.WINE
Daily 8am–9pm (tasting bar Fri 4–7pm)

JV Wine and Spirits is the biggest wineshop in Napa, and according to a recent survey by the *Napa Valley Register*, it is also the one most frequented by local residents. It offers a range of wines that are not confined to the Napa Valley and stocks all sizes and forms, including by the box and the case. JV also offers an opportunity to taste a featured winery's goods every Friday evening at a wine bar set up in the luxury wine section of the store. Whether you're searching for one peerless bottle or stocking up for a big bash, consider checking out JV's selection.

Napa General Store

www.napageneralstore.com
500 Main Street, Napa
707.259.0762
Daily 11am–6pm

The Napa General Store has a beautiful setting that includes a great big bar and an outdoor terrace on the Napa River. The store's selection is small but precise, with lesser-known labels shelved beside quintessential Napa wines. Wines are available by the taste and by the glass; you may consume there or buy a bottle for take-away. Napa General Store's location and its large selection of wine-related gift items combine to merit it a visit, especially if you're looking for a place outside the usual venues to enjoy a glass of wine.

ST. HELENA

Acme Fine Wines

www.acmefinewine.com
1104 Adams Street, Suite 104, St. Helena
707.963.0440
Mon–Sat 9am–6pm

There seems to be a natural progression for Napa Valley wine professionals: moving from working in a restaurant environment to owning their own retail shops. This is true of David Stevens and Karen Williams, Tra Vigne alumni who have partnered up via their business, Acme Fine Wines, to sell a great selection of small-production, cult-status wines.

Acme's office-cum-shop is shared with a couple of other businesses, which adds to the unique layout of its ultramodern space. Juxtaposed against the stone walls of the historic Pritchard building, Acme's interior is all cool stainless steel, blue-tinted corrugated plastic walls, and steel and blue accents that inspire a dreamlike sensation; it feels kind of like you stepped into a magazine cover. The wine "shop" is hidden behind a large sliding steel door. A closet-like space, it has floor-to-ceiling stainless-steel shelves filled with wine bottles, and cases are stacked against the walls.

While Acme's hospitality always shines through, it's intensified at the special events that it hosts every four to six weeks. These events reflect the true passions of wine professionals: the only thing they love more than drinking wine is sharing it with others. Acme makes this happen, and in the process communicates its dedication to bringing great wines and undiscovered gems to like-minded folks.

St. Helena Wine Center

www.shwc.com
1321 Main Street, St. Helena
707.963.1313 or 800.331.1313
Mon–Sat 10am–6pm, Sun 10am–5pm

With its soaring ceiling, cool terra-cotta floors, posh architectural appointments, and pristine collectibles room, St. Helena Wine Center has a refined, clubby interior that feels something like a luxurious wine cellar. For almost three decades, buyers seeking hard-to-find and collectible wines from Napa Valley producers have been coming here and leaving happy. With its diverse and well-stocked inventory, including the large-format bottles (magnums and up) and older vintages on display in the Collector's Room and the large cold case for those who want a chilled bottle, SHWC easily satisfies discerning tastes.

In terms of practical considerations, SHWC's catalog and wine club combine to make shopping easy. The store's Wine of the Month Club is unusually liberal in that it provides members with a monthly choice of wine types and price preferences; this is in contrast to the majority of wine clubs, which generally limit your choices. For out-of-towners who want to shop Napa, the store's user-friendly website—with its direct online ordering capability—allows you to become educated while building your personal cellar. (Before you get out your credit card, be sure to check that your home state allows wine to be shipped from California directly to you.)

And if you're planning to visit in person, first go online to check out the wide array of activities that the store sponsors: everything from charity auctions, dinners, and celebrity tastings to Christmas caroling in the caves. Or stop by any weekend to taste one of the wines it's pouring and chat with staffer Jack Smith, a former surgeon who has studied wine for forty-eight years and is now the resident novelist, weaving tales of wine and intrigue.

St. Helena Wine Merchants

www.shwinemerchants.com
699 St. Helena Highway, St. Helena
707.963.7888 or 800.SAY.WINE
Daily 10am–6pm

If there were a décor test for wineshops, St. Helena Wine Merchants would flunk, with its crudely wainscoted walls, chipped plasterboard, and half-opened cardboard boxes scattered about. But there's more here than meets the eye. Just start talking to Geoffrey Smith, resident wine geek, and you'll quickly realize you've entered a very rarified wine universe. Geoffrey will talk your ear off about growers, vines, fruit, vintages, good buys, special resales of exceptional wines from private collections, and the next hot bottle that's still below the radar. For wine sleuths on the trail of reserve wines and older vintages, this is a good place to start; but it's only fair to warn you that your search might end right here, where it began. You're bound to leave laden with invaluable information—as well as with hard-to-find, allocated, and small-production wines that don't usually make it beyond the state of California; reserve wines and older vintages; and cult wines like *T-Vine*, *Ancien*, *Summers*, *Buoncristiani*, *Melka*, and *Cedarville*. Before you know it, you'll start preaching the gospel about beauty being only skin deep.

A whimsical sculpture at Bistro Don Giovanni.

YOUNTVILLE

Groezinger Wine Shop

6528 Washington Avenue, Yountville

707.944.2331

Mon–Sat 10am–5pm

The best wineshops are like small bookstores in that they reflect the personalities, passions, and tastes of their owners. In this way, Groezinger is Rick Beard: slightly irreverent, broad of focus, and bold of sensibility. The store's walls are lined with rock-and-roll memorabilia, and the shelves are stocked predominantly with wines produced in quantities of less than one thousand cases; a few imported ringers are thrown in for good measure. After a few visits you'll know Rick's taste, and he or his associates will become your reliable source for wines you'll love.

Vintage 1870 Wine Cellar

www.vintagewinecellar.com
6525 Washington Street, Yountville
707.944.2451 or 800.WINE4US
Daily 10am–5:30pm

In 1870, pioneer vintner Gottlieb Groezinger thought the world was his oyster. Acquiring 370 acres in Yountville, he began the extensive construction of his much-admired and well-organized winery, with its brick wine cellar, stables, barns, distillery, steam plant, and mansion. The cellar's capacity was 400,000 gallons, then the largest in California, while the distillery's two stills produced 150 gallons per day. But by 1876, an explosion and fire had destroyed nearly everything.

Today, what remains of the brick complex has been designated a historic structure in the U.S. National Registry of Historic Places. Now it's used as a small, cheerful shopping mall, in which you'll find a pleasing selection of shops, restaurants, cafés, and galleries.

At the back side is Vintage 1870 Wine Cellar, a wine store as dedicated to its historic location as to its excellent selection of wines. Winemaking artifacts are paired with educational panels, so you leave with more than bottles or cases—you leave with an understanding of the inner workings of cork production, barrel making, and more. With the intention to be more than just a wineshop, Vintage 1870 aims to be your personal wine shopper. Customers are encouraged to complete a personal wine profile, making future purchases more of a science than a guess. Choose from a terrific inventory of large-format bottles, boutique-label wines and ports, and domestic sparkling wines and imported Champagnes, as well as hard-to-find imported wines such as *Tignarello*, *Rayas*, and *Château Beaucastle*.

Before you leave, take the time to sit and sip at the back of the store on well-worn stools, around small round tables, or out on the airy patio. Each day's tasting menu offers ten wines and two dessert wines.

SONOMA COUNTY

HEALDSBURG

The Wine Shop
331 Healdsburg Avenue, Healdsburg
707.433.0433
Mon–Sat 10am–6pm (Fri until 8pm), Sun 12–6pm

The Wine Shop is a smallish, slightly cramped, and unassuming shop that is bursting at the seams with excellent inventory on its floor-to-ceiling shelves. You'll find *Brogan*, *Collier Falls*, *Ridge*, and *McIlroy*, among many other well-respected labels.

A "good value" section offers a nice selection for the adventurous taster of more modest means, while a private reserve room has high-end reds for bigger spenders, featuring both European and local names like *Harlan*, *Chapoultier*, *Dashe*, and *Duxoup*. Friday-night in-store tastings star local winemakers, and themed events add a little something extra in terms of wine education.

SANTA ROSA

Bottle Barn

3331 A Industrial Drive, Santa Rosa
707.528.1161
Mon–Sat 9:30am–6:30pm, Sun 9:30am–5pm

It's hard to imagine you'd want anything that Bottle Barn doesn't carry. A warehouse-mini-megastore, Bottle Barn can outfit you in bubbles from Pepsi to Champagne and offers an outstanding collection of local and international wines. All manner of spirits are also well represented. Many prices are below winery retail tags, including high-rent names like *Roederer, Spellitich, Paul Hobbs, Viader, Flowers,* and more. It takes a little elbow work to dig them out of the trough-like bins in which all the wines are displayed, but just a little rifling through the yards of bins will be a rewarding experience for bargain hunters with an eye for great wine. Despite the store's large size, the knowledgeable, cordial staff interact as though they're working in a mom-and-pop shop. Visit them for big deals with a no-big-deal attitude.

SONOMA

Taylor & Norton Wine Merchants

www.taylorandnorton.com
19210 Sonoma Highway, Sonoma
707.939.6611
Mon–Sat 10am–6pm

Taylor & Norton Wine Merchants is a haven for the rare-wine collector. Small and crowded with wooden display boxes, the store is a super-constellation of high- and super-high-end wines, with plenty of older vintages for sale. Just around the corner from the magnums of *Opus* and *Billecart Salmon* Champagne, you'll find a mother lode of fantastic cabernets from eminent producers such as *Bryant Family, Dalla Valle, Ridge Monte Bello, Shafer, J. Phelps Insignia, Dominus,* and *Caymus Special Selection.* If you're a heavy-hitter buyer looking for a heavy-hitter list, this is the place for you.

The Wine Exchange of Sonoma

www.wineexsonoma.com
452 First Street East, Sonoma
707.938.1794 or 800.938.1794
Mon–Thur and Sat 10am–6pm, Fri 10am–6:30pm, Sun 11am–6pm

Harmonious, calm, serene, pretty, and phenomenally well stocked—this
fifteen-year-old institution is everything a wine store should be. The front
room is an ode to aesthetic precision. Lined with evenly spaced bottles of
inspired pedigree, the shelves showcase labels such as *Ridge*, *Paul Hobbs*,
Random Ridge, and *Pisoni*, all well-regarded reflections of their regions.
There's an equally impressive array of European fruit wine, Port, Sherry,
and Madeira.

Stepping deeper into the Wine Exchange, you'll pass a large cigar display
just before reaching the attractive tasting bar, fitted with casual wooden
stools on one side and draft beer taps on the other. A neatly printed chalk-
board (rendered with the same precision as the shelved bottles) tells you
the specials for the daily wine and beer tastings.

Before leaving with your armful of bottles, be sure to look up and around
at the fine collection of vintage oversized posters. Then check out the various oils, vinegars, spices, condiments, and poster postcards for sale, along
with one of the largest and best selections of imported and domestic beers.
And be sure to pay your respects to the barstool with the plaque dedicated to Amy, a whippet who visited frequently with her owner and begged
for biscuits from her well-worn perch.

Finally, rest assured that after your laid-back samplings, you can have a
lovely little nap on a bench in the town square, conveniently located just
across the street.

MENDOCINO COUNTY

HOPLAND

The Wine Reserve
www.thewinereserve.com
13450 Highway 101, Hopland
707.744.1725 or 800.327.3405
Tues–Sun 10am–6pm

In what feels like an almost deserted western town, the Wine Reserve is an oenophile's oasis. Although too small to warrant a drive all the way to Hopland, if you are in or passing through town, this is the place to stop and pick up a bottle or two. Much of the selection is small-production wines, including *Walker Station Chardonnay*, a highly sought-after label with distribution as tiny as the Wine Reserve itself.

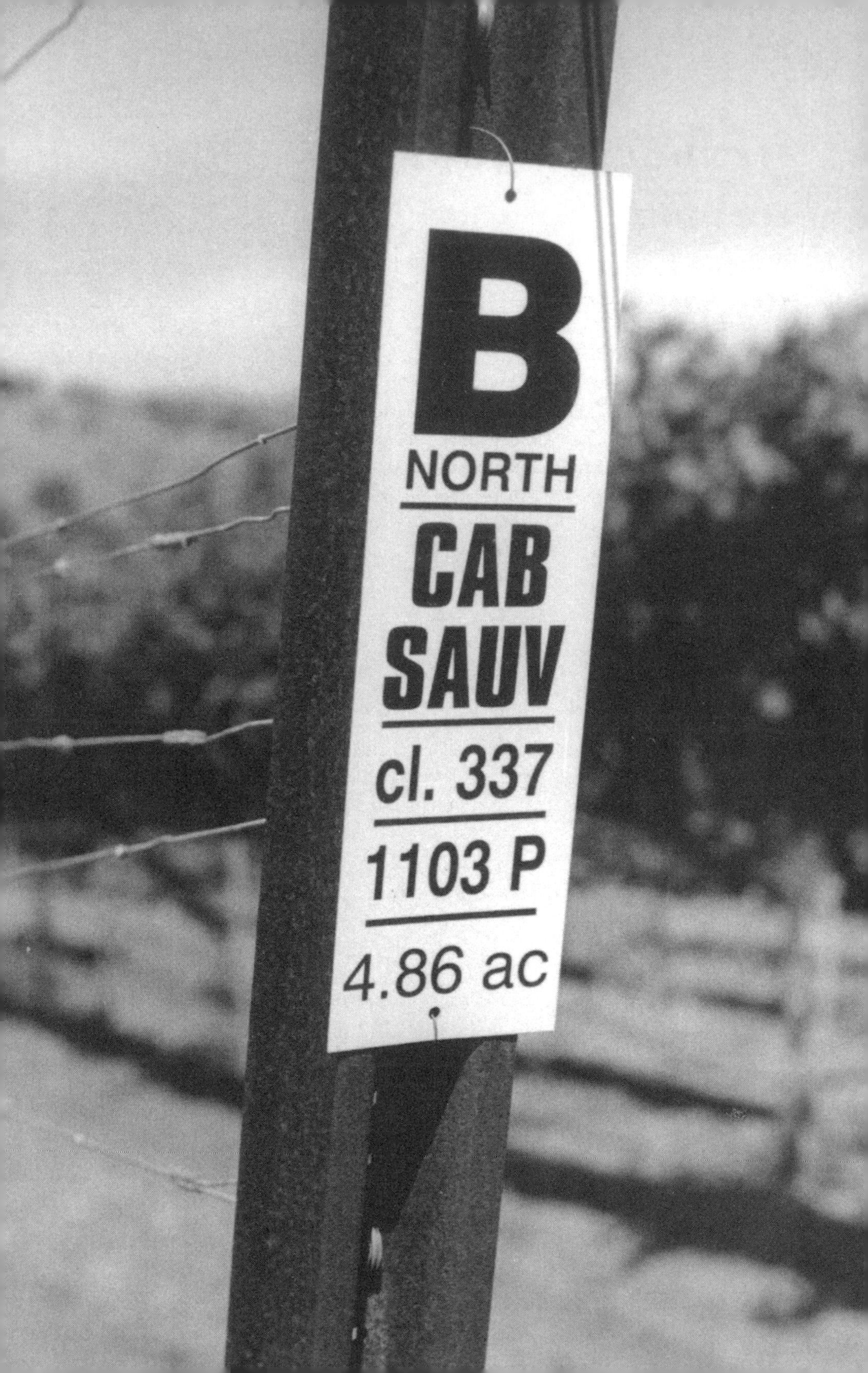
B
NORTH
CAB
SAUV
cl. 337
1103 P
4.86 ac

WINERIES
by REGION

It goes without saying that wineries are the primary reason to visit the wine country. Practically hallowed ground for visitors who flock here every year from far and wide, they stand as a testament to the mystique and prestige that surround wine, and offer enlightenment to those who want to learn the secrets of how wine is made.

In your travels, you will find wineries that range from the ultra-elegant to the rustic and remote, with others of every stripe in between. With so many wineries to choose from, how do you begin to plan your itinerary? By appellation. This approach allows you to parse the wine country into manageable geographical areas that are distinctly different from one another in climate, topography, scenery, history, and even culture. By exploring the wine country appellation by appellation, you'll gain a greater understanding of how and why the wine country as a whole is so utterly compelling.

Napa County Appellations

Napa Valley is the largest appellation in Napa County, and within it are thirteen subappellations. This book explores a major portion of the Napa Valley appellation and eleven of its subappellations, taking you from the lowest elevation in Carneros to the highest in Spring Mountain.

As you visit wineries within each appellation, you'll personally experience how different sun exposures, soil types, and land contours affect the growing season—and, ultimately, the characteristics of the wine produced in each region. As you travel, you'll see how the earth can change color from a light cocoa brown to a fierce red. You'll experience how some Napa County appellations can be so scorchingly hot you'll feel sorry for the grapes, while others are so cool and windy you'll check the skies for flying cows.

Appellation Primer In the 1980s, California vintners began to lobby and receive recognition for designated wine-growing regions, technically called American Viticultural Areas (AVAs), in much the same way that France and Italy have used Appellations of Control for centuries. These defined geographical regions—casually referred to as appellations, districts, areas, or simply as regions—must receive formal designation by the Alcohol and Tobacco Tax and Trade Bureau (TTB).

To achieve this status, vintners or others petition for designation. An AVA is granted to a grape-growing region distinguishable by geographic features when it meets certain criteria. The name of the region must be commonly known, locally or nationally. Its boundaries must be legitimate. And there must be evidence that the area's growing conditions—that special combination of sun, soil, and slope—are distinct.

Today, two decades after the first appellations were granted, California's wine country is almost entirely divided into discrete regions that are determined by the attributes of each. Vintners here have, in turn, gained mainstream recognition for their regional wines, proving the argument that wines are all about place. Sure, you can grow a grape anywhere, but a Stags Leap district cabernet sauvignon will taste entirely different than an Alexander Valley cabernet sauvignon, in much the same way that two producers' wines of the same varietal will differ.

Appellations also come in a variety of sizes and shapes. While some are populated by hundreds of wineries, others don't have a single winery within their borders. Moreover, a winery can make several different appellation-designated wines, as long as each wine is produced with at least 85 percent of its grapes grown in the specified AVA.

As in all other American commerce, the almighty dollar plays a huge role in the world of wine, and subsequently in the inner workings of appellations. Increasing numbers of vintners are planting varietals with higher ticket prices wherever they can be grown; a good example of this is the proliferation of cabernet sauvignon wherever growers can get it to ripen.

DIAMOND MOUNTAIN

Diamond Mountain is a relatively small region with only a handful of wineries within its borders. The Valley's northernmost appellation, it sits on the eastern front of the Mayacamas and is characterized by pockets of dense forest interspersed with vineyards. The soils are primarily tufa—a light, chalky soil that retains heat from the sun. This keeps the vines warm, ensuring that the cabernet sauvignon for which the area is renowned reaches ripeness at an even pace.

Schramsberg

www.schramsberg.com
1400 Schramsberg Road, Calistoga
707.942.4558
By appointment only

Carved out of a hillside at the base of Diamond Mountain by Jacob Schram in 1862, Schramsberg is a singular kind of paradise. In any other setting the fabulous buildings—a Victorian house circa 1889, an old barn, caves, and winery—would be all you'd talk about. But here, despite their beauty, they play second fiddle to the foliage that's so lush it's like Napa in the tropics.

The winery history is rich and full. Speaking of rich, Schram was a major personality of his time whose wealth was a result of a good stock tip. He used his good fortune to buy the property and plant vineyards, and soon he began making riesling and a Burgundian blend. Like most vintners of the time, he hired Chinese laborers to dig out the caves by hand.

Some eighty years later, in 1965, Jack and Jamie Davies, a young, risk-taking couple, moved their family from Los Angeles to Schram's property. They wanted to honor Schram's winemaking efforts but didn't want to compete with the other eighteen wineries in the Valley. So they chose to make sparkling wine. This daring move made the Davieses the first in the United States to produce a blanc de blancs in the style of traditional French Champagne houses. This groundbreaking achievement led to others, such as creating the first non-French Champagne to be poured at an international event (it was the oenophilic highlight of Nixon's visit to China).

Of course, you'll hear many more such stories when you visit Schramsberg—and whether or not you're a sparkling fan, you absolutely must go. The tour is among the very best in Napa Valley, and for sparkling wine it is the absolute best. Led by warm and friendly guides, the tours tell the tale of the winery from its inception through current goings-on. As you walk through the caves and around the winery, you'll gain tremendous respect for the exceptionally time-consuming effort it takes to produce a sparkling wine of Schramsberg's caliber. If you're lucky enough to happen upon riddler Ramone Viera doing his job—forcing the solids in a sparkling-wine bottle into the neck by gently pounding the bottles against a soft surface—you'll understand how painstakingly hands-on this whole enterprise really is. The sound of Champagne bottles being banged with a drumbeat rhythm is unforgettable.

As your tour proceeds, you'll be educated about the vineyards and about where the fruit is grown, clued in to the art of stacking bottles in the cellar, and regaled with tales about how Jack and Jamie Davies made their dreams come true. If the romance of Schramsberg is intoxicating, a sit-down tasting of four sparkling wines is transporting. Each is divine in its own way; they're like liquid jewels in faint tints of amber, ruby, and topaz. In addition to the blanc de blancs, Schramsberg produces several top-notch sparkling wines, including a blanc de noirs, a brut rosé, a crémant demi-sec, a reserve cuvée, and its signature J. Schram—an aged brut that is just now facing competition in the form of the new J. Schram rosé. Any of these wines can rival even the best French Champagne. If all you did was leave home, fly to California, and visit only Schramsberg, you'd go home smiling and content.

von Strasser Winery

www.vonstrasser.com
1510 Diamond Mountain Road, Calistoga
707.942.0930
Daily by appointment only

The wee cabin that serves as von Strasser's tasting room is sparse, reflecting the arid soils that make up the Diamond Mountain appellation. In fact, the best reason to visit von Strasser is to look at the hillside vineyards planted on the property. These winding, undulating rows of vines—set hard into chalky, rocky, light-brown earth—stand in sharp contrast to the neat rows of vines on the verdant Valley floor. Taken together, they offer a great lesson in *terroir*: how place affects the taste of wine.

Rudy von Strasser's wines offer signature mountain characteristics: concentration, dense flavors, and chewy tannins. Among the wines offered for sampling is von Strasser cab, a sterling example of the region's best and a perfect excuse for making the drive up the mountain.

> **Lunchtime** Diamond Mountain is basically a forest- and vineyard-covered hillside composed of strong vines, stronger vintners, and not a single restaurant. But a wine lover's got to eat! Calistoga is your best and closest bet. Try some tasty take-out (fresh sandwiches and a wide assortment of other foods) from **Palisades Market** (1506 Lincoln Avenue, Calistoga, 707.942.9549).

The Best of the Rest You'll wish you had a helicopter to whisk you up to **Constant Diamond Mountain Vineyard** (2121 Diamond Mountain Road, Calistoga, www.constantwine.com, 707.942.0707), because it's way, way up a heavily forested road that finally ends at the peak of Diamond Mountain. The locale is appropriate since visiting Constant offers a lingering peek into how the other half lives—and by this we mean the half with money to burn, style to spare, and no qualms about your looking into their personal (but not so private) home. It's like *Architectural Digest* come to life, and great wines are part of the pretty picture.

HOWELL MOUNTAIN

Howell Mountain was the first area in Napa Valley to be planted with traditional Bordeaux varietals in the late 1800s. Today, the western face of Howell Mountain is home to a multitude of vineyards planted primarily to cabernet sauvignon and zinfandel. The infertile volcanic soils that dominate the region's terrain result in small berries with lots of concentration—and in wines that boast full fruit flavors and chewy tannins.

Forman Vineyard
www.formanvineyard.com
1501 Big Rock Road, St. Helena
707.963.0234
By appointment only

Ric Forman likes to blow things up. At least that's what he did to his Howell Mountain property—before planting it with grapes, of course.

While Ric wasn't the first to move the earth, he may have been the first to do so by drilling holes into seventeen hundred rocks, filling them with dynamite, and sending them sky-high. The evidence of this is on display in the Forman Vineyard tasting room he built using stones recovered from the hillside. Hanging over the room's fireplace are two large photographs that capture Ric's big bang.

At age twenty-one Ric, was hired by Peter Newton to be a winemaker for *Sterling*. Peter sent Ric to France for an informal education; Ric returned with a wealth of knowledge and a burning desire to put it to use. And he has. Over the last four decades (first at *Sterling*, then at *Newton*, which he began with Peter, and now at his own winery), he has initiated a handful of firsts for California's winemaking industry. He was the first to make merlot as a commercial commodity. He was the first to make a nonmalolactic-fermented chardonnay and the first to plant petit verdot.

A one-man show, Ric built every structure on his property, including the cave and winery. While all this is commendable, the most remarkable part is that it's all amazingly well done, both aesthetically and functionally. When you visit, Margaret Harre, Forman's marketing director, will show you around. In addition to praising Ric's career and talent, she'll sit you down and have you partake of a glass of wine. It may be a cab, current or older, made from the Howell Mountain vineyards, or a chardonnay from a Rutherford vineyard that Ric owns with *El Molino Winery*. They somehow taste as if they were imbued with that first flash of dynamite and the perseverance of solid rock; they are truly unforgettable.

Ladera Winery

www.laderavineyards.com
150 White Cottage Road (South), Angwin
707.965.2445
By appointment only

In the 1880s, two French gentlemen, Jean Brun and W. J. Chaix, found their way up Howell Mountain, where they planted Bordeaux-varietal grapes. About 120 years later, Anne and Pat Stotesbury bought the property—which had lain dormant during Prohibition and exchanged hands a couple of times afterward—renamed the winery Ladera (roughly translated from Spanish as "hillside"), and began renovations to return it to its original state.

The stone winery has been restored to include the three floors that were designed to allow the wine to move via gravity flow from crush to barrel. The landscape is being beautified with indigenous plants, and the chardonnay vines planted by the previous owners are being replaced with cabernet sauvignon. The only step the Stotesburys haven't taken, and probably won't need to, is to replace the mirrors that were once used in the cellar window to signal to the Valley how many barrels of wine were ready to be transported down the hill.

Ladera is a nice blend of working winery and historic structure. A tour around the grounds and through the cellar offers interesting information on both topics and culminates in a tasting of a barrel sample of its hillside cab, made by the very talented Karen Culler. With the year 2000 marking the inaugural release of Ladera, it is obviously an old winery with a young heart—one with the potential to grow to great heights. Don't miss it.

Lunchtime The terrain of Howell Mountain is such that the wineries that have chosen this region as home are spread out and tucked into valleys and canyons and on ridges. While there's a town on top of the hill, its options for dining are nearly nonexistent. So it's best to head down to St. Helena for lunch. Check out **Villa Corona** (1138 Main Street, St. Helena, 707.963.7812). It's simpatico, the food is cheap and great, and the winemaker- and vineyard manager–watching is a great side dish.

O'Shaughnessy Winery

www.oshaughnessywinery.com
Howell Mountain
707.965.2898
By appointment only

It takes confidence to name a winery after yourself when your name is so hard to spell. But Betty O'Shaughnessy didn't worry. She knew she had everything it took to inspire people to learn how to spell O'Shaughnessy: great vineyards that produce high-quality fruit, an über-talented winemaker, stellar wines, and a magnificent winery in which to make and showcase them.

A decade-long search for the perfect location came to a happy end on a pristine, extremely remote hillside on Howell Mountain. If the world were flat, you'd think you were on the edge, except for the view of the mountains that never quits. O'Shaughnessy Winery masterfully blends a Japanese tea-house aesthetic with modern California sensibilities and the craftsmanship of Minnesota woodworkers. The fermentation room has been smartly designed (with input by winemaker Sean Capiaux), and is so neat and tidy it looks like a tank showroom. The cave, too, is meticulous, with enough space for it to be used for fermentation as well as for storing the winery's entire production capacity in a single layer of barrels.

A tour will take you through each of the winery's key areas and then back to the reception area to taste the current release. This translates to tasting one or two of the mountain cabs—or both, if you're lucky. O'Shaughnessy produces only cabernet sauvignon, but from two different regions: Howell Mountain and Mount Veeder. Although the wines command your full attention with their perfect balance, luscious fruit, and regional characteristics, don't feel guilty if between tastes the surroundings seduce your focus away from wine.

Every aspect of the winery's nonproduction area is attractive. In the foyer, well-worn grape harvest baskets hang from the wall, and nearby is a stunning credenza, handcrafted from a single slab of wood. In the tasting area, O'Shaughnessy celebrates her home state, Minnesota, with two imported oversized tables and a credenza made from wood salvaged from the bottom of Lake Superior. As for the wine library, enclosed completely in glass, it will make most collectors green with envy. Expect to be wowed, expect to be wooed, and expect to have the spelling of O'Shaughnessy indelibly etched on your brain.

The Best of the Rest Howell Mountain is a funny region in that the famed mountain is divided between the wine industry and a large Seventh-day Adventist population that firmly prohibits the consumption of alcohol. More's the pity, because there's some great juice made on Howell Mountain. ···· At **Burgess Cellars** (1108 Deer Park Road, St. Helena, www.burgesscellars.com, 800.752.9463, retail sales daily 10am–4pm, tastings by appointment only), Tom Burgess has been crafting cab, chardonnay, and zinfandel for more than thirty years on his hillside property. In the barrel cellar, visitors can try those wines plus a few other varietals. The wines are wonderful, but after one look at the view it will be hard to stay inside for long. ···· Down and around the mountain is **Venge Vineyards** (424 Crystal Springs Road, St. Helena, www.vengevineyards.com, 707.967.1008, by appointment only), a collaborative effort between father and son Nils and Kirk Venge. In this very quiet spot, they've restored a century-old winery, added a large cave, and basically created a respite from the crowded valley floor. You'll wonder why it took master winemaker Nils so long to build a place like this for himself. Linger, and help make up for lost time. ···· **Viader Vineyards** (1120 Deer Park Road, Deer Park, www.viader.com, 707.963.3816, by appointment only) will make fans of petit verdot and tempranillo very happy, because this is where Howell Mountain vintner Delia Viader produces both of these varietals, along with syrah and cabernet sauvignon. The view from Viader's tasting room is the perfect stage for savoring its wines on small, private tours.

The Best Appellation Event You must attend the **Taste of Howell Mountain** (location varies, www.howellmountainwineauction.com, biannual in midsummer). The evening starts with a walk-around tasting in a garden-party setting of nearly all the wines produced on Howell Mountain (more than twenty). By the time you're done, you'll have forged an intimate link between a name on a label and what's in the glass. For example, just one sip of Randy Dunn's wine is all it takes for you to understand the area's reputation for producing wines with great tannic structure and age-ability. You'll also discover the full impact of winemaking style on taste when you sample other vintners' younger wines: they show definite structure but are simultaneously soft, supple, and drinkable. Just wait till these babies grow up.

Silent auction items are placed strategically between wine and food tables so that you can shop and savor at the same time. After each silent auction table has closed, the live auction begins. By then you'll most likely be sated from the lavish spread that includes everything from barbecue (a perfect complement to the tasty **Lamborn** zinfandel) to pizza (great with the luscious **Robert Craig** cabernet sauvignon).

But don't let your wine-happy brain forget that this is a charitable event as well, with proceeds going to the Howell Mountain Education Foundation. Both the silent and live auction lots include alluring packages, many of which are lunches, dinners, tastings, and tours at the mountain's most exclusive wineries that are otherwise off-limits to the public.

Have a hankering to dine in the caves at **O'Shaughnessy**? Hungry for a hillside picnic at **Outpost**? Or maybe you'd rather become your own vintner? In 2003, the Howell Mountain Home Vintner Kit provided the top bidder with one thousand pounds of Howell Mountain cabernet sauvignon grapes—one of the first varietals grown here—plus winemaking equipment, bottling supplies, and a consulting winemaker. All these treats and treasures become easy to bid on once you start tasting the outstanding—and rare—wines of Howell Mountain. Finish the evening by indulging in decadent desserts while watching paddles being raised toward the heavens—all for a good cause.

LOS CARNEROS, NAPA

The windswept hills of Carneros have gained worldwide recognition as the perfect location for growing grapes that thrive in cooler climates: chardonnay, pinot noir, and merlot. Although Carneros was once home to grazing sheep, historical documents indicate that vineyards were planted here as early as 1875. But it wasn't until the late 1960s, when Rene di Rosa planted pinot noir, that the region was viewed as valuable for growing premium-quality grapes. As a result, the Carneros region (which is spread across the southern end of both Napa and Sonoma counties) is populated by a substantial number of wineries.

Artesa Winery

www.artesawinery.com
1345 Henry Road, Napa
707.224.1668
Daily 10am–5pm

Not even the breathtaking views along the winding road carved into high green hills can prepare you for the splendor that is Artesa. This is contemporary winery architecture at its boldest and most original. Modernist in its emphasis on function, classical in its relationship to nature, the building's site and design are required viewing for oenophiles with an equivalent love of architecture.

A high-impact entry—two steep staircases flanked by sculpted water fountains and pools—leads to a building that resembles a twenty-first-century Mayan temple. The building's exterior eco-design barely intrudes on the environment. Planted over with native grasses to resume the appearance of the original hill, it is built into an existing knoll with commanding panoramic views. You would never guess the architects excavated to a depth of four and a half stories.

Inside, Artesa is all cool space, clean wood surfaces, soft music, diffuse light, and fresh Carneros breezes. (There is a large terrace, although the mistral may send you back inside for cover.) Standing in the visitor center—with its art-laden walls, sleek tasting bar, expansive interior courtyard, and stylish minimalist tables and chairs—you can't help feeling cheerful. The main floor also houses the Carneros historical center and artifact museum, well-designed restrooms, and an excellent gift shop selling everything from chocolate-merlot fudge, olives, and crackers to pewter tableware, books, and chic jewelry.

While Artesa produces mostly Carneros pinot noir and chardonnay, estate grown on its 160 planted acres, it also produces wines from other regions, notably Bordeaux blends from Alexander Valley. There is a standard tour that explains the winery's Spanish Catalan connections and its history of specialization in sparkling wines. The tour's one unique aspect is the steady hum of chanting monks—sounds piped into the barrel cellar in homage to the monastery down the road from where this Catalan family-owned winery has its roots in Spain.

Finally, for wine and architecture lovers who also happen to be runners, Artesa is where the annual 5K and 10K Carneros Run begins and ends. Our advice: run *before* you start tasting.

Bouchaine Vineyards

www.bouchaine.com
1075 Buchli Station Road, Napa
707.252.9065 or 800.654.9463
Daily 10:30am–4pm

Nestled in the back roads of Carneros, Bouchaine is a gem of a winery—both a lovely surprise for meandering motorists and a worthy destination on its own. A flowered path beckons you from the road to the tasting area with its views of distant hills, softly undulating vineyards, and the last cow-grazing pasture in the area. Interesting outdoor mobile sculptures—made of wine-barrel hoops—gently twist and bob with every passing breeze. In total, it's a bucolic setting, one made even more welcoming by the cozy tasting room and visitor center.

There you may arrange for a customized tour or linger over a glass of wine on the deck, which offers shelter from the strong local winds. While you're tasting, you may wish to ponder the history of the place: in 1875 these hundred acres were bought by Johnny Garetto, who established Carneros's first post-Prohibition winery. Here he grew and made wine from Italian varietals—and made a name for himself by distilling grappa. If these hundred acres of vineyards could speak, what stories they could tell!

Today, Bouchaine is still doing some experimental growing and distilling. Its primary focus, however, is on the core varietals of the region: pinot noir and chardonnay.

Delectus

www.delectuswinery.com
908 Enterprise Way, Suite C, Napa
707.255.1252
By appointment only

The motto of Delectus is simple: grapes don't need a view. In any case, that's the world according to owner and winemaker Gerhard Reisacher, who believes grapes (read wine) just need a nice cool place and a compatible barrel to hang out in. And that's exactly what they get at the Reisachers' winery.

What makes Delectus different from most is that it's in an industrial park south of the town of Napa. But what really sets the winery apart goes beyond location. It's about the heart and soul of the business: a collaborative effort between husband and wife, parents and children, and friends and customers. With this as their basic ethos, Gerhard and his wife, Linda, have grown their business into a well-respected red-wine-only winery with excellent wines.

Every year Gerhard's parents come over from Austria to work the harvest, and even his young daughter, Julia (a future oenophile and the namesake inspiration for Julia's Cuvée, the winery's high-scoring signature cab), lends a hand in the vineyards and the winery. Friends also have had an impact on the business. When Linda and Gerhard first leased their warehouse, it was just that—a warehouse. But with a hand from friends who painted the floors, entryway, and dining room while Linda's mom painted the cellar—with a color named Wine, of course—it was transformed into a warm and fetching space. Everyone who worked on making the space lively and comfortable literally left their mark: their handprints are on the cellar walls.

You'll get to see all this when you visit Delectus, but not before you've met the family (including Flash, the dog) and been poured a glass of wine.

You're likely to be instantly drawn to the table in the center of the dining room. There, under a large pane of glass, are eight trays filled with dirt and rocks from each of the vineyards used by Delectus. This up-close look at soil types is the best way to learn how dramatically soils can vary from location to location, and even from vineyard block to vineyard block.

Once you've finished studying the soils, Linda or Gerhard will take you to the cellar for a barrel tasting and a brief explanation of what's in your glass. While this experience is similar to one you'd have in other wineries, somehow the Reisachers' personalities and fundamental good natures shine through and make an impact. As you come to realize who they are— hardworking, fun-loving, open, warm, down-to-earth people with old-world values—you'll know you're having an interaction that is impossible to duplicate.

Over a Barrel If you're even vaguely interested in where the wine was before it reached the bottle, you'll love a trip to **Seguin Moreau** (151 Camino Dorado, Napa, www.seguinmoreaunapa.com, 707.252.3408). This is where the ancient art of the cooper continues to be practiced—a tradition that merits as much admiration as respect. After all, winemaking would be a messy business without the invention of the wine barrel—and wine itself would be a rather characterless liquid without the cooper's contribution to rich wood and toasted flavors.

The tour here is self-guided and brief. It starts with a ten-minute educational video that explains the basics of coopersmithing. When it's over, take a minute to inspect the sample logs, staves, tops, and hoops—the raw materials of a barrel. Grab some goggles and earplugs and walk a few steps across the courtyard into the barrel-making area. Here you'll get a fun and surprising wake-up call to all the senses: it's noisy with the sounds of artisans pounding hammers; fragrant with the breakfasty aromas of warm brioche, vanilla, baking bread, and coffee (fragrances intrinsic to the process of custom barrel-toasting); and eye-catching with the sight of the barrel maker's dance—coopers circling a barrel that in turn surrounds a small fire that toasts, shapes, and tames the staves.

Follow the numbered stations through every step of the cooperage process, from assembling the staves through the final sanding, finishing, and barrel refurbishing. By the time you're done, you'll have real insight into how a cooper helps to shape a wine.

Domaine Carneros

www.domainecarneros.com
1240 Duhig Road at Highway 12, Napa
707.257.0101
Daily 10am–6pm

If you're not in love when you enter Domaine Carneros, it's likely you will be by the time you leave. The seduction begins the minute you see the winery's exquisitely groomed vineyards and breathe in its beguiling, gardenia-scented gardens. A grand, stately staircase leads to the manor house, inspired by a Louis XV–style chateau in Champagne, France.

Inside, all is elegant, gracious refinement. You're greeted with genuine warmth and seated either inside the large tasting room or at an outdoor table. Weather permitting, choose a seat on the broad, comfortable terrace, where you can overlook mile upon dreamy mile of natural beauty.

But all this is just the backdrop. The real reason to fall in love at Domaine Carneros is the wine: specifically, some of the world's best ultra-premium sparkling and pinot, made by the renowned Taittinger family. The wines combine and balance the best of French and California traditions, using the classic grapes of France's Burgundy and Champagne regions. But what makes Domaine Carneros wines special is the way they seamlessly blend classic practice with the signature, fruit-intense flavors of the Carneros region.

Wines are poured tableside. With each glass comes a detailed but low-key explanation of your selection; it feels intimate and educational at once. Try a glass—better yet, a flight—of the classic Domaine Carneros Brut, stellar Brut Rosé (sold only on the premises and perfect for Thanksgiving dinner), and La Reve, its premium wine. Or taste the pinots. Either way, you'll be served a complimentary snack made with local artisanal foods. If you're hungry for something more substantial, order a cheese plate, designed especially to pair with sparkling or pinot.

The Best of the Rest The Carneros region is a sprawling area that not only sweeps around the entire top of the bay, but also is divided between two counties, Napa and Sonoma. With plenty of Carneros wineries to visit, you may have to pick and choose, but there are a few that you may not want to miss. ···· **Acacia** (2750 Las Amigas Road, Napa, www.acaciawinery.com, 707.226.9991, Mon–Sat 10am–4pm, Sun 12–4pm, tours and tastings with prior appointment) makes wine from some of the oldest pinot noir vines in the Napa Valley. The tasting room is sparse, but the wines are extremely well made. ···· At **Etude** (1250 Cuttings Wharf Road, Napa, www.etudewines.com, 707.257.5300, by appointment only), the tasting room is still a work in progress, but the hospitality is well polished. Your hosts will shepherd you about the property and give a short tutorial on how the making of pinot noir—their signature varietal wine, made under the guidance of wine-maker Tony Soter—varies from that of other varietals. After a personalized tasting of Etude's pinot, cab, and merlot, your thirst will be slaked and your curiosity sated, and you'll be free to walk around the large, flower-filled courtyard. ···· **Carneros Creek Winery** (1285 Dealy Lane, Napa, www.carneroscreek.com, 707.253.9463, daily 10am–4:30pm) is owned by Francis Mahoney, a winemaking pioneer who is widely credited as the father of Carneros chardonnay and pinot noir. Its *Little House on the Prairie* vibe tips you off that Carneros Creek is less about grandiosity than it is about the grandeur of the wine. ···· **McKenzie Mueller Vineyards and Winery** (2530 Los Amigos Road, Napa, 707.252.1086, by appointment only) gives you a behind-the-scenes glimpse into the workings of a tiny hands-on winery with a high-beam focus on red wines.

The Best Appellation Event The greatest advantage of attending **Holiday in Carneros** (www.carneroswineries.com, 800.909.4532, third weekend in November) is that it, like other events of its ilk, provides entry into wineries that are otherwise inaccessible or require an appointment and some tricky arranging to visit. More than a dozen Napa and Sonoma wineries in the windswept region of Los Carneros open their doors for this event, including **MacRostie**, **Adastra**, and **Truchard**. All the participants pour wines otherwise unavailable for tasting, including older vintages, tiny-production wines, and barrel samples. Small snacks are served, and some places offer tours of caves and vineyards. The best way to attend this week-end event is to split it, concentrating on Napa one day and Sonoma the other. (Or do just one county this year and come back next year for the other.) This allows you to fully explore the entire Los Carneros region, indulge in a leisurely lunch, and have enough time to tour around without feeling like you're on a schedule. One of the nice things about this event is that every year it supports a charity, and has done so since it began in 1986.

MOUNT VEEDER

High above the fog line, Mount Veeder is a sun-loving grape's paradise. Despite a wine history that dates back more than a century, it wasn't until the recent past that the region really gained acclaim for the Bordeaux varietals that prosper there. This was the first place that all five classic Bordeaux varietals were planted in the United States, and their success in the Mount Veeder clime demonstrated the region's full potential. Mount Veeder's vineyards expose grapes to extended sunlight but at cooler temperatures than on the valley floor. This climate, combined with infertile soils and meager water supplies, yields smaller crops of grapes with intense flavors. Today the mountain is home to several grape growers but only a few wineries.

The Hess Collection Winery
www.hesscollection.com
4411 Redwood Road, Napa
707.255.1144
Daily 10am–4pm

In its sublime peacefulness and isolated solitude, the Hess Collection Winery is close in feeling to the Mont La Salle spiritual retreat, just down the road. But here the religions are historic winemaking and contemporary art, and the totems of worship are well-made wines and well-displayed paintings, sculptures, collages, digital art, photography, and film.

From the outside, the building is unassuming but made lovely by delicate gardens, interesting sculptures, and a lap-pool-size lily pond. Inside, a historic stone cellar finds its counterpoint in white walls and a blond-wood floor. Your self-guided tour takes you up three floors. As you roam, your eyes fall on art in its familiar form and art in the form of the winemaking process. The former includes an impressive collection of pieces from well-known names such as Morris Louis, Frank Stella, Robert Motherwell, and Francis Bacon, and lesser-known but powerful artists such as Magdalena Abakanowicz (check out her visceral burlap sculptures on the third floor). The winemaking process is viewed from a distance, framed by large glass windows; in a small theater, a video about winemaking is shown regularly throughout the day. From the top floor, you can glimpse the winery's distant vineyards in the Mount Veeder appellation; the layout of the rows is mimicked by the garden beds just below the window. It's yet another example of nature's art: aesthetic creations that are easy to appreciate and require no explanation.

When you complete your tour, stop in the high-ceilinged tasting room, with its glassed-in gift shop and view of the barrel cellar, and its wood bar with soft underlighting. It's a perfect place to discuss the meaning of the burning typewriter sculpture you just saw—and the qualities of the chardonnay and cab you just sipped.

Lunchtime Remote and rugged, Mount Veeder is populated by wineries, vineyards, and city-shy people wanting to live in near-seclusion. It's not too surprising that you'll have to head to downtown Napa for some food. Try **Pearl** (1339 Pearl Street, Napa, 707.224.9161), where the locals fill the place noon and night, dining on California fusion cuisine.

Mayacamas Vineyards
www.mayacamas.com
1155 Lokoya Road, Napa
707.224.4030
Mon–Fri by appointment only

Perched on its own little ridge on the edge of a dormant volcano near the top of Mount Veeder, Mayacamas Vineyards is a place to remember. The ride to this super-remote winery is hair-raising: way up a tough-to-drive road, past red, red soil and giant old vines. When you finally get your shaking knees out of your car, the sound of birds madly chirping in the nearby sky and the astonishing display of earth below—meadows, mountains, flowers, grasses, you name it—make you feel a little insignificant by comparison. If you feel like you've somehow dropped out of real life and been transported into a movie backdrop, it's only because you have: this is where one of the scenes from the film A Walk in the Clouds was filmed.

The old stone winery, dug into the hillside in 1889, today produces about five thousand cases each year. Primarily devoted to cab and chard, Mayacamas also makes smaller quantities of sauvignon blanc, merlot, and pinot. All wines are made from grapes grown on the property from vines that characteristically produce low-yield, high-flavor fruit. A short tour traces the winemaking process via a walk through what is clearly one of Napa's most bucolic wineries, the most interesting part of which is the old-fashioned trap-door fermentation tanks. A tasting follows. Sip slowly, savoring the fine wine—and the knowledge that you're enjoying these noble grapes in one of the most extravagantly beautiful corners of the planet.

The Best Appellation Event Almost all appellations have formed consortiums for marketing their wines and wineries, and, to this end, most host regular tasting events. **The Mount Veeder Appellation Council Tasting** (www.mountveederwines.com, autumn) is a perfect showcase for the wines grown on Mount Veeder, most of which are custom-crushed at Napa and Sonoma Valley wineries. Almost always held somewhere on the hill, it is one of the best-kept secrets of the Napa Valley.

The wineries that have chosen this western mountain along the Mayacamas range as their home include **Random Ridge**, **Jade Mountain**, **Godspeed**, **Mayacamas Vineyards**, **Mount Veeder Winery**, **Rubissow-Sargent**, **Lokoya**, and **Vinoce**. With the exception of a few wineries, most of those with a Mount Veeder address do not have a facility for receiving visitors, so this is a great opportunity to taste their wines. In fact, the set-up is ideal for doing side-by-side tastings of the grapes harvested from the rugged mountain vineyards, since most of what you'll taste are wines made with 100 percent estate-grown fruit.

Due to the event's Indian summer timing, be prepared for warm temperatures. Wear cool clothing and drink lots of water, and you'll be in fine shape to leisurely sip the mountain beauties.

NAPA VALLEY

The Napa Valley is the largest appellation in Napa County, encompassing nearly the entire county. It's more than the strip of land that connects San Francisco Bay to Mount St. Helena; it also includes both mountain ranges that form the main valley, and a handful of smaller valleys that are created by the plethora of low mountains, hills, and knolls.

More than thirty types of soil have been identified in the Napa Valley appellation, and the climate can vary dramatically between the southern and northern ends, the valley floor and the mountaintops. The diverse growing conditions and massive expanse of the Napa Valley yield a broad range of grape varietals.

Calistoga

Barlow Vineyards

www.barlowvineyards.com
4411 Silverado Trail, Calistoga
707.942.8742
By appointment only

When soft-spoken Warren Smith, owner of Barlow Vineyards, first tells you that his tastings usually last two to two and a half hours, you think he must be joking. But within minutes you realize you could easily spend two and a half days chatting with him about everything from how each row is planted in his fifty-acre vineyard to his background (he was a Southern California pharmacologist who visited Napa Valley for the first time with his wife, Jeanne, two years after they got married more than half a century ago).

When the Smiths decided to buy a vineyard in Napa Valley, they partnered up with their son Barr and his wife, Ann. Their joint intention was to grow and sell grapes, which they did for the first few years. Then, on a whim, they produced twenty-five cases of cabernet sauvignon for their own personal consumption. It was so good, the winemaker suggested that they sell it instead. They did—and, as the saying goes, the rest is history. Today the Smiths annually produce almost two thousand cases of sensational single-vineyard cabernet, merlot, zinfandel, and a red Bordeaux blend called Barrouge.

A visit with the Smiths really is . . . a visit. They truly welcome you into their lovely home, with its expansive main room, soaring ceilings, and windows, windows, windows that suffuse the space with light and open to verdant vineyards. The heart of the room is a large dining room table where the important business of tasting the Barlow wines occurs. The wines are wonderful. And the Smiths, well, they're wonderful, too. It's a privilege to be a guest in their home—and a delight to sample their wares.

Chateau Montelena Winery
www.montelena.com
1429 Tubbs Lane, Calistoga
707.942.5105
Daily 9:30am–4pm, tours by appointment only

Chateau Montelena achieved acclaim in 1976 when its wines were entered into a blind tasting in France, judged by nine Gallic high priests of the grape. Imagine their *horreur* when the first prize for whites went to a '73 Chateau Montelena from Calistoga, California!

The winery's award-winning chardonnays, as well as its red wines and sold-only-at-the-winery riesling, are as prized today as they were back then. But Chateau Montelena's fabulous wine is not the only thing to make a Frenchman blush: the winery itself is a European-style object of beauty. The tasting room, where visitors can taste its chard, cab, and johannisberg riesling, is in a cool, damp, three-walled structure, the fourth side being the inside of a mountain. And the façade of the chateau is thoroughly authentic: a castle with spires, regal dimensions, and a mood of serene gravitas.

As for the grounds—254 acres at the base of Mount St. Helena—they're home to Jade Lake, a natural sanctuary filled with fish and wildlife, bordered by dramatic weeping willows, sequoias, and other native plantings. An Asian bridge and pagoda complete the romantic picture. It's all perfectly peaceful—but for the rogue swan who patrols the lake with hostile intensity, all in the name of protecting his girlfriend. If the swan approaches dry land, run like hell!

Clos Pegase
www.clospegase.com
1060 Dunaweal Lane, Calistoga
707.942.4981
Daily 10:30am–5pm

The upside-down terra-cotta exclamation point that heralds the entrance to Clos Pegase offers fair warning that you're about to enter someplace unrivaled. This Michael Graves–designed "temple to wine and art" (the result of an architectural competition cosponsored by the San Francisco Museum of Modern Art) is a unique yellow-, gray-, and salmon-hued structure. With its turrets, spires, and stripes, it can remind you simultaneously of a smokehouse and a playhouse.

Chateau Montelena's castle-like winery.

If the sculptures that dot the property make Clos Pegase seem as much an
art museum as a winery, that's because it is both in equal parts. Walk
toward the tasting room through a tiled outdoor foyer and you'll be transported from the whimsical to the classical. Fifty-two flat-topped cypress
trees (they look cheerfully beheaded and apparently represent each week
of the year) line a path to a formal center garden; at the end of the walkway is an extraordinary three-hundred-year-old oak tree. Isolated from
other trees, it's showcased to take on the character, hauteur, and interest
of the sculptures that surround it—a bow to nature's intrinsic artistry.

A tree-size sculpture of a thumb is at the vineyard entrance—perhaps a
nod to the hand that makes the wine, or maybe just one more visual
exploration of the relationship between nature and art. A priceless
Bacchus fountain of Carrara marble, set into a Renaissance-style niche
and originally from the royal palace in Turin, is a mere stone's throw away
from plebian café tables, which are practically set into the vines. It's all a
perfect mix of high and low culture, serious beauty and bacchanalian
irreverence.

This nervy blend is intensified in the tasting room, where T-shirts and masks mingle with world-class art of many centuries and wonderful wines of many vintages. Clos Pegase is a wine-and-art lover's destination that is not to be missed.

Dutch Henry Winery

www.dutchhenry.com
4310 Silverado Trail, Calistoga
888.224.5879
Daily 10am–4:30pm with prior appointment

Laid-back, casual, and compact, Dutch Henry Winery is also music-loving, dog-friendly, blue-collar—and proud of it. This is the real thing: an actual working winery that's the polar opposite of the Disneylandish, theme-park image some other wineries have cultivated.

Dutch Henry produces about forty-five hundred cases of wine made from Bordeaux-varietal grapes. The wines are available primarily through the winery, which is housed in a simple concrete structure flanked by the Silverado Trail on one side and a wild turkey–filled forest on the other. A bocce court is set between vines and olive trees—the same ones that produce the fruit for the luscious house-made olive oil that's also for sale. After tasting the wines and the olive oil, it becomes immediately clear why the place is such a draw.

Frank Family Vineyards

1091 Larkmead Lane, Calistoga
800.574.9463
Daily 10am–5pm

The old Larkmead Winery is a stone building from 1906—beautiful yet unassuming, quietly doing its job. But now it's become an icon of a time gone by, purchased by Frank Family Vineyards and preserved as a treasure by the National Registry of Historic Places. The old stones probably have great stories to tell. Behind the original winery is a rough-and-tumble, funky building that looks like a cross between a warehouse and a shoe-box; this is home to the Frank Family tasting room.

Emanating from an entirely different era, the tasting room nonetheless conveys an appreciation for nostalgia. This is clear when you are immediately offered a flight of sparkling wines produced solely to honor Hans

Kornell, the late Napa Valley vintner who made his sparkling wines at the same location. Although the gesture is generous, pass up the sparkling and head to the back room for a taste of the still wines. These are what Frank Family makes best, and what you'll want to drink.

Storybook Mountain Vineyards

www.storybookwines.com
3835 Highway 128, Calistoga
707.942.5310
By appointment only

Iron gates silently, mysteriously glide open to welcome you to Storybook Mountain Vineyards, setting the tone for an unforgettable wine country experience. This is a place of extreme natural beauty, set high above Calistoga. You'll start your tour by trekking up one of the steep hills of the extraordinary ninety-acre property, forty-five acres of which are planted. When you reach the top, you'll find yourself lost in a world of zinfandel vines.

Because the vineyard's hillsides are so steep, tractors are out of the question. So all grapes are hand-picked and hand-hauled—backbreaking work that results in admirably high quality control. In fact, this vineyard's growing conditions are so precious that the owners indulge any needs the land seems to have.

The property was farmed originally in 1883 by the Brothers Grimm of Germany; while unrelated to the fairy-tale brothers of the same name, their shared sense of magic and grand imagination permeates the land. Today Storybook is a small, top-notch boutique winery producing seven thousand cases a year.

A century ago it took four years to hand-carve Storybook Mountain's three-hundred-foot caves out of volcanic rock, but the result is a moody, stirring environment, one well suited to house its fine wines. Among the highlights of the caves is a handsome, ornately carved barrel (shipped from Germany in one piece) that depicts the history of the winery in wood-relief images. Its centerpiece celebrates Aesop's fable of the fox and grapes, an apt image with which to end your tour.

> **Lunchtime** Calistoga's wineries are fairly spread out, but no matter where you are, the center of town is only a few minutes away. Have your midday meal at **Buster's Barbecue & Bakery** (1207 Foothill Boulevard, Calistoga, 707.942.5605). Even barbecue snobs agree it's as good as any you'll get in Texas.

Twomey Cellars

www.twomeycellars.com
1183 Dunaweal Lane, Calistoga
800.505.4850
Mon–Sat 9am–4pm

Merlot lovers, your search has ended with the opening of Twomey Cellars, a Napa Valley producer devoted exclusively to making outstanding merlot. The journey to the bottle begins at the winery's Soda Canyon Ranch vineyard, where imported merlot clones from Bordeaux's Pomerol region grow on 148 acres of deep volcanic soil. Owner Ray Duncan (also co-owner of *Silver Oak Cellars*) was so inspired by this vineyard's extraordinarily complex fruit that he decided it called for a winery of its own.

There's something poetic about this enterprise, in that it shows how slow, careful winemaking can eloquently express the essence of a given parcel of earth. The tasting-room experience here is fittingly spare and modern—an appropriate counterpart to the single-minded clarity of the winemaking. With Twomey, Ray Duncan and his sons have created something truly unique.

Vincent Arroyo

www.vincentarroyowinery.com
2361 Greenwood Avenue, Calistoga
707.942.6995
Daily 10am–4:30pm with prior appointment

You won't find Vincent Arroyo wine at your favorite restaurant. And forget about your local wineshop. All eight thousand cases are sold only at the winery, and many are sold as futures.

Housed in a simple gray barn, Vincent Arroyo winery is about as casual as it gets. So casually allow them to pour a wide selection of their wines for you to taste, including their signature petite sirah. Let them share their estate olive oil. And by all means, sit back and let them treat you to their dog show starring JJ, an affectionate black Lab.

Although JJ is just one of several dogs hanging around the winery, he'll likely be the one to follow you into the barn–cum–barrel cellar. At the cue of your host, JJ will climb to the top of the barrels and stand there until you toss a tennis ball for him to catch. While this may not seem like such a big deal, in person it's an impressive feat. You'll be invited to reward JJ's hard work with a biscuit from the giant box that shares shelf space with winemaking equipment. *Your* hard work will be rewarded by the wine you buy.

Not a bad life for a dog, spending his day in the cellar on top of a bunch of wine barrels. And not a bad day for you, playing catch with a good, good boy while sipping good, good wines.

JJ the dog hard at work.

Buehler's ghost winery.

Conn Valley

Buehler Vineyards
www.buehlervineyards.com
820 Greenfield Road, St. Helena
707.963.2155
By appointment only

It's a fabulous ride to Buehler Vineyards, up six winding miles of narrow mountain roads amid captivating scenery that includes grazing horses, old barns, Lake Hennessey, and amazing views.

But the wild ride really begins once you get out of your car and into John Buehler's SUV. This is one tour you definitely want to be on. John takes you around his three hundred acres of hillside vineyards (fifty-five of which are planted), all the while regaling you with stories of his winery (his dad started it in 1972 as a tax shelter for himself and as a career for his son); his family (four kids, all of whom want to continue the family business); his head-trained, dry-farmed vineyards; his vines; and his wines. In between, he'll chat about winemaking history; the rattlesnakes, ospreys, and mountain lions that inhabit his land; hypoallergenic dogs; photography; New York City hotels; and anything else that strikes his or your fancy. John is the urbane, intelligent man's vintner, and his lively patter makes for a totally satisfying visit.

After the car tour, John will take you through the path of the wine, from the vines to the crusher and so on, all the way to the tanks and presses. You'll finish in the exquisite tasting room, located in a French-style castle that's depicted on the bottle labels. Buehler Vineyards is kind of a stealth winery—one that's under the radar but has a large and devoted following.

Last Chance Wineries In addition to seeing working wineries, great views, and pretty scenery along the way, a trip to **Buehler** (see facing page) or **Nichelini** (2950 Sage Canyon Road, St. Helena, www.nicheliniwinery.com, 707.963.0717, Sat–Sun 10am–5pm) offers a little something extra. At the former, you'll find an abandoned stone building that owner John Buehler calls the "second-to-last chance winery," and at Nichelini, you'll find—yep, you guessed it—the **last** last chance winery, still in operation today. Both are on what was once the stage road that was used to travel from Napa Valley over to Lake County and beyond. As their descriptions suggest, these were the last wineries on the road out of the Napa Valley to offer travelers a chance to buy wine. While today neither winery is actually at the end of the road, their remote locations certainly make it feel like they are. Lucky for us wine buffs, it no longer takes all day to reach these historic sites—and you don't have to travel the rocky road by buggy.

Lunchtime The wineries in Conn Valley are so far off the Silverado Trail that the drive alone will make you hungry. All the better for enjoying lunch afterward on the deck at the **Auberge du Soleil** (180 Rutherford Hill Road, Rutherford, 707.963.1211), Napa's only restaurant with a view of the Valley.

Neyers Vineyards

www.neyersvineyards.com
2153 Sage Canyon Road, Rutherford
707.963.8840
Mon–Fri by appointment only

Visiting Neyers Vineyards is all about keeping it real. It's a small set-up, and while it's certainly attractive enough—with a flagstone terrace and pretty cave—there's nothing fancy or awesome about it. But Neyers provides something most wineries don't: absolutely personalized attention. Look inside the clean, efficient winery to see its open-top fermenters, with their inventive, customized pneumatic punch-down device. Learn about Bruce Neyers's affiliation with Kermit Lynch Imports (he is its national sales director) and about his and his wife, Barbara's, various winemaking decisions, like air-drying oak barrels a year before use (to mellow them), eschewing sulphur, favoring use of indigenous yeast, and leaving the wines unfiltered. When it comes time to taste, sit in a spare office, on functional office furniture, to taste Neyers's workhorse chardonnay and signature syrah, along with others. Just as important, you will have the precious opportunity to talk to a real expert, at length and in depth, about what's in your glass and what's in the winemaker's imagination.

The Best of the Rest Although Conn Valley is not a designated appellation, it is a distinct area within Napa Valley. Shaped like a bowl with wide, sloping sides and Lake Hennessey at the bottom, it encompasses the southern side of Howell Mountain and the northern side of Pritchard Hill. Traversing Conn Valley requires patience and good driving skills since there are essentially no straight roads in sight. Instead, wind your way around the narrow country roads. ···· Whichever road you take, only one leads to **Amizetta** (1099 Greenfield Road, St. Helena, www.amizetta.com, 707.963.1460, by appointment only). Clinging to the edge of Howell Mountain, Amizetta offers a spectacular Conn Valley overview. Owners Spencer and Amizetta Clark are former Texans whose southern roots show in their distinctive hospitality. They'll pour you a glass, walk you through the pint-size winery where Bob Egelhoff makes their stuff, and show you the cave where the wines are stored. The Clarks love talking about the cabs they make, the twenty-five-year-old and ten-year-old vines planted in their hillside vineyard, and the adventures of raising a family and living at a winery up on the mountain. ···· On your way back to town, stop in at **Seavey Vineyard** (1310 Conn Valley Road, St. Helena, www.seaveyvineyard.com, 707.963.8339, by appointment only). Seavey is where the Ponderosa meets Napa Valley. It's a ranch environment so convincing, it might make you hungry for campfire beans. Repress this urge, and instead slake your thirst for wonderful wines. Consulting winemaker Phillipe Melka has his fingerprints all over them—in other words, they're handily made.

Napa, Northeast

Darioush Winery

www.darioush.com
4240 Silverado Trail, Napa
707.257.2345
Daily 10:30am–5pm

Darioush Winery brings a taste of Persia to Napa Valley. Owner Darioush Khaledi, an Iranian-born wine lover, combined a piece of his ancestry with the best of California to create a winery that makes superb wines. It is designed to reflect the architecture of Iran's Persepolis (the ancient Persian city built during the dynasty of Achaemenids, rulers of the world's first empire, which flourished between 550 BC and 330 BC). Darioush has the quality of a mirage on the Napa landscape. Its resplendent golden stone, tall decorative columns, and dramatic angles—all set upon one of the Valley's most arid spots—evoke the image of a castle rising from the desert.

Inside, you can quench your thirst with tastes of the notable cab, chard, merlot, viognier, and shiraz—a grape believed to have been first cultivated in the Shiraz region of Persia. The tasting room also offers a peek into other cultural aspects of Persia, with its inventory of Persian cookbooks and a display of Persian art.

Del Dotto Vineyards

www.deldottovineyards.com
1055 Atlas Peak Road, Napa
707.256.3332
Daily 11am–5pm, Fri–Sun barrel tastings by appointment only

What you see on the outside of Del Dotto Vineyards—a solemn, vine-covered stone building erected in 1885—has pretty much nothing to do with what you see on the inside. There, in the large retail room, tasting room, and entrance to the caves, you'll find a peculiar, eclectic assortment of antiques and memorabilia—everything from Venetian masks to oversized abstract sculptures to huge ceramic vases.

Once you get into the century-old hand-dug caves, however, the atmosphere changes radically. Del Dotto offers barrel samples from eight types
of domestic and imported oak barrels. The winery's unusual candlelit cave
tastings are organized around tasting the differences in its connoisseur
series: eight cabs, each aged in a different type of oak. The winery sells
the series (along with the other varietals it produces: merlot, sangiovese,
and cabernet franc), allowing you to conduct your own blind "barrel tasting"
at home.

Farella-Park Vineyards
2222 North Third Avenue, Napa
707.254.9489
By appointment only

Farella-Park feels wild; you'd never believe it's only four miles from
downtown Napa. Set into a quiet, hidden, dreamlike corner of the Valley,
its architecture, décor, and ambience all reflect its owner's passion and
respect for nature. Low stone walls scattered here and there around the
fifty-six acres seem to have been part of the landscape for hundreds of
years (actually, they, unlike the rattlesnakes that inhabit the woodsy terrain, haven't lived here long—Farella-Park was built in 1985). Small windows
and wrought-iron decorations are set jewel-like into the winery's hand-
plastered walls. Adding a touch of modern intelligence to it all is a tall,
organic, three-armed abstract metal sculpture that mirrors the sway of a
nearby black oak and resembles nothing less than a mythical marriage
among a sea anemone, armadillo, and elephant trunk.

In fact, according to winemaker Tom Farella, the sculpture was commissioned to represent the "Trois Amis," meaning three friends; this refers to
the wine-producing cooperative venture among owner Frank Farella, a
local attorney who is also Tom's father; hotelier George Rafael; and Tom
and Mary Elke of Elke Vineyards. For Rafael, Tom custom-crushes cabernet;
for the Elkes, he makes pinot. For Farella-Park itself, he devotes most of its
mere thousand cases to small, individual lots of wine from the thirty-acre
estate vineyard: chard, cab, merlot, pinot, and sauvignon blanc.

The majority of Farella-Park's grapes are sold to elite Napa Valley wineries,
such as Far Niente, and are greatly respected and appreciated by fellow
winemakers. A visit here is in some sense a quintessential Napa experi-

ence: personal attention from a passionate hands-on winemaker whose goal it is to demystify wine. The small, well-organized barrel room is lovely, especially since you walk right into it instead of into a T-shirt retail space. In fact, nothing here is retail-oriented—tastings often take a European approach, showing and sharing what's in the barrel, not in the bottle. But if bottles are what you're after, an intimate, unfussy reception room keeps both wine taster and winemaker on the same side of the bar—exactly as it should be.

Hagafen Cellars

www.hagafen.com
4160 Silverado Trail, Napa
707.252.0781 or 888.HAGAFEN
Retail sales Sun–Fri 11am–4pm, tours and tastings by appointment only

Set back far enough from the Silverado Trail to make it feel like a heart-land farm, Hagafen Cellars marries a homey, no-nonsense sensibility with an artistic spirit. The winery's corrugated-steel structure sits side by side with an unusual mix of materials, textures, and plantings. The overall effect is one of warmth and originality—perfect for a small family-owned and -operated business.

Owner Ernie Weir, who works alongside his Israeli-born wife, Irit, personally tends the tasting-room bar. Humorous and intelligent, he happily converses about anything from winemaking to international affairs. His interest in the latter may be partly due to his peripheral contribution to the Arab-Israeli peacemaking effort: on the occasion of the Palestinian Interim Agreement, Hagafen 1991 Reserve Chardonnay was served. In 2003, Hagafen wines were honored once again by President and Mrs. Bush, who served the winery's pinot at a celebration honoring the opening of an Anne Frank exhibition.

In Hebrew, *hagafen* means "the grapevine"—it's a word familiar to many Jews who chant a ritual prayer before drinking wine. So it's no surprise that Hagafen wines are kosher. But what may be news to many people who still think that kosher wines have the sweet, cloying flavors they remem-ber from their youth is that Hagafen wines are sophisticated, classic, and correct. What's important is not that they're kosher—it's that they're wines you want to drink.

> **Lunchtime** The northeast part of Napa is dominated by rolling hills, vine-yards, and private homes. Unless you have a friend living in the area, the best place to grab lunch is the **Soda Canyon Store** (4006 Silverado Trail, Napa, 707.252.0285), where the deli serves up sandwiches and some hot specials every day.

Jarvis Winery

www.jarviswines.com
2970 Monticello Road, Napa
800.255.5280 ext. 150
By appointment only

The entrance to Jarvis Winery—two oversized gold doors set into a mountain—is one part *Arabian Nights* and one part pure Disney. The interior is just as fantastical, and a tour through the Jarvis winery and cave is as entertaining and fascinating as the man behind it.

William Jarvis was a pioneer in the fiber-optics business. His love for this technology was soon matched by a love of winemaking, and these twin passions come together . . . in the bathroom of the Jarvis Winery! As part of the tour, guests are led into the ten-stall ladies' room, which features a fiber-optic light show on the ceiling. It's funny and peculiar.

William and his wife, Leticia, are also collectors, so the tour includes a viewing of their collection of quartz, displayed in one of the winery's ballrooms. By this time you don't quite know what to expect next, but what comes is something rather traditional: after you explore the entire cave, you're offered a sit-down wine tasting, which showcases Jarvis's estate-grown chardonnay and cabernet sauvignon, crafted by Dimitri Tchelistcheff, son of the legendary André Tchelistcheff.

Jarvis is one of the Valley's most unusual wineries. Some people think it's too much; others can't get enough. Whichever camp you fall into, you'll have to agree it's like no other place you know. We give it points for sheer flamboyance.

Pritchard Hill

Chappellet
www.chappellet.com
1581 Sage Canyon Road, St. Helena
800.4.WINERY
By appointment only

After a phenomenal ride past miles of Spanish moss, grass so soft it looks smudged, vines laid out like mysterious crop circles, oaks, madrones, and moss-painted stone walls, you reach Chappellet. You know you're there when you see what looks like a motel on one side of the road and a secret army bunker on the other. A fixture on Pritchard Hill since 1969, this "bunker" is in fact the winery—which is built into the side of the mountain and shaped like a tetrahedron (which, if you've forgotten your geometry, is a four-sided three-dimensional figure. An abstract bird's-eye view of it is on every label, just in case you need a visual aid).

Your tour at Chappellet starts with a tasting. It's held at a tiny bar beside the barrels in the winery proper. Even if the winery at first seems surprisingly small inside, you'll soon see that the wines pack a wallop. Wine in hand, you'll follow your guide for an outdoor walking tour. You'll head straight into the vines, with their mountain fruit known for its low ratio of juice to skins, dark color, and luscious flavor. You'll learn about exactly what's planted where on the hundred grape-farmed acres; about the history of the forty-year-old vines overlooking Lake Hennessey; about farming practices such as grafting and pruning; about the ins and outs of the crush and other winery areas; and about anything else viticultural you'd like to know, since the winery prides itself on personalized tours.

After time spent touring the vineyard, you begin to realize that each vintner is as unique as each winery, and the thumbprint of a vintner is his or her vineyards: their layout, their rootstocks, their clones, and all the big and small decisions that make them what they are. Out of Chappellet's extraordinary old and new vines come terrific juices. The winery's calling card is its consistently fabulous cabernet: lots and lots of bright fruit wrapped around great internal structure.

The winery encourages visitors to reserve a picnic table to use before or after tours, and you should definitely do it, because it's magical here. The dips of the mountains seem to embrace the clouds; the rocky slopes appear alternately gentle and forbidding; the silence is profound; and it feels like the center of the universe. All you can hear is the birds, the wind, and your own intake of breath. This place is what wine country is all about.

Lunchtime Pritchard Hill is halfway to nowhere. So when you get hungry, turn around and follow Highway 128 west across the Silverado Trail. Just before Highway 29 on the left side of the road, you'll see the sign for **La Luna Market Taqueria** (1153 Rutherford Road [Highway 128], Rutherford, 707.967.3497), an unprepossessing Mexican grocery and deli. Pick up a freshly made burrito or taco. Hang a U-ey, and dine beneath a shade tree beside miles of vines.

The Best of the Rest

Two main roads travel the length of the Napa Valley: Highway 29 and the Silverado Trail. The latter was originally developed as an alternative route for times when the valley floor flooded. Today it's the road less traveled, so it's the less crowded and more scenic of the two. The Trail's thirty-mile-plus path traverses several of the Valley's subappellations, and although the entire length can be driven in under an hour, you could spend days visiting all the wineries that call the Silverado Trail home. As always, we recommend concentrating on one appellation in a single day. Here, from south to north, are a handful of wineries at which it's worthwhile to stop. ···· **Luna Vineyards** (2921 Silverado Trail, Napa, www.lunavineyards.com, 707.255.5862, daily 10am–5pm) specializes in Italian varietals, including a splendid tocai friulano, pinot grigio, and sangiovese, and offers two flights of wine for tasting. Be sure to walk up to the top of the tower for a view of the vineyards. ···· Up the road at **Silverado Vineyards** (6121 Silverado Trail, Napa, www.silveradovineyards.com, 707.257.1770, daily 10:30am–5pm), you'll feel like you're in a tree house when you look out the tasting-room windows. Even if you don't have time to stop for a sip of wine on the terrace, be sure to pick up a bottle of the outstanding olive oil, produced from a stunning, decades-old *oliveto* on Soda Canyon Road. ···· **Miner Family Winery** (7850 Silverado Trail, Oakville, www.minerwines.com, 707.944.9500, daily 11am–5pm) produces some fantastic cabs, served in a tasting room adjoining a windowed hallway with a bird's-eye view down into the cellars. ···· One of Napa Valley's first vintners to produce a pinot noir from the Carneros district was **ZD Wines** (8383 Silverado Trail, Rutherford, www.zdwines.com, 707.963.5188, daily 10am–4:30pm). While only a few bottles of those early vintages may still be in existence, ZD does offer library wine tastings by prior arrangement, as well as tastings of its current releases on a daily basis. ···· Ignore the faux-castle appearance of **Chateau Boswell** (3468 Silverado Trail, St. Helena, www.chateauboswellwinery.com, 707.963.5472, Sat–Sun with prior appointment). What's inside is what's important, and that's the really good wine, crafted in tiny amounts by Drew Neiman; it is available for tasting in the antique-filled, closet-sized tasting room. Drew originally came to Napa Valley to work for John Kongsgaard during harvest and never went back to Ohio. Now he produces Chateau Boswell's wine and his own eponymous label. ···· From the outside, the **Cuvaison** (4550 Silverado Trail, Calistoga, www.cuvaison.com, 800.253.WINE, daily 10am–5pm) tasting room looks like a Spanish cottage. Inside it's homey and small, with a copper bar offering tastings of its Napa Valley cab, zin, and merlot, in addition to the chard and pinot made from its Carneros vineyards. At the northernmost end of the Trail, you'll find **Zahtila Vineyards** (2250 Lake County Highway, Calistoga, www.zahtilavineyards.com, 707.942.9251, daily 10am–5pm). In summer, the short walk from car to tasting room is a rose lover's paradise: a terraced yard is blooming with dozens of roses in a rainbow of colors. The minuscule tasting room looks as though it might have been a former toolshed, but it'll feel a whole lot bigger once you start talking to the amiable staff, which often includes owner Laura Zahtila. They produce—and you can taste—three zinfandels and two cabs, in amounts nearly as small as the tasting-room footage.

OAK KNOLL

Napa Valley's newest appellation, Oak Knoll, is primarily a large plain between the towns of Napa and Yountville. The maritime influences from the nearby Bay keep the region cool in the mornings and evenings, while the afternoon sun provides enough warmth for grapes to slowly ripen. These two predominant conditions permit a variety of grapes, such as chardonnay and cabernet, to thrive here.

Trefethen

www.trefethen.com
1160 Oak Knoll Avenue, Napa
707.255.7700 or 800.556.4847
Daily 10am–4:30pm

A corridor of impressionistic sycamores lines the one-mile driveway leading to Trefethen. Known as one of the "Big Four"—one of only four renowned buildings designed by Scottish sea captain Hamden McIntyre, which include Greystone (the Culinary Institute of America) and the wineries *Far Niente* and *Niebaum-Coppola*—Trefethen dates back to 1886. It was originally called Eschol (the Hebrew word for "valley of grapes") and now remains the only three-story wooden gravity-flow winery in Napa.

Today the building is not only restored to its former beauty inside and out (it was recognized in 1988 by the Department of the Interior and placed on the National Registry of Historic Places), but it's surpassed even its own high bar for unique, artful design. In addition to the pretty tasting room and gift shop (with glass doors that let you peer into the cellar), a second, clubby library room in the back is breathtaking. Masculine and refined, with wood-lined walls, comfortable couches and leather chairs, a big farmer's table with seating for twelve, and a concrete floor made remarkable by wine-stain glaze and trompe l'oeil hardwood planks, it lets you easily imagine a life lived by only the lucky few. With its natural materials, careful appointments, and rigorous attention to detail, the winery itself reflects the chards and cabs that carry its name.

Lunchtime Oak Knoll is on the northern edge of the town of Napa. Your best lunch choice is **Bistro Don Giovanni** (4110 St. Helena Highway, Napa, 707.224.3300), where you'll get great food and the chance to rub elbows with wine industry bigwigs.

The Best of the Rest An appellation that is not on most visitors' radar, Oak Knoll is a region that is easy to pass through. But if you want to explore it fully, drive down Big Ranch Road. ⋯⋯ There you can stop in at **Andretti Winery** (4162 Big Ranch Road, Napa, www.andrettiwinery.com, 888.460.8463, daily 10am–5pm) for a brief retreat at a quiet, shady spot. And yes, Andretti is named for racecar champion Mario Andretti, who teamed up with winemaker Robert Pepi to create a winery that is pleasing in every way. With its ceramic-tiled floor, ocher stucco walls, low arches, and traditional wood-and-iron doors, it looks like it was plucked from the hills of Tuscany and gently placed down in the back roads of Napa. Inside the tasting room, racing lovers will find things of interest—books and other memorabilia from Mario's racing days. ···· **Laird Family Estate** (5055 Solano Avenue, Napa, www.lairdfamilyestate.com, 877.297.4902, daily 10am–5pm) looks like a Howard Johnson's that somehow grew straight out of the vineyards. While it's somewhat visually incongruous, its wines are perfectly consistent with Napa's best. Crafted by esteemed winemaker Paul Hobbs, Laird wines are worth seeking out.

Sleep among the Vines Secluded, tranquil, and luxurious, **Oak Knoll Inn** (2200 East Oak Knoll Avenue, Napa, 707.255.2200) is surrounded by six hundred acres of chardonnay vineyards, for which Stags Leap Mountain provides a stunning backdrop. A hot tub, swimming pool, gourmet breakfasts, and notably large rooms round out the amenities. But the biggest treat here is the intimate daily afternoon wine and cheese tastings with visiting winemakers, which promote learning from the very people who literally put the wine in wine country. The inn staff also will be glad to arrange winery tours, freeing up your time for more important things, like napping.

Trefethen's smudge pots stand at the ready to fight frost.

OAKVILLE

Oakville is not too big, not too small, not too hot, not too cool; and it has just the right soils. Measuring just under seven thousand acres, the region stretches from the slopes of the Vaca range to the Mayacamas. Although Oakville is in the middle of the Valley, the Bay's maritime influences cool down the grapes on even the hottest days. The soil throughout the region drains well, which stresses the vines just enough to produce grapes with full, complex flavors and sturdy tannins.

The Oakville region of Napa Valley is considered the premier appellation in California for growing cabernet sauvignon grapes. This reputation is due in large part to the works of legendary figures such as H. W. Crabb (the area's first vintner), John Bensen (the original owner of *Far Niente*), Robert Mondavi, and Joe Heitz, who have transformed the natural attributes of the area into exemplary wines.

Cardinale
www.cardinale.com
7600 St. Helena Highway, Oakville
707.948.2643
Mon–Fri 10am–4pm with prior appointment

> Atop a knoll east of Highway 29, Cardinale offers regal million-dollar views of nearly the entire Oakville appellation. Given that the winery belongs to Jess Jackson (the owner of the *Kendall-Jackson* empire), its king-of-the-mountain location might be expected. What isn't expected is the pure loveliness of the old stone building, the welcoming mood of the pergola-covered patio, and the simple, dignified furnishings of the tasting room.
>
> Three of Jackson's high-end cabs are offered: Cardinale, of course; Atalon; and Lokoya. Lokoya, produced from Mount Veeder fruit, was originally intended to be the lower-cost cousin of Cardinale, but when it was released, it received such high scores that the price shot up to more than one hundred dollars a bottle! Atalon is now, and will remain, the line-up's (relatively) economical alternative cabernet.
>
> Whichever you taste or purchase, you're going to leave happier than when you arrived. All the wines are magnificent, and all are served in Riedel glassware—appropriately demonstrating Cardinale's commitment to both the wine and your experience in drinking it.

Diamond Oaks

www.diamond-oaks.com
1595 Oakville Grade, Oakville
707.948.3000
Daily 10am–5pm

The Maniar family's vineyard on Diamond Mountain in Calistoga is known for its signature oak trees. So it's fitting that they bought the property where Diamond Oaks resides, given that its most remarkable attribute is the oak-dense picnic area just across from the elegant tasting room.

In fact, this is one of the prettiest places in Napa to revel in a wine-themed picnic. The winery encourages visitors to buy a bottle of its wine (try its signature chard) and amble over to the shaded tables or bocce court, or wander around the side of the property, sit on a bench, and gaze upon the stunning panorama before them. It's impossibly romantic, so be sure to go with someone you like. (However, if you go with more than five people you like, be sure to make a picnic reservation before you arrive.)

Far Niente

www.farniente.com
1 Acadia Drive, Oakville
707.944.2861
By appointment only

When the late Gil Nickel purchased the Far Niente property in 1979, he bought a shell of an estate that had lain dormant for sixty-eight years but was originally designed by Hamden McIntyre (who also designed Greystone, *Trefethen*, and *Niebaum-Coppola*). Nickel devoted himself to renovating the winery and returning it to its former glory. He also brought the gardens back to life—a natural act given his background as an Oklahoma nurseryman.

The name Far Niente means "without a care," and until recently the winery tried to keep things that way by making itself accessible only to the trade and to those who attended the occasional special event. But, lucky for us all, now the mesmerizing building that has long seduced the gaze of drivers-by can be visited. Guided tours lead guests through the historic winery, which features period fixtures (and a few spiderwebs) that evoke images of what it must have been like when Hamden first built it. By the time you've descended to the winery's bottom floor—into the modern and beautifully lit caves with a view into the wine library—you'll share the same envy felt by everyone with an affection for Oakville cabs. Before the tour ends at the house, you'll also have peeked into the barn that holds a small part of Nickel's car and boat collection. And although they're not officially part of the tour, as you walk around you'll be able to appreciate Far Niente's unique gardens—including the largest planting of azaleas on the West Coast. When they're in bloom, they're so colorful they can be seen from nearly a mile away on Highway 29.

Far Niente was created and built with a single focus: to produce just two wines from a single estate, a chardonnay and a cabernet sauvignon. A sit-down tasting at the end of the tour includes the current vintages of both varietals, as well as another Nickel wine, Dolce, a scrumptious sweet nectar. To cap things off, one or two older vintages of the cab are also poured, offering an even broader perspective on the history of this estate and its wines.

Nickel & Nickel Winery

www.nickelandnickel.com
8164 St. Helena Highway, Oakville
707.967.9600
By appointment only

The late Gil Nickel and his *Far Niente* partners, Dirk Hampson and Larry Maguire, had a deep passion for restoration. The culmination of their labors is Nickel & Nickel Winery. So while the winery is devoted to single-varietal wines, Nickel & Nickel offers more than just good juice in its Oakville digs; it also offers the restoration buff a chance to view how the craft of American carpentry can showcase state-of-the-art winemaking.

The property's history can be traced back to 1865, when John C. Sullenger, a prospector who struck gold in the Sierra Nevada, acquired the parcel from the Rancho Caymus land grant. On it he built two barns and a Queen Anne Victorian home in the 1880s; they were still standing nearly 120 years later when the Nickel & Nickel partners bought what was left of the farmstead.

The restoration project began out of respect for the property's farm history (most of Oakville was dairy land in the early 1900s). In the spirit of American farms that are passed from generation to generation, with each generation contributing a new building, Nickel & Nickel decided to restore the existing site structures and enhance the property with additional ones.

On a winery tour here you'll visit the Gleason barn, a striking red barn circa 1770, purchased in New Hampshire and moved to the Valley in 2002.

You'll go into the fermentation cellar, made from reclaimed wood, which exemplifies a kind of carpentry rarely seen in buildings today (check out the wooden pegs used in lieu of metal nails, and the two types of post-and-beam trusses).

From the fermentation room, your tour will take you underground, where the old-fashioned root-cellar entrance is at fascinating odds with the wine cellar's ultra-contemporary design. Unlike all the other structures, the wine cellar was not inspired by an American farmstead, but rather by European monasteries that use below-ground spaces to store wine.

In the Queen Anne house, where you'll end your tour, you'll be treated to a view of what a home might have looked like in the 1880s. It's here where you'll get to experience the best of Napa's past and some of its best present-day offerings: a sit-down tasting of the Nickel & Nickel cadre of single-vineyard wines.

The winery also offers tastings on the back porch. Flights of wine as well as a wine and cheese pairing are served in the splendor of one of the Valley's truly inspirational estates. Surely John Sullenger would approve.

Opus One's grand entry.

Opus One Winery

www.opusonewinery.com
7900 St. Helena Highway, Oakville
707.944.9442
Daily 10am–4pm with prior appointment

Opus One has an image problem. Valley folks tend to accuse it of being inaccessible and a bit snobby. But neither accusation could be further from the truth.

The winery is staffed by a warm and gregarious crew who know their establishment inside out. And while it's true that the wine tasting is expensive, there are free tours offered daily that are a hundredfold more interesting than some that charge a fee. For those wanting to sample Opus One, a Bordeaux-varietal blend, a tasting is not included in the tour but may be purchased afterward.

Whether or not you choose to taste, the building itself is enough of an anomaly to qualify as a bona fide draw. Visitors who are lured by the sight of the grass berms (the walls and roof of the underground cellar) will be delighted to discover what's inside the winery, including the circular courtyard, the light-filled foyer, and the grand staircase, with its reverse-design balustrade. A trip up to the second-floor terrace offers a one-of-a-kind bird's-eye view of the vineyards and uninterrupted vistas of the mountain ranges on both sides of the Valley.

While Opus One offers one of the most comprehensive and intelligent tours in all of the wine country, there are a few tidbits you probably won't learn on a tour, such as the rumors that circulated during and after construction of the building. There was talk about natural springs flooding the hole that was dug for the cellar, causing construction delays and additional costs that were enough to fund a small winery. Although you might learn that Scott Johnson, the architect of record, actually took over after the original architect, William Pereira, had passed away (Pereira also designed San Francisco's Transamerica Pyramid building), you most likely will *not* learn that the wildly inventive Pereira was not only quite the ladies' man, but a three-time Oscar winner to boot. Or that his original design for Opus included huge sails intended to float above the winery. Surely that would have been a sight to see.

All that said, what you *will* learn on a tour is the magnificent history of the partnership between Robert Mondavi and Baron Philippe de Rothschild; what motivated Johnson when he completed the design of the three-story structure; how the vineyards are planted and farmed; and how the wines are produced using a hands-on approach and gravity flow. You'll visit the salon, lab, crush area, tank room, private tasting room, and infamous underground cellar that has inspired imitations by dozens of other wineries.

So if a naysayer nixes Opus One, nod politely as you schedule a tour, splurge on a glass of wine, and decide for yourself if Opus One is worth a visit. We think it is.

Paradigm

www.paradigmwinery.com
800.963.1683
By appointment only

It's easy to understand how Paradigm has risen to cult status. Everything about the wine, the winery, the vineyard, and the owner seems rare and special. Just one visit is all it takes to feel as though you've been placed under a magical spell by the personal attention of proprietor Ren Harris.

A tour will most likely begin outside in the vineyard (on rainy days, you might stand under the eaves or sit inside gazing out the window). Looking at the generously spaced vines, the trained eye might notice that the rows are spaced further apart than in most vineyards. Ren explains why he's bucked the trend to plant vines closer together: his vines produce optimum-quality fruit, which in turn results in wines that sell out instantly upon release. This comes as no surprise given their food-friendly and easy-to-enjoy nature and qualities that include masculine aromas that morph into soft perfume, great fruit flavors that aren't overextracted, and tremendous, enviable balance.

The hundred or so tons of grapes grown in the vineyard are brought into the understated barn-like winery, the simplicity of which belies the stature of the wine. Everything inside is as neatly stored, perfectly spaced, and spotlessly clean as the vineyards themselves. Ren talks you through the process casually but succinctly; he seems genuinely pleased to share what he's learned in his forty-year-plus experience in the grape-growing industry, including the more than two decades he spent brokering sales for seventy-seven wineries (a task he accomplished with fellow vintner Jean Phillips).

By the end of your time at Paradigm, you'll appreciate more than ever the wines made here by Heidi Barrett—and you'd be hard-pressed not to also admire the life- and work-style choices Ren has made: rather than growing more grapes, making more wine, and creating more work, he's chosen to stay small in order to enjoy travel and motorcycling. Of course, after sipping Paradigm's delicious cab and merlot, you'll also wish there were more to go around.

Lunchtime Where dairy farms used to reign, wineries now dominate the landscape of Oakville. The town itself is so tiny you could miss it if you blink, so it's no surprise that there's no real restaurant. No problem, though: the ever-popular **Mustards** (7399 St. Helena Highway, Yountville, 707.944.2424), just a mile or so south, is always serving the scrumptious food on which its great reputation was built.

PlumpJack Winery

www.plumpjack.com
620 Oakville Cross Road, Oakville
707.945.1220
Daily 10am–4pm

Leave your AARP card at home—PlumpJack is all about being young and hip. This tasting room belongs to the jeans-and-black-sweater crowd. There's music with a lively beat, beautiful people on both sides of the bar, and stylized décor that would just as easily fit into a very cool restaurant.

The obvious attention paid to the smallest details inside the tasting room is trumped by the effort devoted to making PlumpJack wines. A few years ago, in a brilliant publicity ploy, PlumpJack gained widespread attention for its high-end Oakville cab when it began bottling half its production with screwcaps. The wine, which superbly exemplifies the region's best characteristics, became fodder for debate because of its controversial closure. Although the screwcap version of the wine isn't usually available for tasting, the winery's estate cab is, along with a selection of chardonnay, syrah, and merlot, all produced by consulting winemaker Nils Venge.

Outside the tasting room is a large courtyard bordered on all sides by low buildings that make up the winery compound. It's filled with cleverly designed fences, benches, and sculptures, and made soft by blossoming flowers, shade trees, and abundant greenery. Redwood tables are scattered here and there for lounging, and a small deck on the north side of the tasting room overlooks the estate's vineyards. Either area makes a great place to sip and contemplate or to make new friends among your fellow tasters.

Robert Mondavi Winery

www.robertmondaviwinery.com
7801 St. Helena Highway, Oakville
888-RMONDAVI
Call for hours

Until recently, it was unthinkable to make a maiden voyage to the wine country without starting at the Robert Mondavi Winery. No other winery is as widely recognized as this mission-style building, with its iconic arch and tower. No other winery has provided the breadth and depth of tours and educational opportunities. No other winery has offered a greater opportunity to experience the culture of wine, food, and the arts set against a backdrop so notably dedicated to aesthetics.

But today, at the time of writing, the winery is in flux, and while we want to recommend it as a must-see, there's no way of knowing what it may offer in the future. So instead, we'll honor it for what it has offered the Napa Valley and the world in the past.

Every square inch of Robert Mondavi Winery is a treat for the eye, from the fountain and statues to the rose gardens and from the To Kalon fermentation cellar, filled with noble oak tanks, to the aging cellar, where barrels are laid out in stunning symmetry. When Robert Mondavi built his winery in 1966, he began more than just a business for himself; he set in motion a legacy. His campaign to increase recognition for Napa Valley resulted in the region's current popularity as a premier wine-growing area and vacation destination. Although others before Mondavi had opened tasting rooms, it was he who defined wine country hospitality by developing celebrated visitors' programs (like in-depth winemaking tours and summer concerts).

Additionally, the Mondavis were known for hosting a slew of special events; their imagination and gracious hospitality can be credited for inspiring many of the other valley's wineries to follow their lead. The Mondavi Great Chefs program was a weekend filled with wine education, cooking demonstrations by the world's most celebrated culinary personalities (Alice Waters, Thomas Keller, and Julia Child all took a turn at the stove), and sumptuous meals served in the candlelit Vineyard Room. Art exhibits continually graced the Vineyard Room; and unforgettable concerts by musical legends such as Dave Brubeck, Etta James, and Aretha Franklin reverberated across the great lawn.

Several venues within the winery offered tastings by the glass or flight, and the beautiful surroundings made you want to take your time when you visited. Guests sat in the shade of the building or soaked up a little sun back by the vineyard, hoping someone special might cross their path—the wonderful Mr. Mondavi himself, or a family member from one of the three generations of Mondavis who for so long carried on the grand traditions he began.

Rudd Vineyards & Winery

www.ruddwines.com
500 Oakville Cross Road, Oakville
707.944.8577
By appointment only

Leslie Rudd, owner of Rudd Vineyards & Winery, is a man who imagines things on a large scale and then builds to his vision. This explains the *Alice-in-Wonderland*–size boulders, chairs, and fountain adorning the front of his winery. Also conveying the idea that this is not your ordinary winery is the brick-red soil on which the vineyards rest. There's a bit of wine lore that says the best red wines are grown in red soil, and Rudd's estate cabernet proves this to be true.

Because wine begins in the vineyard, so do the tours at Rudd, at least on sunny days. On rainy days, guests are led from the handsome foyer into a plush dining room to look out over the tightly spaced rows, which demonstrate the winery's farming philosophy: stress the vines to make them give you small berries with lots of concentration.

Inside, the winery is clean enough to eat lunch off the floor—in fact, the only signs that it's a working winery are the occasional stray bucket or strainer. This art-meets-science room is remarkable for its design and beauty—Leslie Rudd's big vision is matched by his excellent taste. Square gleaming tanks, spotless tank pads built at a tilt, neat hose racks, the blond-wood ceiling, and a press that looks like a sculpture are all enhanced by glass and metal accents; it's an environment meant to captivate anyone with an eye for design.

Downstairs, in the twenty-two thousand square feet of subterranean caves, are barrels as far as the eye can see. Your host—who might be Bill, a gentleman who's worked with Rudd for more than twenty-five years and remembers everyone's name—will lead you through the caves to a spectacular twenty-foot-long table made from a single redwood tree. Again, not a single detail is left to chance: you'll find the table neatly set with the appropriate number of glasses for tasting sauvignon blanc, chardonnay, and one to two cabs. As Bill talks you through the wines, you may come to realize that he's as entertaining as anyone you'll ever meet in this business.

Saddleback Cellars

www.saddlebackcellars.com

7802 Money Road, Oakville

707.944.1305

By appointment only

If you want the experience of drinking in a cellar—a real, down-to-earth cellar—Saddleback is for you. At one end of the cinderblock-and-wood winery is a makeshift bar where guests gather to drink the wines of Nils Venge. With a résumé that includes winemaking at some of the Valley's best-liked wineries—*Groth*, *PlumpJack*, *Del Dotto*, and *Keenan*—Venge's credentials are indisputable and his talent for making great juice widely recognized. His simple winery clearly conveys an admirably nonfussy approach to wine: make good wine, drink good wine, share good wine.

Turnbull Wine Cellars

www.turnbullwines.com

8210 St. Helena Highway, Oakville

707.963.5839

Daily 10am–4:30pm

It's rare to find an establishment that nurtures both the eye and the palate, but if you're as interested in photography as you are in distinctive wines, take a look at Turnbull.

In addition to Turnbull's wide range of varietals—from its signature cabernet sauvignon to its sauvignon blanc, merlot, sangiovese, cabernet franc, syrah, and zinfandel—this winery also houses one of the world's largest collections of photography by Ansel Adams and other photographers, all shown in rotating exhibits in the otherwise modest tasting room. Steichen, Horst, Strand, Kertesz, Man Ray, Weston . . . the list of world-class artists is as impressive as the wines you are served.

With four estate vineyards in the Oakville appellation of Napa Valley, Turnbull creates wines that reflect their distinct *terroir*. Whether the grapes grow on the valley floor, benchland, or rocky hillsides, they all exhibit the right characteristics, and there's a deft hand behind their journey to the bottle. The tasting-room personnel are neighborly—they'll even direct you to other wineries if you tell them what you're most interested in tasting.

Turnbull's nod to times past.

The Best of the Rest Oakville is such a small town that you can barely turn around without bumping into wineries, all of which produce incredibly delicious wine. It's tough to narrow down which wineries to visit, but there's only so much time in a day. If you find yourself with extra time, consider visiting one of these. ···· **Groth Vineyards and Winery** (750 Oakville Cross Road, Oakville, www.grothwines.com, 707.944.0290, Mon–Sat by appointment only) is easy to spot as you drive down the road: it's the giant pink building that looks like the love child of a Middle Eastern mosque and a Franciscan mission. Groth was one of the early Oakville producers that helped build the appellation's renowned reputation for growing some of the world's best cabernet sauvignon grapes. ···· Just across the street is **Silver Oak Cellars** (915 Oakville Cross Road, Oakville, www.silveroak.com, 800.273.8809, Mon–Sat 9am–4pm), a winery that until recently maintained a sleepy dairy-farm image. Now it offers its loyal following a place to taste and genuflect in the shadow of its signature water tower.

The Best Appellation Event Twice a year, at the **Silver Oak Release Party** (915 Oakville Cross Road, Oakville, www.silveroak.com, 800.273.8809, late January or early February and late July or early August), the winery releases its highly sought-after cabernet sauvignon. And in the wake of the wine comes an event of legendary proportions. Throughout the wine world tales buzz and rumors fly of people lining up the night before, of thousands of thirsty people descending on the tents set up for the occasion, and of hundreds of cases of the hundred-dollar-a-bottle wine being poured.

While these stories may or may not be true, they have built up a simple wine release into a near-religious experience. As you begin the trek down the driveway toward the winery, you'll find yourself swept up into what feels like a pilgrimage to Mecca. Despite the long line of cars, everyone is generally affable.

Although you'll see golf carts and buses shuttling people down the drive, resist the urge to catch a ride—the walk down is worth the effort. In winter, when the Napa Valley wine is released (the Alexander Valley cab is released in summer), pay close attention to the vineyard below the road. You'll see still-naked vines lined up like tall, lanky men, arms spread, soaking in the sun on a carpet of soft green grass.

As you get closer to the winery, you'll find tailgaters, picnickers, and frolicking families. You'll also find small hordes of hip urbanites—single folks take note: this is the place to check out other single wine enthusiasts.

Once inside, there's a lot to grab your attention, all tucked into nooks and niches: food stands, clothing sales, coopers making barrels, artists painting, and, at the back of it all, a tasting bar that seems to stretch on forever. As crowded as it is, it's still easy to make your way up to fill your glass with the nectar that started all this fuss. Find a quiet corner and sip with the care it deserves.

Afterward, stay in the area. In the wake of Silver Oak's success, most of the wineries in the area, including **Rudd**, **Groth**, **Cardinale**, and **PlumpJack**, have begun to open their doors and throw parties of their own the same day.

RUTHERFORD

Home to two of California's most influential wineries, *Inglenook* (now *Niebaum-Coppola*) and *Beaulieu Vineyard*, the Rutherford appellation has long been recognized for producing distinctive cabernet sauvignon. Today the region is also well known for producing equally good sauvignon blanc grapes. Rutherford is relatively small, but it's home to many wineries that make use of its diverse microclimates and the alluvial fans that characterize its soil makeup.

Cakebread Cellars

www.cakebreadcellars.com
8301 St. Helena Highway, Rutherford
707.963.5221 or 800.588.0928
Daily 10am–4pm with prior appointment

A private family-owned and -operated winery, Cakebread Cellars was started in 1973 by Jack and Dolores Cakebread. Today it's run largely by their sons, Bruce and Dennis, along with daughter-in-law Karen and a fantastically capable staff.

Cakebread's wines are really terrific. But don't stop here just to taste the cab, chard, and other varietals that the winery makes so well—be sure to also make time for the guided tour. It will take you through the gardens—both flower and vegetable—over to the vineyard and through the very neat redwood winery with ceilings so high and beautifully lit it's been dubbed "Bruce's Cathedral" (in reference to Bruce Cakebread, the former winemaker and current president).

One of the winery's greatest assets is its private chef-in-residence, Brian Streeter. Throughout the year, the Cakebreads host special events for sampling Brian's fare and their wines; join them for their annual open house in February. Or, if you like to cook, sign up for one of the winery's cooking classes, and spend the day cooking with Brian either inside the winery or in the outdoor kitchen. Most classes are hands-on, with topics ranging from the art of sauce preparation to the science of grilling. At the end of each class, you'll sit down to dine on the tree-covered patio or inside the winery house and be treated to one of the best wine and food pairings available in the Valley.

Caymus Vineyard

www.caymusvineyard.com

8700 Conn Creek Road, Rutherford

707.967.3010

By appointment only

"Six degrees of separation" is a way of life in the Napa Valley. Everyone in the wine industry seems to be connected to everyone else in one way or another—a shared winemaker, a traded technique, a borrowed piece of equipment. For Caymus Vineyard, its essential connection to other wineries is genetic: its first vineyard, planted in 1965, used clones from the renowned Fay Vineyard. Sixty acres of those plantings are still a prominent fruit source for Caymus's cabernet sauvignon.

Six years after the first vines were planted, the late Charlie Wagner, a longtime farmer and Caymus proprietor, released his first vintage. In doing so he perpetuated a family tradition of winemaking in the Napa Valley that began when his grandfather was a winemaker at Inglenook. Today Caymus is best known for its cabs and its white wine called Conundrum, a blend whose constituent grapes are difficult for a taster to puzzle out: hence the name. The winery also makes a zinfandel from fruit grown in the Monte Rosso vineyard in Sonoma Valley. Two or three of these wines are offered to small groups in the winery's tasting room.

Given the building's rustic elegance and a sales room that is paradoxically not retail oriented, it comes as no surprise that the tasting room feels like part of a sleepy, historic California ranch. Its walls are lined with photographs depicting the early days of Napa Valley. Antiquey wood furniture is complemented by a Bear Flag that honors Northern California's beginnings, a further reminder that the winery's location was once part of the original Rancho Caymus land grant. The room is a gracious setting in which to learn about the history of the Wagner family, the wines, and the vineyards.

When it's time to leave, stop and smell the roses—literally. The dense planting of climbing roses, along with a multitude of other flowering plants and a large vegetable garden, creates a panoply of all the natural wonders this lovely spot can produce.

Franciscan

www.franciscan.com
1178 Galleron Road, Rutherford
800.529.WINE ext. 73830
Daily 10am–5pm

A lesser-known fact about Franciscan is that it was started in the early 1970s by Ray Duncan and the late Justin Meyer of *Silver Oak* fame.

What's more widely known is that Franciscan has sparked major innovations in the wine industry. For example, Franciscan was the first winery in Napa Valley to ferment chardonnay with wild yeast, thus creating its Cuvée Sauvage. It was also instrumental in creating the name *meritage* as a descriptor for a blended table wine.

Franciscan hosts a repertoire of dynamic programs for wine enthusiasts. The Magnificat blending seminar lets you play winemaker—you get to make your own blended Bordeaux-varietal wine. A wine and cheese pairing seminar experiments with four wines and four cheeses, allowing you to determine the best matches. And an entire seminar devoted to identifying and appreciating wine aromas helps you hone sensory-evaluation skills.

While all these offerings are notable, what makes Franciscan most notable is its wine. So, tour or no tour, seminar or no seminar, by all means make the one stop at Franciscan that is unmissable: the tasting bar.

Frog's Leap Winery

www.frogsleap.com
8815 Conn Creek Road, Rutherford
707.963.4704 or 800.959.4704
Mon–Sat 10am–4pm, tours and tastings by appointment only

With or without a tour and tasting, this is one of the most delightfully enchanting places you'll ever visit. You'll know you've reached Frog's Leap Winery when you see the big, eye-catching Red Barn. Nice as the Red Barn is (it's historic too, built as a winery in 1884 and renovated by Frog's Leap more than one hundred years later), it's just a drop in the pond compared to what lies beyond it.

There you will find an absolutely fresh, happy, surprising, one-of-a-kind world—one filled with flowers on arbors and arches, in gardens and pots: roses galore, daisies, poppies, freesia, you name it. And then there are the grasses, the herbs, and the organic vegetable garden overflowing with hundreds of varieties of tomatoes, peppers, and other succulent treasures.

The fruit trees are laden in season—but with rotating crops that change with the weather, every season is "in season" here. And while a sweet frog pond might be expected, could anybody rightfully expect a water tower with flowing water? Or landscaping as abundant as Eden's? Or a scattering of alluring buildings, from the elegantly somber, dignified brown barn to the beguiling Vineyard House and small cottages?

Reserve your chance to attend a sit-down group tasting. If you come by in summer, you're likely to leave with one arm full of terrific Frog's Leap wine (a wide range of varietals produced from organic grapes) and the other brimming over with fruits or veggies. If you come at another time of year, that works, too—in fact, it leaves both your arms free to carry more bottles home.

Grgich Hills Cellar
www.grgich.com
1829 St. Helena Highway, Rutherford
707.963.2784 or 800.532.3057
Daily 9:30am–4:30pm

Whether or not they realize it, most white-wine drinkers have drunk from the hand of Grgich Hills Cellar's Miljenko "Mike" Grgich. An immigrant from Croatia, Grgich moved to the Napa Valley in 1958, whereupon he began a series of jobs with the top winemakers of his—and any—day: a short stint at *Christian Brothers*; nine years with André Tchelistcheff at *Beaulieu Vineyard*; and then work for *Robert Mondavi* at his eponymous winery. Then came *Chateau Montelena*, where he produced the astonishing 1973 chardonnay—the wine that won a staggering victory in the historic Paris blind tasting of 1976.

Grgich Hills was established on the Fourth of July, 1977, and with it Mike Grgich declared his independence. Since then he's been creating renowned wines. His chard is his signature: creamy, fruity, masterful. His reds live up to the challenge of the whites.

You're likely to see Mike in the flesh when you visit Grgich Hills—he's the short man on the floor or behind the bar, the one with the casual-proper jacket and ever-present jaunty beret. You'll see him, that is, if you can see anything at all in the dark winery tasting room. With no natural light, a cement floor, and winery workers busily racking barrels and warehousing all around you, you might feel like you've fallen into a wormhole and landed straight in Croatia. But rest easy. One sip and you'll know you're in Napa, in the hands of a master.

The entrance to Frog's Leap.

All Roads Lead to BV Beaulieu Vineyard (1960 St. Helena Highway, Rutherford, www.bvwines.com, 800.264.6918, daily 10am–5pm), better known as BV, is the grande dame winery of Napa Valley. With a history that dates back to 1900, BV's impact on the Northern California wine landscape has been profound.

The story begins at the end of the 1800s, when phylloxera devastated the Valley's vineyards. BV founder Georges de Latour responded to the situation by importing rootstock from France, and in the process revitalized a failing industry. Then, during Prohibition, BV was one of only two wineries in California that remained in operation. While the express reason for this was to make "holy" wine for Christian ceremonial practices, it also allowed the winery to perfect its cabernet sauvignon. Today cab remains its flagship wine, one that has been inspirational to generations of vintners.

De Latour made one more decision that far surpassed his other actions in terms of creating an indelible impression for his brand: he hired master vintner André Tchelistcheff, whose name is still spoken in the hushed tones of true reverence. A genius enologist, Tchelistcheff worked for BV for nearly forty years, but his reach extended to nearly every winery in the Napa Valley and beyond. He is credited with teaching such legendary winemakers as Joe Heitz and Mike Grgich their craft, and he consulted with dozens—if not hundreds—of other wineries, sharing his vast knowledge and experience. The standards that de Latour and Tchelistcheff set for BV have spread beyond the winery's easily recognized ivy-covered walls in the heart of Rutherford. The wine industry is better for both these fine men.

Honig Vineyard and Winery
www.honigwine.com
850 Rutherford Cross Road, Rutherford
707.963.5618
By appointment only

A visit to Honig is fun. Sure, the wines are serious, as is the winery's strict adherence to organic farming methods and winemaking practices. But the rest is about having a good time.

Recently Honig created a permanent tasting room to show off its wines, and here you're bound to encounter an enthusiastic staff. As you taste through two sauvignon blancs and one cab—and banter about everything from the bee mascot to the cab vineyards—you'll also have the chance to look at a binder filled with postcards used to announce new releases. Definitely take up the offer—these are not your ordinary marketing materials. Rather, the cards are a statement about the Honigs and their staff: they're playful and downright clever.

Lunchtime In Rutherford, the **Rutherford Grill** (1180 Rutherford Road, Rutherford, 707.963.1792) is definitely the place to see and be seen if you work at one of the area wineries. Either that or everyone's just taking advantage of the no-corkage-fee policy. Have the ribs, and don't pass up dessert—you're on vacation!

Long Meadow Ranch
www.longmeadowranch.com
1775 Whitehall Lane, Rutherford
707.963.4555 or 877.NAPA.OIL
By appointment only

One of the last buildings designed by William Turnbull, the Long Meadow Ranch winery is like an architectural ode to the hillside on which it's built. This description is way more than just a poetic conceit, since the geometrically shaped winery and olive oil frantoio are constructed entirely of rammed earth—the same earth that was dug out to create its cellars.

But rammed earth walls are just the visible aspect of the winery's thorough commitment to ecological sustainability. Recycled materials are used throughout the property; heating and cooling systems are all passive; even the wood beams were color-stained using wine. It adds up to an austere and tasteful environment. The winery is punctuated by attractive yin-yang tables that use different colors on each half to represent Long Meadow's twin passions: wine and olive oil. Before you leave, be sure to check out the twenty-mile view from inside the cave—it's the best winery-cave view in the Valley.

The Ranch offers a selection of experiences for visitors: the Pinzgauer exploration, which takes you through the back roads of the six-hundred-acre property; and the ranch hike, a guided trek through the vineyards, the 120-year-old olive orchard, and on up to Lookout Point. Both tours—which, visitor beware, are very expensive—take you through the frantoio and winery and include private tastings of its two extra-virgin olive oils as well as its estate-produced cabernet sauvignon, sangiovese, and Ranch House Red, a proprietary blend. If you really want the fullest Long Meadow Ranch experience, stay for lunch: a picnic affair featuring the ranch's Highland beef, organic produce, olive oils, and a wine selection that includes something from the winery's library.

Niebaum-Coppola Estate Winery

www.niebaum-coppola.com
1991 St. Helena Highway, Rutherford
800.RUBICON
Daily 10am–5pm

Being at Niebaum-Coppola is like entering another world—or stepping onto a fastidiously appointed movie set. Welcome to the vision of film legend Francis Ford Coppola, who brings to his winery the same studious eye for detail that he brings to his films.

Take, for example, the winery's courtyard, with its picturesque fountain. Does it feel strangely familiar? Maybe that's because it was created by the same set designer who worked on the *Godfather* movies, hired here by Coppola to re-create Paris's Luxembourg Gardens. Everything from the winery's fountain to its lampposts and benches was imported from France to further the illusion. By the time you finish looking around at the property's meticulously restored buildings—such as its glorious, historic Inglenook Chateau, designed by Hamden McIntyre about 125 years ago— you'll see exactly how a filmmaker's vision can create an unsurpassed sense of place.

Coppola entered the wine business in the late 1970s, a couple of years after he moved to the Napa Valley for strictly personal reasons. He purchased the back half of the property—fifteen hundred acres—with profits from the *Godfather* movies, and purchased the front half—one hundred acres and the winery chateau—with the earnings from his movie *Dracula*. (The joke is that the whole winery was bought with blood money.) But before long Coppola was producing wines from estate-grown grapes— including Rubicon, a Bordeaux blend; Edizione Pennino, a zinfandel; and a bevy of varietal wines.

Niebaum Coppola offers three kinds of tours: one about winemaking, one about the vineyards, and one devoted to the history of the winery. But even if you don't sign up for a tour, there's plenty to see on your own. Downstairs in the Inglenook Chateau you'll find the Centennial Museum, with original winery owner Gustav Niebaum's re-created (and shipworthy) Captain's Room, along with a display of zoetropes. Upstairs—the staircase itself is an object of astounding handwrought beauty—is a movie memorabilia museum containing Francis's many Oscar statuettes; a filmography of the movies he's written and directed; and iconic film objects, such as the desk from *The Godfather*, the car from *Tucker*, a bamboo cage from *Apocalypse Now*, and the costumes from *Dracula*.

There is, of course, an equally dramatic venue for tasting and purchasing Niebaum-Coppola's fabulous wines. Set into a retail space whose architecture is as memorable as the items it sells are several tasting bars surrounded by tantalizing objects. You'll find etched glassware and edible treasures, Italian pottery and French trinkets—mostly beautiful props with which to turn your dining room into a magical movie set of your own.

You may leave with stars in your eyes. And perhaps, if you're lucky, you'll have a star sighting to write home about: Francis Ford Coppola himself, sitting in the shade of an olive tree, as unpretentious as a man could be in the place he calls home.

The Days of Wine and Movies Wine lovers with a passion for the big screen can enjoy the best of both worlds at two wine country events. Still in its youth, the **Sonoma Valley Film Festival** (www.cinemaepicuria.org, 707.933.2600) has not yet reached the level of acclaim of Sundance or Toronto, but it shows great promise. Held in Sonoma every April, the festival is a mix of celebrity appearances, parties, and movie screenings hosted by wineries. During the summer, the annual **Wine Country Film Festival** (www.winecountryfilmfest.com, 707.935.FILM) is held at several locations in Sonoma and Napa. Films usually are screened outdoors at wineries and often are accompanied by a meal and wines that match the movie's theme.

Peju Province

www.peju.com
8466 St. Helena Highway, Rutherford
707.963.3600 or 800.446.7358
Daily 10am–6pm

Peju Province is a world unto itself. The entrance road is bordered on one side by an endless row of sycamore trees, aggressively trained to be taller-than-tall and reed-thin; they stand against the sky like serene Asian prayer flags. Beyond them lie sculptured marble fountains, a surreally gorgeous camphor tree (also aggressively trained in the name of beauty), an inviting garden with a stepping-stone walking path, French garden lamps, a tiny bridge over a wee stream, a koi pond, and a reflecting pool.

It's hard to ask for more, but more is what you get: a hand wrought iron gate, ornate iron pillars, even a moat guarding the front door (which, naturally, is of masterfully carved wood). Inside, the tasting room and guest center feel like a place of worship—a secular cathedral devoted to wine. It's a soaring space; the stucco and stone building is one of the tallest towers in the Napa Valley, and its verdigris-finished copper roof is a notable landmark (it's also pictured on every label). From the elaborate stained-glass windows to the carefully curated bookshelves that look as though their copy of Karen MacNeil's *Wine Bible* could easily be replaced by the Old or New Testament, this is a wine lover's paradise. (Don't forget to wander through the second retail room in the back in search of more books, chocolate, and wine paraphernalia.)

Of course, visitors to Peju can't live on beauty alone—they must have wine. And if Peju Province is to your taste, you're not only in the right place, you're in the *only* place; since the winery is not nationally distributed, almost all sales take place right here.

This is one of the best tastings you can attend. A handful of guests is assembled on an ad-hoc basis, and a highly structured adventure begins. The intelligent, impeccably attired pourers here are consummate professionals. They don't just splash some juice in a glass and chat about the weather; rather, they teach you how to think about what you're experiencing. They present a selection of varietals, from chardonnay to zinfandel (current releases and reserves), in a logical sequence and help you create a universe of flavor. By the time you're finished, you've educated your palate, inspired your eye, and—delightedly—lightened your wallet.

Quintessa's innovative architecture.

Quintessa

www.quintessa.com

1601 Silverado Trail, Rutherford

707.967.1601

By appointment only

Wear walking shoes when you visit Quintessa. The tour begins with a short jaunt to the top of one of the property's five spectacular hills—or *coronas*, as they're called in deference to owners Agustin and Valeria Huneeus's Chilean roots. Spread out before you is the entire expanse of Quintessa's unique composition—from the valley to the lake, and the river to the infinite rows of vines that snake through the property.

From your aerie, you'll learn about the Huneeuses' organic, sustainable, and biodynamic farming efforts and how they've divided the vineyard into multiple blocks to take advantage of the unique variety of climate and soil conditions.

When you come down off the hill, you'll get to visit the winery—a structure at once striking and subtle. Built into the curve of the hill, its stone façade blends so seamlessly into the landscape that it's not until you're up close or inside that you can fully appreciate its splendor. The architecture is highly unusual in that the roof is the crush pad; this allows the must to be transferred completely by gravity into the tanks below on the mezzanine level. Eventually the wine travels to the ground level, where the entrance to Quintessa's cave is celebrated with a stunning fountain sculpture.

The visitors' reception area is Quintessa's most dynamic room. Its rough concrete floors contrast with a cork ceiling and wood tables and chairs worn to a satiny patina. Warmly colored paintings of the vineyard in every season hang beside black walnut cabinets. It's dark, mysterious, and seductive.

Quintessa makes only one wine: a blend of Bordeaux varietals. The first vintage was in 1994, four years after the vineyard was planted; a decade later it is beginning to transcend its youthful exuberance and is heading into maturity, greater complexity, and pure grace. Even if you don't have time for the tour, visiting Quintessa to taste the wine will make the Napa Valley deliciously unforgettable.

Going Underground Everyone knows caves are natural places to store wines. Many Napa Valley vintners have turned their functional storage areas into fantastic works of art, creating underground spaces every bit as beautiful as what rises above them. The **Napa Valley Museum** (707.944.0500) offers **Napa Valley Underground**, an annual series of comprehensive tours that explores half a dozen winery caves. Guests are driven by van in small groups to each winery and led through it by the cave designers themselves. It's a full-day event that includes wine tasting and a picnic. Participants have included **Quintessa, Vineyard 29, Hartwell Vineyards, Pine Ridge**, and **Frazier**. Cave dwellers seeking more than just a tour can attend **Carols in the Caves** (707.224.4222), a holiday program of music held in caves throughout the Napa and Sonoma valleys.

Rutherford Grove Winery and Vineyards
www.rutherfordgrove.com
1673 Highway 29, Rutherford
707.963.0544
Daily 10am–4:30pm

Although it is right on busy Highway 29, ivy-covered Rutherford Grove feels far away. It's a low-key, under-the-radar type of place. Winemaker Andy Pestoni makes good red wines, mastering cab, merlot, petite sirah, and sangiovese.

Involved for generations with a family-owned grape composting business, the Pestoni family seems to operate according to a simple and intelligent principle: when the gods give you grapes, make wine; when they give you grapeseeds, make grapeseed oil. Rather than turning this "waste" from other wineries into compost, the Pestonis decided to use it to produce high-quality cold-pressed grapeseed oils. Rutherford Grove's edible oil is joined on the shelves by its lavender body oil. All oils, as well as other local Napa food products, are sold in an airy, uncluttered shop beside the tasting-room bar.

Rutherford Hill

www.rutherfordhill.com
200 Rutherford Hill Road, Rutherford
800.MERLOT.1
Daily 10am–5pm

There's something welcoming and good-natured about the campus of Rutherford Hill. The setting, above the renowned Auberge du Soleil resort, is secluded and quiet; the tasting room is filled with local food products; and the picnic areas are among the very best the Valley has to offer. It's easy to imagine unpacking a picnic basket under the ancient olive trees or on the hillside covered with oaks and manzanita. It's just as easy to imagine never wanting to leave.

Although Rutherford Hill is best known for its flagship merlot, it also produces a wide range of other varietals that are available for tasting on most days. Any of them would be the perfect accompaniment to an afternoon spent lounging in the shady embrace of an old olive tree.

Swanson Vineyards

www.swansonvineyards.com
1271 Manley Lane, Rutherford
707.967.3500
By appointment only

When Alexis Swanson, the public relations diva for Swanson Vineyards, and her mother decided to create a tasting room for their winery, they wanted to design something extraordinary. So they re-created a nineteenth-century Parisian salon—a place where tales could be told, philosophies shared, and libations enjoyed.

The result of their creative efforts is a fabulous room decorated in bold strokes. The walls are painted a deep magenta and covered with whimsical portraits by Ira Yeagar, a well-known local artist. Dark wood doors mirror the solid, handsome table that takes center stage in the room. An over-sized fireplace is flanked by wicker baskets holding ancient grapevines, a reminder of where you are. And an ornate crystal chandelier presides above the table, which accommodates only eight guests at a time. This ensures that every tasting is personal—or, in the language of the Swansons, feels like a party thrown in each guest's honor.

The room achieves its goals so well that it would be easy to sit and talk only about it during an entire visit. Instead, your host will guide you through a comprehensive discussion of Swanson's history and winemak-ing techniques in the company of its wines. As if not to be outdone by the décor, the two tastings offered also have an edge of decadent humor: they are named Jean Lafitte and Harvey (these monikers seem even funnier when you learn they're inspired by the winery's mascot dogs). Both tast-ings are accompanied by nibble-pairings of chocolates and cheese and conclude with a cup of sweet chicory that tastes like it's straight out of a New Orleans parlor.

Both tastings showcase a unique assortment of Napa Valley wines. Jean Lafitte is composed of four wines, such as rosato, pinot grigio, merlot, and Alexis, a proprietary blend named after (who else?) Alexis Swanson. Harvey is a seven-wine flight that includes some rare limited-production wines and a barrel sample as well as current releases.

While there may be places of equal substance, Swanson holds the title for the most daring.

Tres Sabores

www.tressabores.com
707.967.8027 (email is best: jaj@tressabores.com)
By appointment only

When Julie Johnson purchased the Rutherford property she lives on, she became the instant owner of a planted ten-acre zinfandel vineyard. For the first twelve years she lived there, she sold the fruit to another winery. Then, in 1999, she decided to keep a little for herself and make her own wine. And this is where the story gets interesting.

Rather than hire one winemaker to turn the grapes into wine, she recruited three—and three of the best. Every year Rudy Zuidema, Karen Culler, and Ken Bernards each determine when their grapes will be picked; then, handling every step to bottling, they each produce their lot of wine.

It would be easy to conclude that tasting these three wines is the highlight of a visit to Tres Sabores. But given the ingenuity that inspired such a bold idea, it turns out that the wine is just one piece of a fascinating visit. In fact, Tres Sabores offers a unique vineyard education. The first thing Julie does when you arrive is point out that you're standing in a canyon and on the edge of an alluvial fan—it's a little like looking through a megaphone as the view broadens into the Rutherford bench.

In summer, when there's fruit on the vine, the lesson on alluvial soils is made simple by tasting grapes from different rows, graphically demonstrating just how much the soil can vary from foot to foot. Julie also discusses every aspect of her certified organic farming methods, including showing off Larry, Leo, and Louie, the winery's three angora goats, whose job it is to keep the grasses under control. Julie explains how cover crops are cut and how certain birds play certain roles in the health of a vineyard, and, if you're lucky, you'll meet "Amigo Bob," the organic guru who makes a monthly visit to the winery.

Julie talks about the vineyard in an easy-to-understand manner, making it seem as simple as tending a home garden. As the vineyard tour winds down, you'll be encouraged to stop and smell the roses—lots of them, since the aroma variation from rose to rose echoes the differences in the wines you'll taste. It's an aromatherapy aperitif.

Tres Sabores is tiny. The low-slung winery building is tiny, the cave is tiny, and the production is tiny. But what is huge is Julie's generous spirit, which shines through every time she welcomes a visitor to her vineyard and winery.

The Best of the Rest Rutherford is a tiny hamlet in the heart of the Napa Valley, concentrated along a two-block stretch of Rutherford Road. The appellation of the same name extends north and south of the town's epicenter and consists primarily of valley floor acreage. Rutherford wineries stretch from the foothills along the Vaca range on the east to the Mayacamas on the western side, creating big decisions for visitors. With so many wineries to visit, there are bound to be a few relegated to "next time" or "if you have time." ···· If you *do* have spare time this time, consider stopping in at **St. Supéry** (8440 St. Helena Highway, Rutherford, www.stsupery.com, 800.942.0809, daily 10am–5:30pm), at the southern end of the region. A lovely white Victorian is what you might notice first, which can lead to a sense of disappointment when you realize the tasting room and winery are actually in a far more corporate-looking building.

This aside, St. Supéry has always been a local favorite because of the self-guided tour through its Wine Discovery Center, its art gallery, its garden programs, and its annual harvest adventure. Basically, what St. Supéry may lack in compelling décor it makes up for in a cordial staff, interesting wine exhibits, and visitor programs. ···· **Esquisse** (1155 Mee Lane, Rutherford, www.esquissewines.com, 707.963.9999, Mon–Thur 10am–4pm, Fri–Sun 10am–5pm) is right on Highway 29, but the entrance is off Mee Lane, next door to a veterinary hospital and animal farm. This pretty much guarantees that there will be stray chickens clucking around the parking lot. ···· Drive around them and head into the sparse collective tasting room to try Dennis Johns's *White Cottage* wines. Johns has been producing outstanding cabs from his Howell Mountain vineyards for years, and now, at Esquisse, they're available for tasting along with *Voss*, *Esquisse*, and *Moss Creek* wines. ···· Across the street is **Provenance** (1695 St. Helena Highway, Rutherford, www.provenancevineyards.com, 707.968.3633, daily 10am–4:30pm), Tom Rinaldi's excellent venture. Provenance promises to meet the level of excellence that Rinaldi made the benchmark at Duckhorn during the more than two decades he spent making wine there. ···· **Sullivan** (1090 Galleron Road, St. Helena, www.sullivanwine.com, 877.244.7337, by appointment only) is somewhat off the beaten track but worth a stop. The entire winery, including the tasting room, is in one room, offering a unique perspective on the goings-on inside the cellar on any given day. ···· Finally, at the foot of the Mayacamas rests **Livingston-Moffett** (1895 Cabernet Lane, St. Helena, www.livingstonwines.com, 707.963.2120, by appointment only). It's tiny in all ways but one: its giant cabs, including its cult label, Gemstone.

ST. HELENA

The St. Helena appellation prides itself on having some of the most venerable wineries in California, from *Joseph Phelps* and *Heitz* to *Spottswoode* and *Beringer*. Yet the region itself is rarely promoted. Shaped like the boot of Italy without the heel, St. Helena stretches several miles north of the town that shares the same name; to the east and west it rises up into the Vaca and Mayacamas ranges. Many kinds of grapes are grown in the Valley's warm-weather spot, including cabernet, zinfandel, syrah, and sauvignon blanc.

Beringer Vineyards

www.beringer.com
2000 Main Street, St. Helena
707.963.4812
June–Oct daily 10am–6pm, Nov–May daily 10am–5pm

Okay, it's a terrible cliché, especially here in California, but Beringer Vineyards is—in a word—awesome. A visit here is practically mandatory, if just to pay homage to the oldest continuously operating winery in Napa Valley, established by Jacob and Fredrick Beringer in 1876. Or to witness the towering, half-mile tunnel of elm trees that stand as sentries guarding this magnificent wine country estate.

Beringer was placed on the National Registry of Historic Places as a "Historic District" in 2001. But even without this stamp of recognition, it's obvious that this compound has a rare assemblage of buildings more than a century old. The landmark Rhine House Mansion, completed in 1884, is a stellar architectural marvel, marked by Gothic accents; its original detail includes extraordinary stained-glass panels. The Old Stone Winery, built in 1877, has hand-dug caves, ornately carved 150-year-old German barrels, and a private family cellar with wines older than sixty years. The painstakingly restored Hudson House serves today as Beringer's Culinary Arts Center. The impressive *Artist's Fountain*, dedicated in the early 1980s, celebrates the centennial of Beringer: it's covered with scenes of the evolution of wine, Napa Valley wine history, and more (see if you can spot the reference to Marvin Gaye's "I Heard It through the Grapevine"). And for pure natural wonder, check out the more than two-hundred-year-old California valley white oak or the breathtaking Redwood Grove (call to ask about the three-course al fresco lunches with wine pairings that are offered here in the summer).

While all this sounds interesting enough, it's anemically pale compared to the actual experience of walking around the property under the intelligent gaze of a Beringer guide. Three tours and tastings are offered: "Introducing Beringer," the basic tour; the phenomenal "Historic District" tour, which is filled to bursting with inside stories and fascinating information; and the "Vintage Legacy" tour, which is longer, more educational, and geared toward current-release, barrel, and private-reserve tastings. All tours are well worth the fee.

Following your tour, you can stop into the two tasting rooms. One is in the old winery; the other, featuring Beringer's reserve and limited-production wines, is in the Rhine House.

Genius for a Day Okay, here's a little secret about how to win friends and influence people while taking winery tours. The hosts will invariably ask a question about wine, usually some obscure fact that they don't expect anyone to know. If you're asked the 95-85-75 question, you'll be able to answer with confidence that a bottle of wine must contain at least 95 percent of the vintage printed on the label; 85 percent of the fruit from the appellation noted; and 75 percent of the grape varietal declared. It might not get you into Harvard, but it's guaranteed to win you admiring glances from your fellow tour members.

Duckhorn Wine Company

www.duckhornvineyards.com
1000 Lodi Lane, St. Helena
888.354.8885
Daily 10am–4pm

Duckhorn's newly finished visitor center is a tribute to all things water-fowl and to the superior wines that Duckhorn has been crafting for more than three decades. Every day, the winery offers tastings of its current releases plus a couple of limited-production wines. You can do your wine sampling at the round bar, at a table in the light-filled room, or in the foyer in the company of the huge collection of ducks in nearly every still-life form imaginable, from sculptures to pictures.

If this seems like mere quackery, Duckhorn offers two opportunities to do more than taste. Wine-serious visitors can schedule an estate tasting, which includes a discussion about the winery and the wines—primarily cabs, merlots, and pinots—and showcases Duckhorn's limited-production wines; it even includes a food pairing. There's also a more comprehensive educational series that focuses on the seasonal activities of the vineyard.

If you don't have time for these in-depth experiences, there's still plenty to do at Duckhorn. Walk through the gardens, peek into the cellar, and get to know the staff behind the bar. They can talk wine with you for days, and nothing you ask will ruffle their feathers.

Ehlers Estate

www.ehlersestate.com
3222 Ehlers Lane, St. Helena
707.963.5972
Daily 10am–5pm with prior appointment

Red wine is good for the heart. No place is this more true than at Ehlers Estate, where all the proceeds from its wine sales are donated to the LeDucq Foundation to benefit cardiovascular research.

Just visiting Ehlers Estate will improve your state of being. Walking through the grassy olive grove will calm you. Exploring the tasting room's historic photos, original equipment, and sensory-evaluation table will pique your imagination. The estate-made olive oil and vinegar will make your tastebuds sing. And tasting the wine made by winemaker extraordinaire Rudy Zuidema—especially the cabernet sauvignon—will definitely make you smile.

Sue, who will most likely be the person on the other side of the tasting bar, will make you feel right at home. She'll tell you about the joys of working for such a philanthropic owner, the wonderful wines, and the history of the estate. She'll chat about the wine business and life in the Valley, and she'll turn you on to the winery's next event. If she gets you to promise that you'll attend it, it won't be by twisting your arm. Sue's friendly vibe, Ehlers's superb wine, and the owner's heartfelt endeavors will be all the encouragement you'll need.

Hall Winery

www.hallwine.com
401 St. Helena Highway, St. Helena
707.967.2620 or 866.667.HALL
Daily 10am–5:30pm

If you want to learn how to make a fortune and buy a winery or two, check out the self-help and real estate books by Craig Hall, who with his wife, Kathryn, owns Hall Winery (Craig's books are for sale in the tasting room). Looking around the cheery digs, you gotta figure he knows what he's talking about.

A pretty archway of roses sitting right on the St. Helena Highway marks the entrance to the winery. Turn onto the property and follow the walkway between the sycamores, roses, and grapevines; it will lead you to a joyful red metal sculpture that looks like oversized ribbon candy. Two more modern

sculptures flank the front door, inviting you into a tasting room with a back wall made of glass, and magnificent views of the mountains and of more gigantic contemporary sculpture. Look out the side window to a grove of fruitless mulberry trees, with sweet red-trimmed tables and chairs beneath; sit for a while.

"Primary Colors," Hall's wine club name, slyly refers to the use of the color red as a decorative accent throughout the property; to Kathryn's strong political roots (she was ambassador to Austria during President Clinton's second term and has run for political office); and, of course, to the three reds that the winery is known for: cab, merlot, and cab franc. (There is also a Hall sauvignon blanc.)

An anteroom off the tasting room is devoted to extolling the Hall family history in words and pictures and running a short video about winemaking. After a glass of this estimable wine, after viewing the video, and after reading one of those how-to-make-money books . . . who knows? One day, this, too, could all be yours.

Heitz Wine Cellars
www.heitzcellar.com
500 Taplin Road, St. Helena
707.963.3542
By appointment only

In 1961, when the late Joe Heitz purchased the A. Rossi winery, which had been in operation until Prohibition, it was a property of little distinction. Then Joe stepped in, a young man with less than a decade of winemaking experience (although most of it was gained working at *Beaulieu Vineyard* under André Tchelistcheff). Christening the winery Heitz Wine Cellars, Joe soon set into motion a family-operated winery that today is as strong as ever, despite his absence.

A tour begins in the old stone winery, where it's easy to imagine Joe crafting his wines in the two-story gravity building. As you're guided to the newer building, which has a definite 1970s look and feel to it, you'll learn the small details that make Heitz Wine Cellars so unique. The business has built its reputation on two vineyards, neither of which it owns. Martha's Vineyard and Bella Oaks supply Heitz with grapes for the wines Joe released as Napa Valley's first single-designate cabs. Not only do these vineyards belong to other people, but there is no contract between the two parties— just a handshake, a remnant of a time when a gentleman's word was a way of doing business.

In the winery warehouse, you'll find a library of extraordinary wines dating back to 1961; they're sitting in the most utilitarian and plain room you could imagine. This complete lack of pretentiousness is exhibited by every member of the Heitz family. Everybody is happy to stop and answer questions from visitors. There's no pretty tasting room here (tastings are held at a separate location in St. Helena; see page 50); this is all about making the wine in the house that Joe built.

Joseph Phelps Vineyards

www.jpvwines.com
200 Taplin Road, St. Helena
707.963.2745
Retail sales Mon–Sat 9am–5pm, Sun 10am–4pm,
tours and tastings by appointment only

There are many reasons to visit Joseph Phelps Vineyards: the sprawling horizontal redwood winery with its shingled roof and somber demeanor; the big wooden entry trellis, entwined with vines so beefy they nearly seem muscular; and the six hundred acres of rolling, hilly ranchland, populated by native oaks and one hundred and sixty acres of tended vines. But two reasons stand out above all others: the wines themselves and the wine education to which the winery is devoted.

Joe Phelps began making California wines back in 1973, when the first Phelps wine, a johannisberg riesling, was introduced. Soon afterward, the winery presented its—and California's—first commercial syrah, thus setting the stage for pioneering Rhône-style wines, including viognier and the acclaimed Mistral, Phelps's proprietary blend.

Today the Phelps portfolio encompasses cab, chard, sauvignon blanc, merlot, and—when weather permits—dessert wines made from johannisberg riesling, semillon, and muscat. The well-known Insignia label is a blend of cab and other Bordeaux grape varietals from a handful of vineyards; it also represents yet another of Phelps Vineyards' firsts, this being the first California winery to create such a blend under a proprietary label.

You can taste these wines at a tasting bar that resembles a cashier's counter. It's in a small foyer area outside a larger room used for Phelps's atypical "tour": a video presentation that is shown to interested visitors. Geared toward beginners, it's a fine way to cut your wine-education baby teeth. You can follow up with the daily seminar that's offered here on a variety of subjects, from sensory evaluation of wine to food and wine dynamics to the blending of Phelps wines.

Louis M. Martini Winery

www.louismartini.com
254 St. Helena Highway South, St. Helena
800.321.WINE
Daily 10am–4:30pm

When *Gallo* acquired Louis Martini, a lot of people wondered if the change in ownership would be positive for the generations-old winery. The answer is a resounding yes. The completely renovated Martini tasting room is themed in black, gold, and red and is sumptuously, dramatically, impossibly gorgeous. From the highway it resembles a modern motel—but open the door and you'll wish it were your home.

The moment you enter the foyer (with its plush, gray velvet–covered furniture, Persian rugs, large circular table, and blown-up black-and-white photos of Louis M. and Louis P. Martini), you're greeted by a well-dressed server who offers you a tasting in a crystal glass; it's like you're at a posh private party. Go through the doors into the main tasting room, which has polished black wood shelving on one side and a super-sophisticated tasting area on the other.

This is no ordinary tasting room—it's a bona fide sexy bar, the kind with red velvet–upholstered barstools, flattering lighting, and the promise of something exciting in the air. Sit and enjoy a taste of one or more of the wines that Martini produces, from barbera to zinfandel. Look up at the skylights made of barrel staves. Look out at the serene, ivy-walled garden, with its wooden chairs and tables set with freshly cut flowers. Smile at the red umbrellas. Choose from the three- or four-wine flights, pick indoors or out, and relax.

Merryvale Vineyards

www.merryvale.com
1000 Main Street, St. Helena
707.963.3018
Daily 10am–6:30pm

Merryvale is right in St. Helena, making it a convenient stop while you're in town. Its unfussy visitor center is smack in the middle of the winery. The plain redwood walls are a stark contrast to the sumptuous merchandise the winery sells: candles, etched platters, and handcrafted items such as trays, baskets, and benches made from sanded and polished barrel staves.

The tasting bar offers three to six flights of wine in several categories: classic, reserve, prestige, all white, and all red. Nearly all of its wines—even the high-end cabs—are included in the flights. The folks behind the bar are extremely hospitable and quick to laugh; they seem to love their jobs. They'll gladly step out from behind the bar to walk you over to the dramatically arranged cask room or guide you to the library to explain its contents. In short, Merryvale goes that extra step. It's evident in its wines and in the way it treats visitors. This great service, combined with the staff's good nature, goes a long way toward making Merryvale the end-of-the-day gathering place for folks who work in other tasting rooms. Join them for a bit of local color.

Lunchtime St. Helena has wineries on both sides of town, and all are easy to reach from the center of town. So that's where lunch should be eaten. Try **Taylor's Automatic Refresher** (933 Main Street, St. Helena, 707.963.3486), a burger joint with a full menu of sandwiches, salads, and other tasty treats as well as a fantastic wine list.

Spottswoode Estate Vineyard and Winery

www.spottswoode.com
1902 Madrona Avenue, St. Helena
707.963.0134
By appointment only

With a barrel thief in one hand and a bottle of wine in another, your Spottswoode host will lead you to the barrel cellar to start your tour. She'll have you bring along your glass of "breakfast wine"—that sauvignon blanc you've been sipping on the porch of the beautiful 1880s Victorian house that is now home to the winery office.

The cellar is exemplary. Built in 1884 as a winery, the stone structure eventually devolved into a tractor barn. It was rescued by the Novak family, who purchased and restored it as the first part of realizing their dream of having their own winery. The story of how the Novaks finally achieved this dream is what makes the tour of Spottswoode so compelling. Yes, the winery is sensational; yes, you'll learn how its highly acclaimed cabernet and sauvignon blanc are produced; and yes, you'll float blissfully through the estate's utopian garden. But it's the guide's candid story about the family that you will remember best—second only to the wines. You'll be instantly infatuated by the sauvignon blanc and totally taken by the cabernet barrel sample, and when you finally sit down poolside to savor a glass of the current-release cab, it will be a full-blown love affair.

The Novaks are special people. They take care of the land by farming organically, take care of the workers who tend it, and ultimately take care of the people who drink their wine.

Vineyard 29
www.vineyard29.com
2929 St. Helena Highway North, St. Helena
707.963.9292
By appointment only

Vineyard 29's owner, Chuck McMinn, might have made his money in the high-tech industry, but today his life revolves around an interest in high-end wines and environmentally friendly winemaking. McMinn has created a flashy winery environment that's kind of James-Bond-meets-South-Beach, replete with shiny catwalks, smooth red cave floors, motion-sensor lighting, and Dale Chihuly glass art.

People interested in winemaking technology will be interested to see a rather unique Rube Goldbergish system for doing pumpovers, whereby an empty tank is lowered into the ground, filled with juice, and raised via a unique elevator; juice then flows back down into a waiting tank. The wine thus avoids bruising; berries and skins are left whole and unblemished; and everybody goes home happy.

What's especially great about this winery is that McMinn's commitment to green-energy principles has resulted in energy that is better for the environment, less expensive to produce, and more reliable than commercial energy. He starts by taking in natural gas and, using microturbines, converts it into electricity that heats and cools water; the cool water, in turn, becomes cooled air (very cool, in fact; bring a sweater into the caves). This is clearly not the simplest way to get these jobs done, so it's particularly refreshing to see somebody putting the environment first.

Of course, Vineyard 29 is not just a big green machine—it's also a rare-wine collector's Mecca. The winery produces only miniscule amounts of its own label every year; the rest of its production capacity is devoted to custom crushing. Since it releases only five hundred cases of its signature wine, Vineyard 29 cabernet sauvignon; barely more of its Aida line; and much, much less of its late-harvest zin, buy what you can when you're here—you may never get your hands on that bottle again.

Right: Spottswoode's iconic garden gate.

The Best of the Rest St. Helena is both an appellation and a town, and both have extraordinary wineries within their boundaries. It would take days to see them all, but along the St. Helena Highway (named for the mountain, not the town) are several wineries that can be visited in a single day. ···· On the southern end is **Corison Winery** (987 St. Helena Highway, St. Helena, 707.963.0826, daily 10am–5pm with prior appointment). Cathy Corison's winemaking domain is a large barn in which she makes wine for herself and for clients (she consults for, among others, the renowned sommelier Larry Stone). ···· **Sutter Home Winery** (277 St. Helena Highway South, St. Helena, www.sutterhome.com, 707.963.3104, daily 10am–5pm) is practically the inventor of white zinfandel, and has been one of the most influential wineries on the American wine landscape. Stop by the tasting room next to its picturesque Victorian mansion to taste the wine it's made famous— or head straight for the Trinchero Reserve Room to taste the wines that help make Napa Valley famous. ···· Just past Sutter Home is **Prager Winery** (1281 Lewelling Lane, St. Helena, www.pragerport.com, 800.969.PORT, daily 10am–4:30pm). This tasting room is a curiosity, known as much for the thousands of domestic and international currency bills stuck to the walls as for the well-liked port it offers. ···· **Salvestrin Winery** (397 Main Street, St. Helena, www.salvestrinwineco.com, 707.963.5105, by appointment only) has a cute tasting room on the second floor of a redwood winery that looks out over one of the first vineyards planted in Napa Valley, by pioneer George Crane. ···· On the other end of town is **Charles Krug** (2800 Main Street, St. Helena, www.charleskrug.com, 800.682.KRUG, daily 10:30am–5pm), a required stop for wine historians since Krug was the first commercial winemaker in Napa Valley. Of course, the winery reached greater acclaim via its association with Robert Mondavi. Robert's father, Cesare, purchased the winery in the 1940s; it was run by Robert and his brother Peter until the 1960s, when Robert—spectacularly—struck out on his own. ···· Farther north, stop in at **Freemark Abbey** (Highway 29 at Lodi Lane, St. Helena, www.freemarkabbey.com, 800.963.9698, summer daily 10am–6pm, winter daily 10am–5pm), a winery with a large tasting room that has an indoor sofa area and an outdoor patio where you can picnic along with a glass of wine. ···· Finally, on the fringes of St. Helena is **Benessere** (1010 Big Tree Road, St. Helena, www.benesserevineyards.com, 707.963.5853, Fri–Sun 10am–4pm), where sangiovese rules the roost, although the winery also offers zinfandel and syrah in the tasting room. It looks like a house in a Mediterranean suburb, with neat boxes of herbs and flowers, cute bistro tables, fresh blue and white paint, and long, low stone walls. Quirky fact: Benessere's location was the original home of *Charles Shaw* wine—better known as Two Buck Chuck.

SPRING MOUNTAIN

Spring Mountain's heavily wooded vineyards are hidden among a profusion of oaks, redwoods, and madrone. The region is without a doubt one of Napa Valley's most beautiful, and remains one of the less traveled. There are only about twenty wineries in Spring Mountain, but they are some of the Valley's most prominent producers and growers; they include *Paloma*, *York Creek*, and *Cain*. Cabernet sauvignon and merlot make up nearly 75 percent of Spring Mountain planting, with zinfandel, cab franc, chard, and a few other grapes filling the remainder of the vineyards.

Barnett Vineyards

www.barnettvineyards.com
4070 Spring Mountain Road, St. Helena
707.963.7075
By appointment only

> There are views and then there are views. And the *view* at Barnett would make a visit worthwhile even if you didn't drink wine. Clinging to the eastern front of Spring Mountain, Barnett looks down on the valley floor, some two thousand feet below.
>
> If you find your way to the top of the hill, the folks at Barnett will graciously share their delicious cab, merlot, pinot, and chard. In fact, weather permitting, you'll be led to the very highest point in Rattlesnake Vineyard: an open redwood deck where your host, Tyson, will share tales of how winery owners Hal and Fiona Barnett found the property, what the growing conditions are like, and the differences between valley and hillside fruit.
>
> Tyson will also pour you wines to taste up on the hill or in the cellar, and, if you like, he'll send you off on your own to explore the vineyard and the other vista points. You'll be enchanted by this stunning location where lizards, wildflowers, and grapevines live in perfect harmony.

Cain Vineyard & Winery

www.cainfive.com
3800 Langtry Road, St. Helena
707.963.1616
By appointment only

It's a loooong ride up to Cain, but worth every minute it takes. This exceptional bowl-shaped site sits on the absolute western edge of Napa County. This creates a variety of exposures in a single microclimate, making for interesting grapes and wines—and also making you feel like you're sitting on top of the world (you sort of are: you're at eighteen hundred to twenty-one hundred feet above sea level, at the top of the Mayacamas range). In spring and winter you may actually feel as though you're closer to the top of Mount Everest because it can get so cold and windy from the Pacific breezes. Bring a sweater so you can enjoy the astonishing view without catching cold.

Bring, too, your thirst for knowledge as well as your thirst for fine cabernets, because if you're on a tour, you won't sate one without the other. The tour here is superior. Thorough without being pedantic, it's technical enough to keep you on your toes and broad-based enough to be entertaining. Your highly competent guide will take you through the property, crush pad, fermentation area, and barrel room, although where you go will depend somewhat on the season. If the winery is racking and bottling, for example, you'll see that, too; if it's blending, you're really in luck.

Finally, you'll be invited to a sit-down, structured tasting held in a glassed-in room overlooking dogwoods, rhododendrons, azaleas, and a flurry of other flowers (could be the owners' southern roots are showing). Here you'll taste Cain's four wines: Cain Musqué, a pure sauvignon blanc; Cain Concept and Cain Cuvée, both cab blends; and Cain Five, the winery's signature blend of the five classic Bordeaux varietals. The people at Cain like to use the word *flow* to describe their wines, and it's apt: these are seamless wines, very balanced and very worth taking back down the mountain.

Guilliams Vineyards
3851 Spring Mountain Road, St. Helena
707.963.9059
By appointment only

Just as the road to good intentions is sometimes lined with pitfalls, so the road to Guilliams Vineyards is lined with rust—rusted cars and car parts for the most part, although some pieces of detritus are so old and abandoned as to be unrecognizable. But don't worry; everything you see belongs to antique car collector/restorer and winemaker John Guilliams, and spending time with him and his wife, Shawn, is about as interesting as it gets.

John started his career as a cooper; after studying the techniques of his enologist friends, he decided to become a home winemaker. While clearing out the woods on their land to plant vines, the Guilliams discovered grapevines already in the ground. It turned out that in 1875, theirs had been the site of the first Spring Mountain vineyard. Before long, the Guilliams were making fifteen hundred cases per year, all produced in a winery in the basement of their home. The first in the area to plant cab franc, they now grow 80 percent cab, 10 percent merlot, and 10 percent cab franc. They blend based on taste—every bottle reflects their commitment to the best expression of their land.

The Guilliams are earnest, intelligent, honest, and intense. They are ready to discuss anything having to do with their location and profession— from the politics of monoculture to the challenges of forming a winery association. They are kind of Renegade Lite winemakers: progressive thinkers who are accessible, challenging, and definitely engaging. This is home winemaking with a Ph.D.

Newton Vineyard
www.newtonvineyard.com
2555 Madrona Road, St. Helena
707.963.9000
By appointment only

Newton Vineyard has something no other winery does: a bright-red British telephone booth. If the gate's closed, you'll have to announce your arrival by entering the booth and calling the winery. Then you'll weave your way up the southern side of Spring Mountain on a road peppered with weeping cherry trees. Resplendent when in bloom, these trees are the first indication of the gardens that await you.

As you reach the peak of the hill, a line of cypress trees distracts you from seeing the winery. This is an intentional camouflage by owner Peter Newton, in response to criticism he received previously for the design of *Sterling Vineyards*, which was built under his management. Accused of having built an ostentatious structure, Newton took a different direction when it came time to build his own winery: he turned the entire campus into a garden. The effect is marvelous.

Behind the hillside cypress sits an office building covered entirely in brightly colored flowering vines blooming in a burst of white, purple, and orange. The parts of the winery that are not dug into the mountain are covered with greenery. On top of the chardonnay cellar is a formal English parterre, a tribute to Newton's birthplace. A lavender-filled garden imbues the air with perfume, and creeping fig adorns one entire side of the cellar. Adding even more drama to the landscape are bright-red Asian lamps, a welcome gate, and a cedar pagoda that reflect Peter's wife's Chinese heritage. And everywhere you look, you'll notice juniper trees shaped into corkscrews, a whimsical nod to the true nature of the property.

With so much garden to look at, it might be difficult to divert your attention to the vineyard, but do: it's a great example of hillside planting. Rows twist and turn to follow the contours of the land, creating a beautiful portrait of mountain farming.

Your visit culminates with a chance to taste the merlots, chards, pinots, and cabs that have brought the Newtons their greatest acclaim. This is truly the place of wine and roses.

Pride Mountain Vineyards

www.pridewines.com
4026 Spring Mountain Road, St. Helena
707.963.4949
By appointment only

The hills surrounding Pride Mountain Vineyards are a crazy quilt of crosshatched grape plantings that are masterfully designed to take advantage of the various exposures. Here on Spring Mountain, in a place where sun, wind, and rainfall make the difference between a good vintage and a great one, it's clear that Pride has met the demands of the soil with the discipline of a scientist and the eye of a painter.

Weather permitting, a tour will take you through the vineyards and then through twenty-two thousand square feet of caves. On your way into the caves, you'll have the unusual experience of straddling the county line between Napa and Sonoma.

Your tour ends with a tasting at the mountain cabin—persimmon and green on the outside, dark and casual on the inside. Expect to be served two to three wines from a selection of merlot, cab franc, viognier, chardonnay, and cabernet sauvignon—whatever is not already sold out. After you're done comparing and contrasting, hike through the property to the tables at the top of the hill, and enjoy the glorious views.

On your way out, be sure to visit the abandoned winery that's on the property. All that's left is a few stone walls, but it is still a pretty site.

Ritchie Creek Vineyard
www.ritchiecreek.com
4024 Spring Mountain Road, St. Helena
707.963.4661
By appointment only

If the junk on the side of the road sends out one kind of signal (it looks like nothing's been moved off the mountain since Ritchie Creek's vineyard was first planted in 1967), the fertile red soil that surrounds it sends out another. Tune in to the earth vibrations, and close your eyes to the rest. Because this is the real thing: an eight-hundred-case winery that makes wines great enough to have deservedly achieved praise from some very picky aficionados.

The winery was begun in a Berkeley garage by Peter Minor, a dentist by profession and an oenophile by passion. While he remains the winemaker of record, his son Tad is likely to be the one to meet you for a tasting, which is held on a plank between two barrels. We dare you to leave without at least one bottle of the Ritchie Creek Blaufrankisch, an unusual—and luscious—varietal that may remind you of Grandma's blueberry pie.

Sherwin Family Vineyards

www.sherwinfamilyvineyards.com
4060 Spring Mountain Road, St. Helena
707.963.1154
By appointment only

Since the opening of Sherwin Family Vineyards, Steve and Linda Sherwin have been like new parents, and the excitement they exude about their venture is contagious. Visiting the Sherwins is like stopping in to say hi to friends of the family. They are warm and jovial, genuine and generous, and all-around nice. You'll feel like old pals within minutes. Steve, a former commercial real estate developer, will show photos of the land being cleared, talk about the tractors he used to remove the thousands of rocks and boulders in the red, red soil, and explain how the irrigation pond was ingeniously drained and lined. Linda will cheerfully recount the evenings spent with Steve in their all-terrain driving cart, traipsing across the entire property to check on the sixteen hundred newly planted vines.

Sherwin is set up on Spring Mountain in its own bowl carved out of a forest of redwood, madrone, and oak trees, and could pass for a luxury mountain retreat as easily as it does a vineyard and winery. It's infused with the dreamy, aromatic fragrance of earth and foliage; one deep breath is all it takes to know you are someplace you'll want to stay for a while. The winery building is filled with plush, elegant furnishings. A large deck looks out over the vineyards and a pond big enough to seem like a lake. Every detail is accounted for, from the antique winemaking equipment to the open kitchen; when you enter, it's love at first sight.

On a typical visit, the Sherwins will welcome you into the winery with a glass of their mountain cab and offer to walk you around the property (be sure to wear sturdy shoes). As you tour, you'll hear how the Sherwins found the property, decided to make wine and expand the existing vineyard, adapted to mountain living, met their neighbors, chose to raise squab in an old pigeon coop, laid out the vineyards to provide the best sun exposure for each row, and took pragmatic and logical actions every step of the way. They'll tell you about Spring Mountain's climate and growing conditions and what varietals are planted in each of the blocks named after their three children. You'll get to see the vines, the soil, and the mountain up close and at a leisurely pace.

After you've seen the better part of the property, you'll return to the winery. Prepare not to recognize the crush pad—it's neat and clean, with the tops of the tanks hardly noticeable, set as they are into the gray floor. When you finally go downstairs into the cellar, it's almost a relief to see the obviously well-used everyday winery tools and hoses scattered about. Tanks, barrels, and equipment are all in one room. Again, you'll notice Steve's efficient mind at work when he explains a few of the smart techniques he's implemented.

After you've finished the tour, drained your glass of the Sherwins' terrific wines, made a purchase, and taken one last peek at the property from the porch, you'll leave with two overriding and lasting impressions: the Sherwins love what they do, and you can taste it in the bottle.

Lunchtime Spring Mountain has lured some righteous winemakers up the hill, but so far not a single chef. So travel back to downtown St. Helena and take advantage of **Martini House**'s (1140 Oak Avenue, St. Helena, 707.963.2233) three-course price-fixed lunch. It's the best deal in town, and its wine list is as entertaining to read as a good book.

Spring Mountain Vineyard
www.springmountainvineyard.com
2805 Spring Mountain Road, St. Helena
707.967.4188
Mon–Sat by appointment only

If the property of Spring Mountain Vineyard seems familiar, that's because it probably is: the historic Victorian house was used as the setting for the 1980s prime-time drama *Falcon Crest*. While Spring Mountain Vineyard may have gained notoriety as the fictional home of Angela Channing and her feuding television family, the estate's real-life history is just as dramatic.

Developed in the 1880s by Tiburico Parrot, the illegitimate son of John Parrot, the U.S. consul in Mexico, the homestead was very typical of the Victorian era, with lush gardens that included an abundance of tropical palm, citrus, and olive trees. Parrot cleared the land, planted the vineyards, and built a home, naming it Miravalle. He also began to tunnel into the hillside to create a personal wine cellar, but died before its completion.

The property sat dormant until the 1970s when Mike Robbins, a real estate developer, bought the property and began producing wines from the vineyards. They received critical acclaim, but Robbins was in over his head; he sold it in 1991 to Jacob Safra, a London banker, who began restoring it to its original luster.

With the completion of the winery and caves, the restoration of Miravalle and the gardens, and the expansion of the vineyards, Spring Mountain was made available to the public in 2004. Small, intimate tours are led by Valli Ferrell, the winery's public relations director and wife of general manager Tom Ferrell. The Ferrells know the property as well as anyone: they were instrumental in its purchase by Safra, guided every detail of its restoration, and lived here for a short time. Valli's first-hand experience makes the tour feel all the more personal as she leads you on a comprehensive exploration of the winery. She begins in the barn, which holds antique equipment and artifacts from Parrot's time, takes you through the glorious caves and tropical garden, and ends in the house for a sit-down tasting of Spring Mountain wines.

Two to three wines are poured to showcase the property's breadth, depth, and potential. You may try a sauvignon blanc, a syrah, a cabernet sauvignon, or even Elivette, Spring Mountain's reserve cab blend—a wine as intriguing as the winery's past.

Stony Hill Vineyard

www.stonyhillvineyard.com
3331 St. Helena Highway North, St. Helena
707.963.2636
Mon–Fri by appointment only

In a part of the world so lovingly devoted to cab and zin, it's rare to find an all-white-wine producer. Stony Hill is such a place. This petite winery, built of stone and stucco on the outside, gives way on the inside to a world filled with estate-grown white Burgundy.

In business for more than fifty years, Stony Hill is best known for its superior chardonnay, but you should also be aware of its excellent riesling, gewürztraminer, semillon, and tocai friulano. To get to this tiny winery, you have to travel two miles up a winding road bordered by chardonnay vines. The road is as steep as it is shaded and shrubby, and when you finally get there, it's as if you've driven into an authentic part of Europe you just never knew existed.

Let your guide walk you around the barrel room, where you'll learn about the rigors of producing and bottling five thousand cases of five different varietals; about the process of noninterventionist winemaking; and about the challenges of gently taming the strong mountain fruit into a food-friendly beverage. It's a personal, one-on-one visit you'll have here, and you'll come away with great insight into these Spring Mountain white beauties.

Terra Valentine

www.terravalentine.com
3787 Spring Mountain Road, St. Helena
707.967.8340
By appointment only

Fame and fortune do strange things to people. After Fred Aves invented the curb feeler to protect whitewall tires, the automatic rear-view mirror, and the rustproof Volkswagen tailpipe, he packed his bags and headed for the hills.

A divorced self-made millionaire in the 1960s, Fred settled on Spring Mountain. He brought with him five laborers, who helped him hand-split and place stones until they formed a two-story winery. Fred named that winery Yverdon and set up shop as a reclusive artist and winemaker. He hand-molded concrete columns for the cellar, made stained-glass windows depicting mythical and astrological scenes and placed them throughout the entire building, built spiral staircases featuring grapevine-shaped rails, and constructed wrought-iron steps with grape leaves to indicate foot placement.

Today, Fred Aves's property is known as Terra Valentine, and here you can see his apparently limitless capacity for creating unusual wood, metal, and concrete art. Three years after this strange, reclusive genius passed away in 1996, the property was purchased by its current owners, Angus and Margaret Wurtele. The Wurteles updated the winemaking equipment— Fred produced a cab under the Yverdon label, but it never developed much of a following—and made a few other upgrades to the structure, careful to preserve the ornate doors, hinges, windows, and woodcarvings.

After an in-depth look at the art and craft that Fred left behind (Fred might not approve of all the people touring about his creation, but he would have to be—rightly—proud of the attention his work garners), a tour of Terra Valentine finishes in a room paneled with ornate wood that

was originally destined for William Randolph Hearst's San Simeon Castle. A sit-down tasting features cheese and chocolates as welcome accompaniments to the winery's hillside cabs. The Wurteles see that four wines are poured, including older vintages made from their Spring Mountain vineyards. With just a few sips, you'll see that winemaker Sam Baxter's talent elevates this extraordinary and unusual winery, which turns out to be as much a treat for the palate as it is for the eyes.

The Best of the Rest To drive from the center of St. Helena to the most remote winery on Spring Mountain takes only about twenty minutes, and yet it seems much longer because it's so different up here. There are a dozen or so great vintners nestled into the mountain, making scheduling a challenge if you don't have a few days to play with. ···· If you can arrange it, visit **Schweiger Vineyards** (4015 Spring Mountain Road, St. Helena, www.schweigervineyards.com, 707.963.7980, by appointment only). A family-run winery, Schweiger makes mountain wines that you'll want to cellar to let their character emerge over time. ···· The long road that leads to **Robert Keenan Winery** (3660 Spring Mountain Road, St. Helena, www.keenanwinery.com, 707.963.9177, Sat–Sun 11am–4pm) is dusty and narrow, making you wonder if the drive is worth it. It is. Crafted by Nils Venge, Keenan wines are great.

STAGS LEAP

Among the oldest vines in Stags Leap are the petite sirah vines on the *Stags' Leap Winery* property. Like the cabernet sauvignon that grows here prominently, petite sirah thrives in the dry, warm daytime conditions and benefits from the Pacific Ocean's cooling breezes. Characterized by a mix of volcanic soils and river sediment soils, vineyards in the Stags Leap district produce grapes with elegant tannins and bright, vibrant fruit flavors.

Chimney Rock Winery

www.chimneyrock.com
5350 Silverado Trail, Napa
707.257.2036 or 800.257.2641
Daily 10am–5pm

Designed in a seventeenth-century Cape Dutch style—with distinctive chalk-white stucco walls, heavy wooden accents, arched gables, stepped roofs, and colorful flower beds—Chimney Rock Winery is as close as the Napa Valley gets to looking like South Africa.

Left: Chimney Rock's courtyard.

The appealing, antique-filled tasting room has a marble-topped bar and nice light. It leads out to a feminine, arbor-covered garden and patio area where you sit at tables situated a stone's throw from a second, equally interesting structure: the first winery building. Its ornate, massive roof relief—an allegorical frieze of Ganymede, cupbearer to the gods—adds yet another dimension to the destination's architectural significance.

The wines here are really well-made cabs, merlots, chards, and fumé blancs. Tasting them, you'd never guess the vineyard on which their fruit grew was once a golf course.

Clos Du Val

www.closduval.com
5330 Silverado Trail, Napa
707.259.2225 or 800.993.9463
Daily 10am–5pm

Clos Du Val—a "small estate of a small valley"—was founded in 1972 on 150 acres of land. Before long, the winery's winning combination of old-world winemaking and Napa fruit was making headlines: its first vintage was one of only five California cabs selected for the legendary 1976 Paris tasting, in which a California wine, shockingly, took first place among a panel of blindfolded French judges. In a rematch a decade later, Clos Du Val's same 1972 vintage took first place. It's fair to say that Clos Du Val helped put California on the world's wine map.

Visiting the winery is informative. A detailed plaque gives a row-by-row explanation of the vineyard details, from trellising and training methods to rootstock and spacing; graphic and "eyes-on," it's a helpful learning tool.

The tasting room—ivy-covered on the outside, high-beamed, dark-wooded, and tile-floored on the inside—has pretty louvered windows that overlook the vineyard. As for the winery's retail marketing, it's raised the bar for branding. You'll find Clos Du Val's tasteful, loopy signature swirl on everything from silk pajamas and boxers to frosted glasses and sleep masks. Buy anything at all, and you'll take home a remembrance of a nice visit.

Hartwell Vineyards

www.hartwellvineyards.com
5795 Silverado Trail, Napa
707.255.4269 or 800.366.6516
Thur–Sat by appointment only

A driveway flanked by graceful Italian cypress trees that stand like sentinels leads you to Hartwell Vineyards. Surrounded by oak trees and longhaired Scottish Highland cattle, Hartwell is a small, exquisitely appointed winery with fantastic views of the Stag's Leap Palisades. Devoted mostly to cab (with some merlot for good measure), it produces little more than four thousand cases a year made from exclusively estate-grown, hand-picked fruit.

Purchased in 1985, the Hartwell Vineyards estate was immediately planted with clones given to Bob Hartwell from friend Dick Grace of *Grace Family Vineyards*. True to the vineyard's noble lineage, Hartwell's first harvest, in 1990, was an immediate success. This and everything else you want to know about the Stags Leap district, the winery's history, and winemaking in general will be explained to you during your enjoyable tour with Barbara. Hers is a tour worth taking. A farmer's daughter, she not only understands the business, she also has the inside scoop on the goings-on of the whole Valley and doesn't hesitate to entertain as well as inform.

After your tour, you'll enjoy a tasting in a voluptuously round room set into the heart of the cave. There you'll sit at a large octagonal table, radiant in the glow of a multitude of candles, tasting the full portfolio of wines. It's a heavenly experience.

Regusci Winery

www.regusciwinery.com
5584 Silverado Trail, Napa
707.254.0403
Daily 10am–5pm with prior appointment

Entering the grounds of Regusci Winery begins a journey back in time. Walnut trees line one side of the road, and a dry streambed lines the other. Adjacent hillsides are covered in lavender, natural grasses, and low stone walls. Olive and citrus trees dot the landscape, and large lawns beckon. The sum of such splendor is a setting that feels like a return to a simpler and much more leisurely era.

The historic winery structure was built in 1878. Somehow its hand-cut lava-stone façade, rough-hewn timber beams, and shapely arched windows convey a kind of Wild West–Mediterranean feel; it's like a scene-stealing set taken from a classic spaghetti western. You get a starring role when you belly up to the bar to taste.

Owned and operated by the Regusci family since 1998, the winery produces excellent cab, merlot, zin, and chard. Try the Angelo's Vineyard cabernet sauvignon, a limited-production wine, or its fantastic zinfandel. They're all as impressively genuine as the place they are made.

Robert Sinskey Vineyards

www.robertsinskey.com
6320 Silverado Trail, Napa
800.869.2030
Daily 10am–4:30pm, tours and weekend seated tastings by appointment only

Horses graze near the stone-pillared entrance of Robert Sinskey, and why not? This is an Edenic plot of land, bursting forth with flowering vines and sensual trees, made aromatic by a rose-and-wisteria-covered pergola, and rendered even more tempting by bountiful vegetable and herb gardens.

But this is more than just pretty gardens: it's a perfect place for a serious lesson in farming and geology. Look closely at the lavender in the front yard, and you'll discern the growth pattern differences within a contained section of land—the bigger plants indicate more fertile soil, and the smaller plants indicate soil that's naturally less nutrient-rich. It's an object lesson in how soil patterns affect plant growth—including the variation of vine vigor within different blocks of a vineyard.

Within the warmly lit, redwood-ceilinged tasting room—decorated with antique French kitchen furniture—other lessons apply. Cooking lessons, for example, given in the fully stocked professional vineyard kitchen run by Maria Helm Sinskey. Learn about the importance of location when you taste the different varietals Sinskey produces from vineyards throughout Napa Valley, such as pinot from Carneros and cab from Stags Leap.

And when it comes to touring at Sinskey, be prepared to make some tough choices: select among the culinary tour, the cave tour, and the library wine tour. Some include food, and each has its individual merits. Or call in advance to reserve a private seated tasting on the terrace (weather permitting). It's a complete destination winery, guaranteed to be the stuff of good memories.

> **Lunchtime** Spread out along the western foothills of the Vaca range, the Stags Leap district is lined with great wineries but devoid of eateries. Take the Yountville Cross Road into Yountville, and pick up ham sandwiches (cold or hot-pressed) at **Bouchon Bakery** (6528 Washington Street, Yountville, 707.944.2253). The artisanal bread wraps itself deliciously around butter, Dijon mustard, and ham; it may be among the most fantastic sandwiches you've ever eaten. (And don't forget peanut butter cookies or chocolate bouchons for later.)

Shafer Vineyards

www.shafervineyards.com
6154 Silverado Trail, Napa
707.994.2877
Retail sales Mon–Fri 9am–4pm, tours and tastings by appointment only

Shafer Vineyards is hands-down one of the best wine producers in the Napa Valley. Its vineyards' shallow volcanic soil is the starting point for creating its celebrated high-end cabs, including Shafer Hillside Select, its signature wine. The winery also crafts meticulous chard, merlot, syrah, and Firebreak, a sangiovese-cabernet blend.

To snag a coveted place in a tour and tasting here, you must call about three weeks in advance of your visit. Friendly canine greeters Jake, Tucker, and Pinto usher you into a hosting area called the Big Dog room, which refers less to your escorts than to you, the VIP guest. Tours begin outside, where you can see all the way down through the Valley to the Bay. You are then guided through the production areas, caves, and state-of-the-art barrel cellar—the latter being Shafer's pride and joy. It looks like an industrial art exhibition, with its blond-wood cathedral ceiling, clean slate colors, smooth concrete walls, and shiny pressed-gravel floor.

As you walk through the property, ask your informative guide about the winery's sustainable agriculture practices and the history of the Stags Leap district. If you are unable to get a spot on the tour and tasting, you can still stop by for retail sales; however, even for that, it pays to call before you come to make sure they have on hand the bottles you desire.

Stag's Leap Wine Cellars

www.CASK23.com
5766 Silverado Trail, Napa
707.265.2441 or 800.422.7523
Daily 10am–4:30pm, tours by appointment only

It's hard to determine where the hill ends and Stag's Leap Wine Cellars begins. This winery is a paean to the very soil on which it stands. The spare adobe structure, adorned only by tree roots and weathered rock, imparts a pueblo-like sense of humble purity and metaphysical mystery. It's as sedate and serious as the wines are spectacular.

In the middle of the winery's vast network of caves is the Round Room, graced by a Foucault pendulum at its center. Winemaker Warren Winiarski thinks of it as "the beating heart of our cave" and considers its movement "a metaphor for the passing of time and aging of our wines."

Stag's Leap Wine Cellars is an extremely worthy place to visit. Established in 1972, the winery came to public attention—and extraordinary public acclaim—when its 1973 cabernet sauvignon from S.L.V. (formerly known as Stag's Leap Vineyard) won top honors at the famous 1976 Paris tasting. Today the winery is known for a small handful of wines made with grapes from other vineyards, including the renowned Fay Vineyard. In the tasting room, you can sample wines from each vineyard, along with estate wines. As you drink from your glass, you'll quickly understand why the French had to swallow their pride—along with their cabernet—more than thirty years ago.

Stags' Leap Winery

www.stagsleap.com
6150 Silverado Trail, Napa
707.944.1303
By appointment only

Ne Cede Malis—"Don't give in to misfortune"—was the motto of Stags' Leap Winery founder Horace Chase, and his belief in this adage was so strong he had it etched into the stained-glass window that adorns the winery's Manor House.

Stags' Leap has changed hands a few times since Horace commissioned the window in 1893, but the Manor House has retained its glory and so have the caves, the vineyards, and the view of the Palisades, where the legendary stags that gave the region its name were first discovered.

Today, *Ne Cede Malis* is also the name given to a proprietary Rhône-style blend that includes petite sirah from seventy-year-old vines grown on the estate. This is one of the wines you might have the opportunity to taste, along with Stags' Leap's signature petite sirah and its viognier, merlot, and cab.

Tasting the wines concludes a tour that begins in the renovated cave, travels through the grounds, where the in-ground swimming pool (rumored to be the first in Napa Valley) was installed, and runs into the stone house built like a castle, turret and all. Anyone with porch envy will turn green with jealousy when they eye the large one attached to the northern side of the house. Not only is it so big that it dwarfs most New York City apartments, it is filled with wicker furniture that evokes images of the times past when guests traveled up from San Francisco to spend the weekend with the second owners, the Granges. The tour gives you the inside scoop on the lore surrounding the estate—everything from the importance of the apostrophe placement in the winery's name to the monkey that lived on the property to the location's history as a post office. This is a tour that merits the effort to schedule.

YOUNTVILLE

The Yountville appellation is where the first grapevines were planted in the Napa Valley by pioneer George Yount, one of the original land grantees. Today the region is planted heavily to a variety of red grapes and a few white grapes, including pinot grigio, sauvignon blanc, and viognier. Despite its relatively large size and numerous vineyards, only a handful of wineries call Yountville home.

Domaine Chandon

www.chandon.com
1 California Drive, Yountville
707.944.2280
May–October daily 10am–6pm,
November–April Sun–Fri 11am–5pm, Sat 10am–6pm

Imagine a genteel, spirited private park filled with luxurious lawns and majestic trees gaily dappled by sunlight. Imagine spring-fed ponds and outdoor sculptures that are as beautiful as they are provocative or amusing. Imagine people chatting happily or wandering about in contented silence over grassy knolls. Now picture yourself in the middle of it all, lounging on a shaded terrace, sipping from a glass filled with sparkling bubbles.

No, it's not a dream—it's Domaine Chandon. Start off at the visitor center, with its attractive retail space and murals that celebrate winemaking. Enter the tasting area, with its wine barrel–vaulted ceiling. Behind the bar, massive plate-glass windows slide open to bring the outside in, bathing the whole room in soft breezes and natural light. It all elevates the concept of "extraordinarily pleasant" to a whole new level.

Perhaps the best time to come and linger is on a balmy Sunday evening, since this winery is open later than most. Buy a bottle or order a flight (or, if you're with friends, share two or three flights for side-by-side comparisons). The staff is smart and thoughtful and will be glad to help guide your tasting. Since you might not ordinarily have the opportunity to taste the reserve and vintage wines, this could be a good occasion to learn the nuances of different varietal compositions and the effects of aging, and to really see what you like.

The Best Winery Restaurant in Napa Valley It's true: there's only one. But it's hard to imagine there could be a better winery dining spot than the ultra-plush restaurant at **Domaine Chandon** (1 California Drive, Yountville, www.chandon.com, 707.944.2892). Think soft candlelight, understated elegance, and the finest china and crystal in service of a California-accented French menu that's created to be paired with wine. In fact, the restaurant rightfully prides itself on having mastered the fine art of food and wine pairing, as evidenced by a stupendous wine list—a real wine **lover's** list—with many delectable choices and some extraordinarily rare wines (like old **Domaine de la Romanée-Conti**). Since it opened its doors in the '70s, the restaurant at Domaine Chandon has been adding to its highly praised cellar. As for the dining room's location, it's simply breathtaking, built into the small slope of the same hill on which the winery sits, with windows that open to the California countryside. Domaine Chandon is the quintessential wine country restaurant in which to celebrate a special occasion.

Right: Hay barn in Yountville.

Elyse

www.elysewinery.com
2100 Hoffman Lane, Napa
707.944.2900
Daily 10am–5pm

Elyse's teeny-tiny winery looks a little like the home kitchen of a science nerd. But the results taste a lot bigger than you'd first imagine. These are sturdy, robust wines made by owner Ray Coursen and winemaker Nancy Cuthbertson, who together create "spice-rack" blends (a little bit of this and a little of that—mostly instinct, taste, and hard work).

So while you won't find a single cookie-cutter wine, you will find two labels, each named for the owner's children. The Elyse label includes zins, cabs, syrahs, and a marsanne, its token white, while the Jacob Franklin label is dedicated to three single-vineyard petite sirahs. Line up the latter for a tasting, and see for yourself how different the Chavez/Leeds, Howell Mountain, and Hayne vineyards really are. By the time you're done, you'll be your own science nerd—and you'll fit right in.

Havens Wine Cellars

www.havens.com
2055 Hoffman Lane, Napa
707.261.2000
By appointment only

Michael Havens single-handedly put California merlot on the map. Yes, there were others who transformed the grape into great juice, but when Havens began making it from Carneros fruit, Parker started raving about it and *merlot* became a household word.

That was nearly twenty years ago. Since then, Havens Wine Cellars has carved out its niche and expanded its repertoire. Today, in addition to merlot, it produces outstanding syrah, a proprietary red blend called Bourriquot, and albariño, a white grape originally grown and used in Spain and Portugal; Havens was the first to commercially offer albariño in America.

The sole purpose of a visit to Havens is to taste the wine line-up. There's no horse and pony show, just an unpretentious, personalized tasting opportunity. In warm weather you can sit outside at sun-dappled tables beneath the ancient oak trees; in winter, you'll gather around a table inside the barrel room (wear a jacket—it can get awfully cold in there). Your wine-savvy host will pour and chat with you as though you're old friends who've stopped by for a visit. Even if you intend to stay for only a minute, don't be surprised to find yourself whiling away the time, soaking up the good wine and relishing the good company.

Lunchtime Yountville is often called the Gourmet Ghetto of Napa Valley because it's bursting with absolutely fantastic restaurants. Per capita, it probably rivals New York. With so many choices, it's difficult to pick just one place for lunch, but if you must, you must. So go to **Bistro Jeanty** (6510 Washington Street, Yountville, 707.944.0103) for the quiche. Or the frisée salad. Or maybe the tomato soup. . . .

Right: Champagne maker's riddling rack.

Sonoma County Appellations

Sonoma County is composed of more than a million acres, sixty thousand of which are planted with grapevines. There are twelve appellations within the county, which itself is an appellation. The whole shebang is bordered by the Pacific Ocean coastline on the west, the Mayacamas on the east, Marin County on the south, and Mendocino on the north.

ALEXANDER VALLEY

Alexander Valley is composed of more soil types than any other wine-growing region in California. The region's history of dramatic geologic activity—from an ancient mudflow that changed the course of the Russian River to earthquake upheavals that redistributed whole sections of earth—created tremendous soil diversity and influenced the contours of the land. These characteristics, combined with a range of microclimates, make Alexander Valley ideal for growing cab with powerful flavors, texture, and tannins. Other grapes that have proven successful for growers in the region are syrah, sangiovese, zinfandel, and sauvignon blanc.

Chateau Souverain

www.chateausouverain.com
400 Souverain Road, Geyserville
888.80.WINES
Daily 10am–5pm

> Francophiles will think they're California dreaming when they set foot on the grounds of Chateau Souverain, a winery that combines the body of a typical grand French chateau with the heart (and roofline) of Sonoma's rustic hop kilns. Built in 1973, it won an American Institute of Architects Design of Excellence Award.
>
> Chateau Souverain is organized around two prominent towers. One tower, with breathtaking views of the estate vineyards, the Alexander Valley, and Mount St. Helena, is dedicated to the winery's tasting room and restaurant. The tasting room sells older vintages, large-format bottles, and limited-release wines. But you're better off doing your tasting in Chateau Souverain's restaurant, where excellent food will complement your wine selections. Before or after dining, walk around to take in the full effect of the chateau.

Jordan Vineyard and Winery

www.jordanwinery.com
1474 Alexander Valley Road, Healdsburg
707.431.5250 or 800.654.1213
By appointment only

> If it weren't for the American flag waving in the breeze, you'd think Jordan was a French aristocrat's private country manor—in France! The traditional chateau stands alone on a hill, vast and noble, surrounded by more than a thousand acres, almost three hundred of which are meticulously tended

Right: Welcome to Jordan.

vineyards. Sculpted hedges sit comfortably among towering trees, and the winery is luxuriously draped in crawling vines. It all immediately telegraphs the delicate balance that has been achieved here between man and nature.

Founded in 1972 as the first ultra-premium winery in Alexander Valley, Jordan offers one of the best tours anywhere. A well-informed guide begins your tour outdoors with a lively history of the region, the life of owner Tom Jordan, and the winery. Your walk around the property takes you from the vineyards, man-made lakes, and kitchen garden to the stainless-steel fermentation tanks, symmetrically arranged classic oak storage tanks, and private dining room. Along the way you'll sample Jordan's Tuscan-style olive oil (luscious, peppery, and acidic), learn about the winery's native connection to prune orchards, and come to understand and respect its legacy relationship with *Lafitte Rothschild*.

The tour ends in a plush drawing room, where you'll sit on comfortable sofas to taste ooh-la-la current releases of chardonnay and cabernet and discuss wine impressions with your small group of fellow tasters. In this room you'll also find library and large-format bottles for sale, as well as a range of sterling silver pieces, furniture, blankets, and more, all designed by Tom's wife, Sandy Jordan.

Lunchtime Smack in the middle of Alexander Valley is the **Jimtown Store** (6706 Highway 128, Healdsburg, 707.433.1212). An oasis of yummy sandwiches and other lunch treats with a good dose of country kitsch thrown in, Jimtown is the place to stop for lunch. Have it packed to go or take it out back and eat in the shade on the patio.

Robert Young Estate Winery
www.ryew.com
4960 Red Winery Road, Geyserville
707.431.4811
Wed–Sat 10am–4:40pm, Sun 12–4:30pm

Robert Young looks like it could have been Betsy Ross's summer home. This traditional white pillared house with prissy lawns is a bit incongruous—it's like a little piece of Americana plunked down in the rugged Sonoma countryside. It's just enough out of place to make you pause before parking.

But inside the small tasting room, all misgivings quickly fade away. This is the real thing: a winery run by a family that's now in its fourth generation of farming and living on the ranch. The walls of the tasting room are sweetly decorated with old-time memorabilia: clothing artifacts, Sears catalogues, and photos that tell the story of the times in pictures. More recent history includes the facts that Robert Young, an innovative farmer, pioneered the conversion of California prune orchards into vineyards and, in 1963, was the first to plant cabernet sauvignon in Alexander Valley. Spend some time chatting with the genuinely enthusiastic, knowledgeable tasting-room host, whose good-natured passion for the history and wines of the area is impressive. And be sure to taste all the wines. One sip and you'll understand why so many other wineries have prospered using the chardonnay, cab, and merlot grapes grown by Robert Young—the quality of the fruit is superb.

Sleep among the Vines In Alexander Valley, the **Robert Young Estate Winery** (4960 Red Winery Road, Geyserville, www.ryew.com, 707.431.4811) offers for rent a luxurious two-bedroom home in the middle of the vineyards. Bring the kids or spend a weekend with friends.

Simi Winery
www.simiwinery.com
16275 Healdsburg Avenue, Healdsburg
707.473.3231
Daily 10am–5pm

Simi is Sonoma County's most historic and storied winery. Founded in 1876 by two Tuscan-born brothers, Giuseppe and Pietro Simi, the winery evolved in epic fashion.

The brothers chose the spot on which Simi stands because it reminded them of their homeland. They quickly began planting vineyards and building a gravity-fed stone cellar. The first half of the cellar was completed in 1890 by Chinese laborers, who were working at the time on the railroad line that bisects the winery property. The second half of the cellar was built by Italian masons, whose work clearly contrasts with the earlier portion; you can see the difference in just a glance.

As the cellar neared completion, the brothers both passed away unexpectedly, leaving Giuseppe's fourteen-year-old daughter, Isabelle, in charge. A remarkable character in every way, Isabelle worked at the winery until her death in 1981, even though she had sold the winery a few years earlier.

During Prohibition, Isabelle saved Simi by cellaring wines, which were then available for sale when the ban was repealed. Her head for business led her to open Sonoma County's first tasting room. She achieved this with quite a splash, rolling a twenty-five-thousand-gallon Champagne cask down to the street and opening a shop inside it!

Isabelle left her mark all over the winery, from her rose garden to her self-planted redwood grove. But her greatest legacy is the quality of wines Simi produces. Throughout Simi's long history, it has employed terrifically talented winemakers, including Zelma Long and Paul Hobbs and consultants André Tchelistcheff and Michelle Roland. Today, Steve Reeder, one of Sonoma's most acclaimed and awarded winemakers, is at the helm of Simi's winemaking team. With Simi's fantastic Alexander Valley vineyards, Reeder is sure to take Simi back to its glory days of producing unbeatable cabernet sauvignon—and forward to a future of well-deserved praise.

While Simi can be visited on a stop-by basis for tasting or sitting on the deck and enjoying a wine and cheese pairing, its tour is so chock-full of interesting stories and historical details that you'll be robbing yourself if you pass it by.

Stryker Sonoma

www.strykersonoma.com
5110 Highway 126, Geyserville
707.433.1944 or 800.433.1944
Thur–Sun 10:30am–5pm, Mon–Wed by appointment only

Wine lovers with a taste for architecture and design will be drawn to Stryker Sonoma. In addition to producing a wide range of reds and whites in varying styles, the winery is constructed from an eclectic blend of materials. The result: a visit that's as much a feast for design lovers as it is for epicures.

Beneath an expansive and moody Alexander Valley sky, a half-moon-shaped stone wall embraces a well-tended lawn with inviting benches and picnic tables. Vineyards stretch in all directions. A terra-cotta and wood walkway, topped by a trellised arbor, leads to the tasting room. Concrete walls punctuated by steel details give way to an all-glass tasting room, its bar flanked by a brick and cement fireplace and a huge window overlooking the pristine barrel room. Overall, it's a fabulous fusion that creates a hyper-modern warehouse look. It's original and artistic without being ostentatious.

The Best of the Rest Alexander Valley is a long stretch of land that is easy to visit in a day or two. ···· In the southern end of the region, **Alexander Valley Vineyards** (8644 Highway 128, Healdsburg, www.avvwine.com, 800.888.7209, daily 10am–5pm) is situated on the original homestead of Cyrus Alexander, whose name inspired the appellation. The winery feels slightly nostalgic. With its covered porch and redwood picnic tables, the tasting room could be someone's home, and the inside décor looks like it hasn't changed much in twenty years. It's all rather endearing. The wines are delicious, and the Two Barrel, a blend of syrah and cab, is a good wine with a good story. Ask about it when you're there. ···· Not too far south is **Lancaster Estate** (15001 Chalk Hill Road, Healdsburg, www.lancasterestate.com, 800.799.8444, by appointment only), a winery devoted primarily to red table wine made from a blend of Bordeaux varietals. With the recent addition of a few single-block cabs, there's more reason than ever to visit. ···· In the other direction, almost in the center of the appellation, is **Murphy-Goode** (4001 Highway 128, Geyserville, www.murphygoodewinery.com, 707.431.7644, daily 10:30am–4:30pm). Started in the 1980s by Tim Murphy and Dale Goode, the winery has consistently produced great Alexander Valley wines. Its signature sauvignon blanc is one of the best made in Sonoma County.

BENNETT VALLEY

Bennett Valley is a small appellation hidden between Santa Rosa and Glen Ellen. With only a couple of wineries within its bounds, it remains a sleepy, quiet region ideal for visiting without worrying about crowds. Merlot and chardonnay receive ample marine-influenced fog and breezes, resulting in well-balanced fruit and delicious wine.

Matanzas Creek Winery
www.matanzascreek.com
6097 Bennett Valley Road, Santa Rosa
707.528.6464 or 800.590.6464
Daily 10am–4:30pm

If you breathe deeply as you enter Matanzas Creek Winery, you'll soon be swooning in lavender-intoxicated delight. Set into the magnificent hills of Bennett Valley, the winery is known for its estate-grown lavender products as much as it is for Journey Meritage, its high-quality blend of merlot and cab.

The gardens, the winery, and the gift shop all smell and feel like quintessential California. Outside, it's all subtly chromatic serenity: native grasses, plants, shrubs, and trees in muted yellows, greens, wheats, grays, and purples blending into an artfully landscaped composition. Wherever you look or wander throughout the gardens, you'll find the perfect place to meditate or simply close your eyes and daydream. The winery and gift shop, housed beneath a vine-covered roof, are equally peaceful and intimate. You almost expect somebody to invite you into a room for a spa treatment. While no such service is actually available, you can buy enough luscious lavender creams, oils, perfumes, sachets, bath salts, soaps, pillows, and the like to set up your own spa when you return home.

The tasting bar is in keeping with the nonhippie yet high-organic vibration. Try all the excellent wines, and hope that the Gods of the Grapes smile on you when you're here—the signature Matanzas Journey is produced only in those years when the sun, wind, and earth conspire fruitfully.

CHALK HILL

On a map, Chalk Hill appears to be quite large, but the accessible area is limited to a two-lane road that offers a scenic route through countryside. The volcanic-ash soil and sunny hillsides cooled by afternoon ocean breezes benefit the cabernet, merlot, sauvignon blanc, and chardonnay vines grown here.

Chalk Hill Estate Vineyards and Winery

www.chalkhill.com
10300 Chalk Hill Road, Healdsburg
707.838.4306
Mon–Fri by appointment only

Chalk Hill Estate is a private world set in an amphitheater of oak woodlands, grassy meadows, and sky so close you want to reach out and touch it. In 1972, Frederick Furth found the property by flying over it in a rented plane. He purchased it and slowly developed it into a winery and more.

The name Chalk Hill was chosen in reference to the white, ashy volcanic soil left by Mount St. Helena's last eruption, thousands of years ago. The image is reinforced by the omnipresent gray tones that appear on everything from the winery exterior to the logo on the label. It's also the color of the giant Suburban you'll jump into to take a spin around the property with Diana, Chalk Hill's estate tour concierge.

This is no ordinary winery property. It includes a home, three guest houses, four lakes, a culinary garden, a private park, a massive equestrian center, and a private dining room complete with an estate chef and an estate sommelier. And every grape varietal produced by Chalk Hill is grown on the estate. The vineyards are planted on hillsides so steep it's hard to imagine walking up them, much less working on them.

The world according to Frederick Furth is extremely neat and well behaved, almost too much so. That is, of course, until you look behind the scenes. As you walk through the lab, the storage room, the fermentation and barrel rooms, and so on, you see that this is indeed a working winery, with real people and real challenges. It's kind of a relief.

When you've fully explored the estate and chatted with Diana about anything that strikes your fancy—the soils, the weather, the views, the horse center crafted from Alaskan golden cedar—you'll finish your tour in the tasting room. It's here you'll taste the Furths' efforts to produce great wines unique to each vineyard on the property, such as the chardonnay for which the winery is best known. While you may not taste each clone and rootstock—all of which were painstakingly selected to grow grapes to their fullest flavor profile—you will taste the care of the land on which the Furths have built their reputation. When you get right down to it, what more could you ask?

Lunchtime Chalk Hill is essentially a one-road appellation between Alexander Valley and Windsor. It's pure country back here, so you'll want to eat before you arrive. The best place to do this is the super-delicious **Willi's Wine Bar** (4404 Old Redwood Highway, Santa Rosa, 707.526.3906). With its roadhouse feel, seasonal wine list that includes a variety of pour sizes, and absolutely scrumptious small plates of wine-friendly food, you'll want to put Chalk Hill (or anyplace else in the vicinity) on your A-list just for a chance to eat at Willi's.

DRY CREEK VALLEY

Dry Creek Valley is most widely recognized for old-vine zinfandels. Most of these are produced from century-old vineyards that were planted by the region's large population of Italian immigrants. Although other varietals are produced in the area, it is the wines made from these old, preserved vineyards—planted with a traditional field blend of zinfandel, carignane, petite sirah, alicante bouchet, and mourvèdre—that are the backbone of Dry Creek. Long, warm days are tempered by cool mornings and evenings, combining to create ideal conditions for these grape varietals to ripen slowly; in the process they develop full flavors and terrific balance.

Bella Vineyards and Winery

www.bellawinery.com
9711 West Dry Creek Road, Healdsburg
707.473.9171
Daily 11:30am–4:30pm

At the very end of West Dry Creek Road you'll find the down-and-dirty Bella Vineyards and Winery. Park your car in the shade of the giant oak tree and head over to the cave that looks like an upside-down swimming pool.

There's not much to do at Bella besides taste and buy the wines, but you'll want to do a lot of both, because the wines are fantastic. Crafted by consulting winemaker Michael Dashe of *Dashe Cellars*, each of the five zinfandels and the single syrah is a perfect example of what great wines should be: balanced, fruity, smooth, and irresistible.

The wine quality is no accident. The fruit comes from fantastic vineyards nearby. One vineyard is Big River, a brilliantly farmed old-vine zinfandel site in Alexander Valley that produces coveted fruit that is shared with only a few other producers (including *Dashe* and *Ravenswood*, both of which make a single-vineyard zin of the same name). Two other vineyards are under the care of Bella owners Lynn and Scott Adams: Belle Canyon and Lily Hill. Both are in the Dry Creek region, and both are sources for exceptional fruit—as is absolutely proved—by Bella wines.

At the makeshift tasting bar in the cave, try the selection of wines they've opened that day. It's fun to hang out here, soaking up the vibe of authenticity and tasting the commitment one family has to the land and to the bottle.

Ferrari-Carano's bronze boar greets visitors.

Ferrari-Carano Vineyards and Winery

www.ferrari-carano.com
8761 Dry Creek Road, Healdsburg
800.831.0381
Daily 10am–5pm

A thirteen-hundred-pound bronze sculpture of a wild boar—demurely holding a mouthful of freshly cut flowers—embodies the over-the-top spirit of Ferrari-Carano. In addition to its well-known fumé blanc, this immaculately kept estate is a travel destination in its own right. Its extravagant Italianate Villa Fiore (which houses the tasting rooms) and its five acres of glorious gardens are a striking contrast to its bucolic surroundings.

This is not a place to picnic, but rather to admire the waterfalls; the fountains; the single-variety planted beds so vast, consistent, and well groomed they practically redefine, say, *tulip*; the small bridges over perfect ponds; and the mixed plantings that here recall Asia and there remind you of Tuscany. Tons of annuals—from Iceland poppies to marigolds and pansies—along with amazing, fragrant perennials, shrubs, and trees together form a splendid mosaic that weds the best of nature with the best of landscape design.

Be aware that Ferrari-Carano is not our own little secret, so if the weather is nice and the winery is sponsoring a special event, it may get a little crowded. In this case, skip the ground-floor tasting room and head downstairs to the very pretty barrel room and somewhat pricier reserve tasting—it's worth it.

Frick Winery

www.frickwinery.com
23072 Walling Road, Geyserville
707.857.3205
Sat–Sun 12–4:30pm

The voluptuous, dark, gnarled old vines beside the visitor parking lot at Frick Winery are reason enough to visit; they're an Italian field blend bursting with the grapey goodness of carignane, zinfandel, alicante bouchet, petite sirah, and more. Coming to this Tobacco-Road-ish destination feels like dropping in to see an eccentric country neighbor—one who lives in a wee house with a bright-red door and a front porch with a playful, clown-like drawing to greet you.

Inside, the whimsy continues, with wall space devoted largely to vivid, humorous paintings by Judith Gannon, the late winery co-founder. Her husband, Bill Frick, is still the owner and winemaker, and it's him you'll meet behind the tasting-room bar (made of recycled wood and metal drainpipe). Bill will be glad to tell you all about growing grapes in the Dry Creek Valley and about how he became known for specializing in syrah. But don't stop your tasting there: sip onward and upward through the whole line-up, from viognier to cinsaut rosé to cinsaut to C2 (Frick's proprietary Rhône blend) to merlot and that superb syrah. They're all small-quantity wines with huge-quality taste and value.

Lambert Bridge

www.lambertbridge.com
4085 West Dry Creek Road, Healdsburg
800.975.0555
Daily 10:30am–4:30pm

You don't quite know whether to order an après-ski hot chocolate or ask to sample a well-made wine when you arrive at the mountain chalet that is Lambert Bridge. (One look into the barrel room that spans the length of the tasting room and you'll quickly figure it out.) Tucked neatly into the forested hillside, this is a extremely peaceful environment. Decades-old wisteria is fragrant and welcoming—an inviting hello that is easily matched by the warmth of the gracious staff.

This may be Dry Creek Valley at its prettiest. A glorious picnic area is irresistible, with nicely spaced tables and unmatched views of wilderness and farmed land. Heed your hosts' unpressured invitation to wander around with or without a tasting—but do yourself a favor and try the wide range of wines they pour every day, from sauvignon blanc, chardonnay, and viognier to zin and merlot.

Preston Vineyards

www.prestonvineyards.com
9282 West Dry Creek Road, Healdsburg
707.433.3372 or 800.305.9707
Daily 11am–4:30pm

Only the most hardened of hearts won't instantly fall in love with Preston. It's inviting, comfortable, homey, and pretty: pure Sonoma country, all the way down to the rockers and wicker chairs on the wide porch. As winery experiences go, this is one of the best there is.

Arrive on a warm afternoon and wander through the tasting room. It's like a large, warm country kitchen—in fact, there is a large kitchen, and most weekends something good is being baked in its wood-burning oven by owner Lou Preston. Don't stop there. Taste the olive oil. Read the literature—especially the story about Lou's neighbor Jim Guadgani and the origins of Sunday's jug wine tradition. (On Sundays you can bring a jug and, in the same manner that wine was sold for generations, fill it up and take it home.) It's not only a tradition, it's great wine. In fact, all of Preston's wines are fantastic.

How did Preston achieve such high quality? Through Lou Preston's clear-minded decision to be better, not bigger. After nearly three decades of building the winery into a sizable operation, Lou and his wife, Susan, deliberately scaled it back. In doing so they returned to doing what they loved most: making wine, not selling wine.

For such a tiny production, the Preston wine list is long. It includes cinsault, vin gris, rousanne, sauvignon blanc, viognier, mourvèdre, carignane, barbera, syrah, sangiovese, petite sirah, a late-harvest semillon, a superb Rhône blend called L. Preston Red, and, of course, the almost-mandatory Dry Creek zinfandel.

So find your way to Preston. Sample the gastronomic gifts of the old-fashioned, farm-minded hosts, and kick back on the porch. You won't just be in love—you'll find yourself wanting to make a commitment.

Ridge Vineyards/Lytton Springs

www.ridgewine.com
650 Lytton Springs Road, Healdsburg
707.433.7721
Daily 11am–4pm

Ridge is one of those rare wineries that you have to love and respect in equal measure. In addition to its general contribution to the industry in helping to put zin on the map, Ridge's earth-friendly winery at Lytton Springs makes it appear easy—and beautiful—to be green.

The brand-new barrel and tasting rooms, built around the existing Lytton Springs winery, which Ridge acquired in 1991, are masterful expressions of environmentally conscious architecture. Since a high winter water table prevented the excavation of caves, the builders used compacted rice straw bales, covered with smooth, thick adobe made of vineyard clay, sand, and straw, to construct an aboveground cave with low environmental impact, good temperature insulation, and tremendous natural beauty.

The new building appears on the landscape as a kind of modern, over-sized barn. It looks almost like a peculiar natural outcropping, with its subtle buff and sand colors and intimate proximity to the winery's thirty-five acres of vines (a traditional field blend of zinfandel, with some petite sirah, grenache, and carignane thrown into the mix). Walking from your car to the entrance on a handsome slate walkway, surrounded by rolling hills in the near distance, you are almost close enough to reach out and touch the vines.

The spare tasting-room interior is like a tall, cool glass of California essence: light and airy, with a spectacular wood bar made of recycled tank staves from the original Lytton Springs winery. Five wines are poured daily, along with two extra weekly special wines. Try them all—you'll be glad you did.

Lunchtime When in Dry Creek, do as the locals do: lunch at **Zin** (344 Center Street, Healdsburg, www.zinrestaurant.com, 707.473.0946). A hit since the day the doors opened, it features casual California cuisine and a wine list that, naturally, showcases some of the area's most delicious zinfandels.

Yoakim Bridge Vineyards and Winery
www.yoakimbridge.com
7209 Dry Creek Road, Healdsburg
707.433.8511
Sat–Sun 11am–4pm, Mon–Fri by appointment only

Expect to turn green with envy when you first lay eyes on Yoakim Bridge Vineyards and Winery. Even if you've never before entertained a fantasy of being a small-winery owner, once you see these perfect four acres of old head-trained, dry-farmed zinfandel vines—alongside an 1886 Victorian farmhouse with stunning views of giant oaks and redwoods—you just may find yourself jonesing for your own place.

At the northern end of Dry Creek Valley, Yoakim Bridge is quintessentially Californian. Outside, the tasting room is decorated with bright potted geraniums. Inside, it is so small you can barely turn around, but it's an especially feminine and elegant space, done up with Parisian flair: its creamy white walls, large mirrors, and antique crystal chandeliers are whisperingly seductive.

This refined boudoir feeling may grow into something a bit more lustful, however, once you taste the earthy, award-winning zins. Fortunately, owner Virginia Morgan and winemaker David Cooper are right there to satisfy your cravings. Virginia even makes and bottles her own zinfandel sauce, a smoky, tangy concoction that she serves with homemade meatballs. Meatballs are the last thing you'd imagine having at a winery—and one thing you wish you'd find more often.

Right: Yoakim Bridge's decorative gate.

The Best of the Rest On a map, Dry Creek Valley looks huge and spread out. In reality, it is an easy-to-navigate thin strip of land filled with narrow roads and wonderful wines and wineries. In addition to the destinations we've described in detail, it's a great idea to tool around Dry Creek, taking advantage of all the excellent wineries within easy reach. ···· Neighboring wineries **Dry Creek Vineyards** (3770 Lambert Bridge Road. Healdsburg, www.drycreekvineyard.com, 707.433.1000, daily 11:30am– 4:30pm) and **Passalaqua Winery** (3805 Lambert Bridge Road, Healdsburg, 877.825.5547, daily 11am–5pm), offer enough contrasting architectural style, picnic areas, and history to make dropping into both for comparison's sake worthwhile. ···· Where Lambert Bridge Road intersects Dry Creek Road, you'll find **Teldeschi** (3555 Dry Creek Road, Healdsburg, www.teldeschi.com, 707.433.6626, daily 12–5pm), a winery worth stopping at to see one of the region's most acclaimed vineyards. While founder Frank Teldeschi built his business selling grapes to home winemakers, today his vineyard is a source for Teldeschi wines, as well as *Thumbprint* and *Ravenswood*. ···· At the far end of Dry Creek Valley, just south of Lake Sonoma, you'll find a winery appropriately named **Lake Sonoma Winery** (9900 Dry Creek Road, Geyserville, www.lakesonomawinery.com, 707.473.2999, daily 10am–5pm). Set on top of a ridge with a spectacular view, the winery has a large patio that can easily fit groups that want to soak up a little sun, gaze out to the horizon, and sip some terrific zinfandels. ···· **Quivira** (4900 West Dry Creek Road, Healdsburg, 800.292.8339, daily 11am–4pm), one of the first wineries in the region to produce a Rhône-style blend, is also known as a premier producer of zinfandel. ···· **Everett Ridge** (435 West Dry Creek Road, Healdsburg, www.everettridge.com, 707.433.1637, daily 11am–4:30pm) is an unpretentious winery with a small tasting room and friendly staff. Syrah, zinfandel, and cab are its signature wines, made from remarkable vineyards throughout Sonoma and Mendocino counties, including its own organically farmed hillside vineyard. ···· A bit further down the road is **Alderbrook** (2306 Magnolia Drive, Healdsburg, www.alderbrook.com, 707.433.5987, daily 10am–5pm), a winery so at ease in the country, it could just as easily be a horse ranch. Alderbrook wines are made under the guidance of Doug Fletcher, who has received tremendous praise for the wines he's been crafting for years at Napa's *Chimney Rock*. ···· On the very edge of Dry Creek Valley is **De La Montanya** (999 Foreman Lane, Healdsburg, www.dlmwine.com, 707.433.3711, Sat–Sun 11am–4:30pm), a pastoral, very California-looking winery that has a small tasting room with big wines. It's a great place to spend some time on a summer afternoon.

GREEN VALLEY

A fertile region within the Russian River Valley appellation, Green Valley is revered for its cool-climate grapes, primarily chardonnay and pinot noir. The area is also considered Sonoma County's salad basket due to the large number of fruit and vegetable growers that share the land with vineyards. The Pacific Ocean's maritime influences temper the heat with fog and breezes.

Hartford Family Wines

www.hartfordwines.com
8075 Martinelli Road, Forestville
707.887.1756
Daily 10am–4:30pm

As wine country landscape goes, the far reaches of Russian River Valley can be pretty rugged, so the last thing you'd expect to find on the furthest-off-the-beaten-track road is the very civilized and grand Hartford Family winery.

The French country–like estate rests amid tall trees and hills and is at once stately and enticing. The aristocratic mood continues indoors, with pale-yellow walls, marble tile, and authentic antiques. Off the foyer is a subtly decorated tasting room, and just outside it an agreeable terrace begs you to sit and sip on warm days.

Everything about Hartford is aesthetically understated. But don't be fooled: this low-profile appearance is in complete contrast to its absolutely high-prestige wine. Its list consists primarily of pinot noirs and chardonnays, almost all of which are single vineyard bottlings—there are eight single-vineyard pinots and nearly that many single vineyard chards, and all are produced from vineyards in cool areas of Sonoma County, Mendocino, and Marin. To keep things interesting, a small-production old-vine zinfandel is on the list.

As the wines are poured, the incredibly nice staff live up to their reputation of being among the friendliest in the area. They're knowledgeable about the vineyards, the high ratings and praise from critics, and the winery itself. The moral of the story? It may look French, but it's pure Russian River in all its unpretentious manner. You're bound to look forward to your next visit long before you even leave.

Iron Horse Vineyards

www.ironhorsevineyards.com
9786 Ross Station Road, Sebastopol
707.887.1507
By appointment only

Given the Russian River and Green valleys' prime conditions for growing chardonnay and pinot noir grapes, it makes perfect sense for a winery here to turn them into bubbles. Iron Horse's sparkling wines are supreme examples of the exemplary fruit that can be grown in the region.

One of the first things you notice at Iron Horse is the grand line of palm and olive trees on top of the hill that borders the driveway. But banish all thoughts of coming upon an equally grand building, because what you'll find instead is a modest set of ivy-covered barns. On the eastern side of the farthest barn is an outdoor tasting room that's as minimal as it gets: a couple of planks atop some barrels underneath a tent. You'll never forget you're outside because of the cool Pacific fog and afternoon breezes that keep the grapes happy, but tasting through the winery's delicious still and sparkling wines will keep the elements at bay. Don't worry, you won't be outside on stormy days; when it rains, the entrance to the winery floods, so no one can get through! Don't ever forget this is the country, and nature rules supreme.

From the vantage point of the tasting room on top of the hill, you'll be able to gaze out to the winery's vineyards, which stretch on forever. The verdant vineyard blocks, the profusion of trees, and the all-around lush landscaping will answer the question of how the Green Valley region got its name.

Lunchtime Green Valley is a treasure trove of agricultural riches, from berries to mushrooms—a chef's dream backyard. The chef at **Willow Wood Market Café** (9020 Graton Road, Graton, 707.823.0233) obviously enjoys cooking with the area's fresh, seasonal food, as is evidenced by the eclectic menu that includes salad plates, open-faced sandwiches, and bowls of polenta topped with vegetables and local cheeses.

Marimar Torres Estate

www.marimarestate.com
11400 Graton Road, Sebastopol
707.823.4365
By appointment only

Marimar Torres is like a Catalan outpost on the back roads of Sonoma County. The winery is a cheerful golden building with blue trim, designed in the image of a Catalan farmhouse—but with pure California landscaping.

A tour begins in owner Marimar Torres's home. You'll feel right at home while watching a video about the winery's winemaking practices, after which you'll explore the winery and the vineyards. You'll learn all about their organic growing methods—including the making of their own compost to provide nutrition for the soil—and about how the vines are planted using traditional European methods.

There are all the things you'd expect, like the large fermentation room and the barrel cellars, and then some that might surprise you, like the kitchen that Marimar frequently cooks in and the warm dining room filled with classic and antique Spanish furniture and objects. This is where you'll enjoy a sit-down tasting of the winery's signature chardonnay and pinot noir, along with a well-chosen selection of the Torres family's wines from Spain.

In an area so overwhelmingly dedicated to all things Italian and French, Marimar Torres's distinct Spanish influence is a refreshing change of pace.

LOS CARNEROS, SONOMA

Once valued for its proximity to the Bay and the commerce it allowed, Carneros is once again treasured for its liquid assets. This time around it's for the advantages the Bay provides to grape growers. Morning and evening fog combined with afternoon breezes create the always-cool growing condition that is necessary for premium chardonnay and pinot noir grapes. With thin soils and just enough warmth to ripen merlot and syrah, Carneros is an increasingly prestigious appellation.

Cline Cellars

www.clinecellars.com
24737 Highway 121, Sonoma
707.940.4000
Daily 10am–6pm

A flowered entryway, blooming madly in every shade of purple, yellow, and fuschia, leads to an 1850s farmhouse surrounded by a wraparound porch, well-groomed lawn, enticing picnic tables, and graceful willow trees offering a welcome respite from summer sun and heat. It's all clean, bright, and cheerful—maybe too cheerful, once you realize those men in the porch rocking chairs are corny, life-sized soft sculptures.

Inside Cline Cellars' small, casual tasting room, you'll find all the impeccable taste you desire. Rhône fanciers may already know Fred Cline as the pioneer behind California's Rhône varietals. He began by producing wines and restoring ancient vines from California's Contra Costa region; of the six hundred acres of existing Contra Costa vineyards, Cline owns and controls half, including some of the oldest surviving vines in the state.

In 1991, Cline relocated to the Carneros region. Today he produces zinfandel, carignane, and mourvèdre from these ancient vines. Here in Carneros he's planted chardonnay, pinot noir, and merlot, in addition to Rhône varietals such as syrah, viognier, marsanne, and rousanne.

To complement your wine research, the Cline tasting room serves and sells local bread, cheese from the Sonoma Cheese Factory, and a variety of other snack foods.

Lunchtime If you're looking for a lunch that will stick to your ribs, the **Schellville Grill** (22900 Broadway Street, Sonoma, 707.996.5151) is the place to get it. This country-style restaurant is where locals and farmers fuel up for a hard day's work. The menu is practically made of meat, from steak sandwiches to smoked tri-tip, from burgers and grilled chicken to a protein platter. Luckily, there are plenty of tantalizing carbs, too. Breakfast is as hearty as lunch, making this a good place to come before you start some serious wine tasting. The inventive breakfast ensembles are as delicious as they are gigantic—big enough to keep you sated for hours.

Right: Larson Family's cowboy legacy lives on in the winery's art.

Larson Family Winery

www.larsonfamilywinery.com
23355 Millerick Road, Sonoma
707.938.3031
Daily 10am–5pm

What do Seabiscuit, rodeos, and chardonnay all have in common? At various times, each has called the site of Larson Family Winery home. Seabiscuit trained on the Carneros property when it had a racetrack. Sonoma's first rodeo was held here—an event that became a two-decades-plus tradition. The property's most recent incarnation is this winery run by Tom Larson, the great-grandson of Michael Millerick, who bought the property in 1899. Under Larson's stewardship, the same land that once nurtured horses and corralled livestock now has given way to organically farmed chardonnay.

Although Larson Family Winery rests at the end of what appears to be a deserted road in the very center of Carneros, its proximity to the Bay has always played an important role in the life of the property. In the early days, Carneros was easily reached by boat, making it convenient to bring in rodeo and racing stock as well as the folks who attended the events. But nowadays Carneros is better known for its climate: the cool maritime conditions are ideal for growing high-quality chardonnay and pinot noir grapes. Larson takes good advantage of these natural gifts.

Wines made from Larson Family's grapes can be tasted in a barn that takes seriously the Larson family's hundred-year heritage. The walls are covered with horse gear, cowboy paraphernalia, and framed articles chronicling the rodeos. Even the wine label features a horse in midstride. At the tasting room, you can try both the winery's varietal wines and its reserve wines. Your hosts' warmth and sincerity allow you to taste the wines at a leisurely pace, read about the rodeos, play a game or two of bocce—and just hang out in what's left of the Wild West.

Sleep among the Vines In Carneros, **Larson Family Winery** (23355 Millerick Road, Sonoma, www.larsonfamilywinery.com, 707.938.3031) rents out a turn-of-the-century farmhouse for folks wanting to travel with family and pets. Four bedrooms offer plenty of space to spread out.

Schug Carneros Estate Winery

www.schugwinery.com
602 Bonneau Road, Sonoma
707.939.9363 or 800.966.9365
Daily 10am–5pm

Driving up the long, barely paved road that leads to Schug, you'd never guess that you'll soon enter Bavaria-on-Carneros. But there it is: the slightly rough-hewn European-style winery that looks like Heidi's summerhouse. Set off on a path, a picnic area overlooks winemaking-in-progress on one side and verdant hills on the other. Birds galore—from turkey buzzards and eagles to red-tailed hawks, starlings, and red-winged blackbirds—make their presence known with all manner of chirping and soaring flights.

Equipment and barrels are everywhere at this winery owned and run by Walter Schug. A native of Germany, Schug was raised on a pinot noir estate near the Rhine River. He made his name as winemaker for Napa Valley's *Joseph Phelps Vineyards*, producing cabernet sauvignon and riesling. But his dream was to re-create his success with pinot noir, the grape of his childhood home.

Schug launched his own brand in 1980; by 1983 his quest for an outstanding California pinot had become serious, and he left Phelps to focus on his own wines from the then newly emerging Carneros region. Today he grows both chardonnay and pinot on his estate, and both are available for sampling in the winery's utilitarian tasting room. Schug is one of the few California producers exporting to Europe, where an impressive 30 percent of its production is sold. With wine lovers on both sides of the Atlantic enjoying his wines, it appears that Walter Schug has attained his goal.

RUSSIAN RIVER VALLEY

The Russian River Valley is a large, rambling, rather flat region that is admired for its high-quality pinot noir and chardonnay grapes; this fruit prospers from its closeness to the Pacific coast. The area has remained remarkably unspoiled in both land use and the casual atmosphere of the more than fifty wineries that reside here.

Belvedere Vineyards & Winery

www.belvederewinery.com
4035 Westside Road, Healdsburg
800.433.8296
Daily 11am–5pm

It's a fact that taste is largely predicated on smell. So what could be better than a winery with an aroma garden to enliven your senses?

It's obvious that Belvedere agrees with this concept. Its exceptionally beautiful terraced garden is planted to hundreds of aromatic herbs, blossoms, and fruit trees. Fine-pebbled paths crisscross the garden, gently leading you to such delectable flora as chocolate cosmos and lemon thyme.

Fetch yourself a glass of the pinot, chard, or gewürztraminer that the winery makes from the region's grapes, and bring it back with you to the garden. There, compare the aromas of the wine with the complex perfume of the garden plants and flowers. Or park yourself at one of the redwood tables or benches and watch the butterflies, bees, and hummingbirds perpetuate the life cycle of plants. You'll feel connected to the earth, the wine, and the beauty of Mother Nature.

Foppiano Vineyards and Winery

www.foppiano.com
12707 Old Redwood Highway, Healdsburg
707.433.7272
Daily 10am–4:30pm

The American dream is alive and well at Foppiano Vineyards and Winery. Founded in 1896, it's one of the oldest continually owned family wineries in Sonoma County, and everything about it feels authentic to the Italian-American experience. Being here is like stepping back a few generations to a simpler time; if you grew up with a *nonna* who cooked pasta for Sunday dinner, you might feel a twinge of nostalgia when you peek at the tables in the back and the jugs of vinegar that undoubtedly make a mean salad dressing.

From the red Northwest Pacific train car to the red barn and red pickup truck to the country music playing in the tasting room, the place has soul. Best known for its dynamite petite sirah, the winery encourages visitors to take a self-guided tour through the vineyard and then hang out at the picnic tables. The tasting room usually pours two to four petite sirahs, including its reserves. The Bacigalupi single-vineyard petite sirah is as much fun to drink as it is to pronounce. One taste is all you need to get back to your—or the Foppiano family's—old-world roots.

Hop Kiln Winery

www.hopkilnwinery.com
6050 Westside Road, Healdsburg
707.433.6491
Daily 10am–5pm

Wineries, like life, evolve in unpredictable patterns. Who would have guessed when it was completed in 1905 that the Sonoma Hop Kiln building, used to dry hops for making beer, would one day become a place for winemaking?

When you see Hop Kiln Winery's stone wall, rusted conveyor belt, and kiln tops, it's easy to forget it's a winery—come to think of it, it's easy to forget what century you're in! The building, which was completely restored by owner Marty Griffin after he purchased it in 1960, is a valuable monument to an industry that no longer exists and to the innovative architecture that was created to dry and prepare hops. While there are a few other original hop kiln buildings still in existence, Hop Kiln Winery is the grandest of those available to the public.

The Hop Kiln tasting room has an outdated, dark interior that would seem out of place anywhere else, but here it's perfect. If it weren't for the wine-tasting bar, mustard, vinegar, and olive oil sampling, and cheerful staff happy to pour you one of the zins made from one-hundred-year-old vines on the property, you'd think you were in the Old West. Enjoy the pretty grounds, complete with picnic tables.

Joseph Swan Vineyards

www.swanwinery.com
2916 Laguna Road, Forestville
707.573.3747
Sat–Sun 11am–4:30pm

The "tin shed" that is Joseph Swan Vineyards belies the star stature of the late pilot-turned-winemaker who founded this eponymous business. As you approach the oversized garage, with its graying lattice and green corrugated plastic hiding tanks, crushers, and barrels, you think you must be in the wrong place. You aren't. It's simply that Joseph Swan was a man concerned more with making fantastic wine than he was with image. And his legacy—a funky shack winery—has been carefully preserved in its original state.

Raised by teetotaler parents in North Dakota, Joe followed an indirect path to winemaking. It began with fermentation experiments at home, developed into home winemaking efforts during his stint as a Navy pilot, and came to fruition in 1967, when he purchased the thirteen-acre old-vine zinfandel vineyard property on which the winery sits today.

While Joe initially made wine using those grapes, he ultimately replanted the vineyard to cool-climate pinot noir and chardonnay. Today Joseph Swan pinot is still among the very best, as are the zinfandels, produced with fruit from other vineyards. The winery also makes really terrific chardonnay, pinot gris, mourvèdre, and syrah.

A self-made winemaker who was generous with his time and knowledge, Joseph Swan was a mentor and friend to many of today's most revered winemakers. A visit to his down-and-dirty winery is a nice reminder that men like Joseph Swan had the best values a winemaker could have: he knew that what is most important is what is in the glass.

Lunchtime If you get a hankering for something other than Californian-Mediterranean-Italian while you're in the Russian River Valley, go straight to **Pho Vietnam** (711 Stony Point Road, Santa Rosa, 707.571.7687). It's a bustling noodle shop that locals love, hidden in the corner of a strip mall.

J. Rochioli Vineyards and Winery

www.rochioli.com
6192 Westside Road, Healdsburg
707.433.2305
Daily 10am–4pm

Hidden behind green trees and even greener shrubs is J. Rochioli Vineyards and Winery, Valhalla for pinot lovers. Rochioli's low-key environment is proof positive that great winemaking doesn't need bells and whistles.

The Rochiolis have a long history in the Russian River Valley, starting with Joe Rochioli Sr., who purchased 130 acres of land along the Russian River in 1938. This was, and remains, a prime area for growing cool-climate grapes. Second- and third-generation Rochiolis Joe Jr. and Tom are keeping up Joe Sr.'s work. Splitting their responsibilities, Joe Jr. nurtures the land as carefully as his father did, while Tom makes wines to match the superior quality of the grapes the family grows.

With the exception of these remarkable wines, the tasting bar and huge plate-glass window are the primary attractions of the simple tasting room. Given Rochioli's penchant for selling out every vintage nearly as fast as the wine can be made, there's never much wine available for purchase, but you can count on being offered a sip of sauvignon blanc, chardonnay, and pinot noir.

Antique farm equipment adorns the landscape.

J Vineyards & Winery

www.jwine.com
11447 Old Redwood Highway, Healdsburg
707.431.3646
Daily 11am–5pm

Put some sparkle in your life by crossing over a lily pond on a wood-plank bridge; on the other side you'll find the low-slung concrete bunker that is J Vineyards & Winery. Inside the sleek modern structure, bubbles abound. The back wall of the wood and glass tasting bar is made of steel, punctuated by what appear to be mighty crystal bubbles (but are, in actuality, rugged chunks of glass cleverly lit by fiber optics). Just past the tasting room's stepped ceiling you'll find the Bubble Room: the private tasting room with seating, table service, and fine food and wine pairings; it's open only on weekends, and only by reservation.

But the bubbles you'll care most about are the ones in your glass, since in addition to its excellent still wines, J's sparklings are outstanding.

One of the many things that set this place apart from some other wineries that give mere lip service to the idea of food and wine pairing is that J puts its money where your mouth is. Every wine-flight tasting is served with a small selection of plated hors d'oeuvres—interesting combinations of foods that are specifically paired to each wine. Menus change often, but each features local, seasonal, and organic ingredients. Imagine a vintage brut with (to name just a few dishes) pink grapefruit salad with red onion . . . ahi tuna tartare . . . spiced almonds . . . or wild mushroom duxelles. It's all so delicious, you just may pop your cork. (If you can't get to the winery, at least check out its recipes online.)

Martinelli Winery

www.martinelliwinery.com
3360 River Road, Windsor
707.525.0570
Daily 10am–5pm

When you see the big red barn on River Road, stop. The historic hop kiln may look like an outdated country store, but actually it's Martinelli Winery, home to the infamous Jackass Hill Zinfandel, made by stealth winemaker Helen Turley.

You won't be able to buy or even taste Jackass Hill (so named because the slope it's grown on is so steep that when founder Giuseppe Martinelli decided to plant vines on it, his wife, Luisa, was rumored to have said only a jackass would do such a thing). Only 170 cases are produced annually and are sold to longstanding customers. But if you get on the mailing list, you will be able to get a bottle—in *ten* years!

Fortunately, there are other wines to try at Martinelli: pinot noir, gewürztraminer, chardonnay, and other zins. In fact, one hundred years after Jackass Hill vineyard was planted, Lee Martinelli Sr. grafted budwood from the century-old vines onto rootstock in another steep hillside vineyard just above the winery. The zinfandel made from these vines is called Giuseppe and Luisa, in honor of his grandparents. It's sometimes offered for tasting in the hop-baling barn–cum–tasting room, but with the high ratings it receives, it tends to sell out quickly.

Roshambo Winery

www.roshambowinery.com
3000 Westside Road, Healdsburg
707.431.2051 or 888.525.WINE
Daily 10:30am–4:30pm

When Roshambo was built, its designers must have looked around the wine country at all the mission-style, Tuscan-villa, redwood-barn wineries and decided to go in a completely different direction. What a great, refreshing change.

Roshambo is about as aesthetically different as it gets out in Sonoma's countryside. The minute you see the wavy green roof, you know that this place is going to be unusual. And when you pass a large fountain—really more of a concrete-backed waterfall—you know you've begun your transition from road to tasting room/art gallery.

Everything here is cool. Here are some details: the tasting bar—anchoring one end of a long room that is all glass, air, and curves—is made of Plexiglas. Glass display cases hold odd art exhibits; on previous visits they were filled with dental tools. Contemporary art, framed by lots of open space, offsets a terrific view of the valley-floor vineyards. The staff is a bunch of hip urbanites. The concrete patio is peppered with bright furniture. The shirts and caps are clever. Even the all-steel gray bathrooms are striking.

Bottom line: Roshambo has personality in spades, an ultra-cool appearance, and great zin, syrah, merlot, and gewürztraminer made from local grapes. Can't ask for more.

The Best of the Rest The Russian River Valley doesn't feel like a valley. There are no immediately visible mountain ranges forming a telltale V shape. Instead, this sprawling appellation (it's so big that the Green Valley appellation lies within its boundaries) seems more like a huge plain. For the most part, Russian River Valley is laid out like a grid. While it may seem initially daunting to navigate, it's actually quite accessible and can be traveled from one end to the other in about thirty minutes. With so many wineries in the region to visit, you might want to spend a couple of days here to see as many as you can. ···· If you start at the northern reaches of Russian River Valley, at the end of Highway 101, you can visit **Acorn Winery** (12040 Old Redwood Highway, Healdsburg, www.acornwinery.com, 707.433.6440, by appointment only). Acorn is minuscule but produces five wines: the syrah-based Axiom; dolcetto; Medley, a proprietary blend of nearly everything in the vineyard; sangiovese; and zinfandel. A visit to the winery won't take long since there's not a lot to see or do, but it's a great chance to taste the wines and talk to Bill and Betsy Nachbaur, Acorn's owners. They're a nice couple with a good product. ···· **Christopher Creek** (641 Limerick Lane, Healdsburg, www.christophercreek.com, 707.433.2001, daily 11am–5pm) is a teeny winery up on a knoll south of Healdsburg. The exuberant tasting-room staff pour a range of varietals, including zinfandel, syrah, and petite sirah. Ask about food pairings and they'll share recipes and tips about cooking with wine, and even send you on your way with a gift of Meyer lemons picked straight off the tree beside your car. ···· To the west is **Davis Bynum Winery** (8075 Westside Road, Healdsburg, www.davisbynum.com, 800.826.1073, daily 10am–5pm). Davis Bynum feels like a summer cabin tucked away in the countryside, especially in winter, when the wood-burning stove is lit. The estate-grown pinot is superb. You won't find any tchotchkes here, just great wines. ···· Not too far away is **Russian Hill Estate Winery** (4525 Slusser Road, Windsor, www.russianhillwinery.com, 707.575.9428, Thur–Mon 10am–4pm). Surrounded by some of the area's most prestigious vineyards—Saralee's Vineyard and Dutton Ranch are just across the road—Russian Hill's location provides a panoramic vista of the Russian River Valley, including neighbor Sonoma-Cutrer's old hop kiln structure. Russian Hill's staff will gladly share what they know about the area's history while you taste the sublime wines they produce from the region's great vineyards. ···· **Pellegrini Family Vineyards** (4055 West Olivet Road, Santa Rosa, www.pellegrinisonoma.com, 707.575.8463, by appointment only) has been growing grapes in Sonoma County since 1933. Originally the grapes were shipped to San Francisco, where the wines were produced and distributed. Eventually, as later generations took over the family business, the wine-making bounced to Sonoma County but was accomplished at leased wineries. Then, in 2004, the third generation of Pellegrinis to run the company completed their own winery, where they now greet visitors for tastings and tours. ····· Chardonnay lovers should be sure to visit the **Walter Hansel Winery** (5465 Hall Road, Santa Rosa, 707.525.3614, by appointment only). Renowned for its Burgundian-style chard, the winery also produces pinot noir in its large barn-style winery that sits, plain and simple, in the center of its vineyards.

The Best Appellation Event The Russian River Wine Road

(www.wineroad.com, 707.433.4335 or 800.723.6336, January, March, and November) organizes several comprehensive themed events throughout the year for the Alexander Valley, Dry Creek Valley, and Russian River Valley appellations, each taking place over an entire weekend. Prior to each, Wine Road provides a full list of wineries and what they will pour and serve. This allows you to plan your weekend according to your tastes and desired route. Bear in mind that the best way to make the most of these events is to concentrate on one region per event, and on visiting wineries not otherwise open to the public.

Wine Road kicks off every new year with **Winter Wineland**, in January. Russian River, Dry Creek, and Alexander Valley wineries open their doors for three days, offering wine tasting, winemaker meet-and-greets, and food and wine pairings. March's annual barrel-tasting weekend features barrel samples and the opportunity to buy futures from many participating wineries. And in November, Wine Road hosts **A Wine and Food Affair**, during which all participating wineries have wine and food pairings; a cookbook is included in the ticket price.

Well organized and high-spirited, Wine Road events are a memorable way to focus on a region, study a wine varietal, or discover the perfect excuse to spend a weekend in the wine country.

SONOMA COUNTY

A sprawling appellation that is about as diverse in *terroir* as any you will find in the world, Sonoma County has been planted with nearly every grape varietal in existence. Warm weather, cool climes, fertile soil, weak soil, plains, and steep slopes all share the land, each equally contributing to the potential of the appellation.

Paradise Ridge

www.prwinery.com
4545 Thomas Lake Harris Drive, Santa Rosa
707.528.9463
Daily 11am–5:30pm

> Paradise Ridge claims to have the most beautiful view in Sonoma County. Arriving at just the right time of day, with the light shining down on the Russian River Valley spread out below you, you'll be inclined to agree.
>
> But Mother Nature has some competition, since Paradise Ridge is also an art lover's haven. Its outdoor sculpture garden is awesome, as are the large pieces of art that punctuate the drive up to the visitors' building. The tasting "room" itself is primarily a small bar at one end of a large room that can be rented for weddings and private parties. Although the room itself is unremarkable, there's a large porch that wraps around the building, and there is that view that launched a thousand sips.

SONOMA MOUNTAIN

Its location above the fog line keeps Sonoma Mountain relatively warm. But low-temperature Pacific breezes prevent the fruit from becoming overheated, promising well-balanced and flavorful grapes. Cabernet sauvignon and zinfandel are the primary varietals of this region, which hosts only a few wineries within its borders.

Benziger Family Winery

www.benziger.com
1883 London Ranch Road, Glen Ellen
888.490.2739
Daily 10am–5pm

> Don't run over the noisy, cock-a-doodling roosters and clucking chickens as you drive onto the grounds of Benziger Family Winery, nestled in the bosom of the Glen Ellen hills. But do make a point of taking a leisurely self-guided tour through Benziger's Vineyard Discovery Center. Set amid

towering trees and terraced plantings (it feels a little like you fell into a green well), the Discovery Center takes you through every step of the grape-growing process, from rootstock to grafting to ripe, juicy fruit. Combining detailed illustrations with hands-on demonstrations and actual artifacts (like tractors, soil specimens, and grapes—yes, you can squeeze the fruit), the center is anything but slick; it's like a brilliant but homespun science project that won first prize in the county fair.

To get to the winery proper, cross a sweet bridge and pass a white clapboard private house, built on the former site of the 1898 Wagnerville Resort. Your path will be marked by various artifacts, such as a hand-operated wine press and vintage barrels. Kids can play on the shaded wooden jungle gym. The tasting room and wineshop are surprisingly commercial in feel given the generally rural environment, but still quite pleasant. Do your tasting at a shiny, well-lit wooden bar, and consider taking one of the winery's frequent tours that guide you through the vineyards via a tractor ride.

In addition to the winery's country surroundings, modern tasting room, and long, long Sonoma Valley history, there's one more reason to visit: to learn about its biodynamic viticultural practices. While you might not be able to drop in during the dead of night to watch ground bone being distributed in the soil, you can learn what characteristics this type of farming imparts to the wine and why it's important not only to wine, but to the environment as well.

Lunchtime Glen Ellen is a small town with an amazing number of good restaurants, making it the ideal place to have lunch while visiting the Glen Ellen, Sonoma Mountain, or Kenwood areas. Try **Olive and Vine** (14301 Arnold Drive #3, Glen Ellen, 707.996.9150), which serves gourmet take-out that can be enjoyed in its pretty storefront location. It shares space with Eric Ross's tasting bar, and you can shop next door at the Olive Press, a cooperative olive oil producer. Or, for a bite of Mediterranean cuisine, try the **Fig Café** (13690 Arnold Drive, Glen Ellen, 707.938.2130), a sibling of the Girl and the Fig in downtown Sonoma.

SONOMA VALLEY

Sonoma Valley is often called Valley of the Moon for its crescent shape and for the local folklore that insists that when the moon is full it rises more than once over the Valley due to the mountain range formation. A large appellation, it stretches far enough from south to north that the range of climate and soils provides good growing conditions for nearly every type of grape. Cool-climate varietals thrive both in the lower end of the Valley and on the high mountaintops. Heat-loving grapes grow exceedingly well in the upper end of the Valley, where century-old vineyards are still planted with zinfandel and field blends.

Sonoma Valley has the historical distinction of introducing wine grapes to the region and its neighbors, thanks to the Franciscan priests who built the last of California's missions here. It is also home to *Buena Vista*, California's first commercial winery.

Glen Ellen

Arrowood Vineyards & Winery
www.arrowoodvineyards.com
14347 Sonoma Highway, Glen Ellen
800.938.5170
Daily 10am–4:30pm

When it's summertime (or any time), the living is easy at Arrowood. Sipping a glass of wine while sitting on the winery's wraparound porch and admiring the astounding vistas can make you feel like landed gentry—especially if you are sipping one of Arrowood's superb chards, syrahs, or cabs.

Inside, it feels like a rich man's living room, with its clerestory ceiling, tons of clean white surfaces, marble bar, and cushiony, comfortable wicker furniture. Make that a rich man with a considerable size anxiety: "How big is big?" reads a sign near a rather impressive bottle collection. Ranging from half bottle through standard bottle, magnum, and double magnum to the freakishly large Imperial, Salmanzar, Balthazar, and the steroidal Nebuchadnezzar, the bottles are set up like nesting Russian dolls that escaped the belly of Momma-doll only to line up in size place. After seeing this array, tasting just a wee glass may feel a little wimpy, but when you're enjoying the wine, size rarely matters.

B. R. Cohn Winery

www.brcohn.com
15000 Sonoma Highway, Glen Ellen
707.938.4062 or 800.300.4064 ext. 24
Daily 10am–5pm

The B. R. Cohn Winery is like Graceland for Doobie Brothers fans. So single-minded is it in its devotion to the group, it should consider renaming itself the Doobie Brothers Fan Club and Winery. Bruce Cohn, the Doobie Brothers' former manager, has lined the walls of his winery with gold records, photos of the band in all its incarnations, and other memorabilia of life on the music-tour road.

But fair is fair. Just as Michael McDonald and Jackson Browne left the group and went on to great solo careers, so did Bruce Cohn. He's one of the first vintners anywhere to see—and exploit—the positive synergy between olive oil and the wine harvest, and he was instrumental (no pun intended) in helping to create the California olive oil industry. He sells his fine oils here, along with his fine chardonnay, cab, merlot, and zinfandel. So stop by next time you're rockin' down the highway.

Bucklin

www.buckzin.com
8 Old Hill Ranch Road, Glen Ellen
707.933.1726
By appointment only

The essence of Bucklin wine is Old Hill Vineyard in Sonoma Valley—an organic, twenty-four-acre, dry-farmed vineyard. Old Hill is such a prominent vineyard that most local vintners can recall at least one significant moment in their lives that took place there. What makes it so special? Ask Will Bucklin, who tends the vineyard owned by his mother and makes Bucklin zinfandel from its grapes, a traditional old-vine field blend.

Will is happy to tell you about the property's history—and there's a lot to tell. It was planted first in 1852 by William McPherson, an innovative man who was ahead of his time. By the time the vineyard was purchased in 1982 by Will's stepfather, Otto Teller, it seemed to be everybody's (but Otto's) opinion that the vines should be ripped out. But Teller, who was an organic farmer before there was "organic farming," decided to follow his own advice. He rejuvenated the old vines, preserving their confusing field mix of varietals—and a terrific plot of land was reborn.

In an average year, Old Hill Vineyard's ultra-small yield is currently enough for only about five hundred cases of Bucklin (and about the same of *Ravenswood*, the only other winery that gets its grapes). But as Will walks the property with you, he'll tell you about some of the techniques he's using to increase yield and make the most of this great old vineyard.

The tour isn't fancy. There's no winery to look at or tasting room to shop in, just a few houses, a car or truck here and there, and the vines, the vines, the vines. If only they could speak! If you haven't already begun to understand the profound attraction of the vineyard, when Will opens a bottle of Bucklin for you to try on his back porch, you'll take one sip and it will be clear.

Imagery Estate Winery

www.imagerywinery.com
14335 Highway 12, Glen Ellen
707.935.6203
Fri–Sun 10am–4:30pm

If winemaking is a blend of science and art, it stands to reason that art should be part of the winery experience—and so it is at Imagery Estate Winery. Owned by Joe Benziger (of *Benziger Family Winery*), Imagery Estate is based on what he calls "a coalescence of the arts, showcasing the artistry of the grower, the winemaker, and the fine artist." In addition to producing meticulous ultra-premium wines, the winery also commissions extraordinary, one-of-a-kind wine bottle labels reproduced from original art.

The end result is a compelling winery–cum–art gallery that houses, on permanent display, the largest single-themed (wine label) international art collection in existence—more than 125 acquisitions, to be exact. Media used range from Magic Marker to oils, from photography to collage. Contributing artists commissioned by Benziger and curator/fine artist Bob Nugent include some of the most celebrated and recognized names in the world, such as America's Sol LeWitt and Japan's Shoichi Ida. The only requirement for participating artists (numbering roughly one hundred) is that somewhere in their image they include an interpretation of the Parthenon symbol, which serves as the winery's logo.

The winery was begun in 1985, when the Benziger family found themselves with two lots of exceptional chardonnay and zinfandel too small for national release but fine enough to demand special treatment. Thus Imagery wines were born. By the second vintage, the Imagery concept had evolved to focus on only esoteric grape varietals not generally available in most winery offerings. This combination of limited-production varietals and unique art labels continues to define Imagery today.

Imagery's chic gallery and tasting room are buoyed by the tones of cool jazz on the sound system; happy people sit around the bar for tastings. In sum, this is a total destination winery, which also boasts formal gardens, an "insectory," bocce ball on the lawn, self-guided tours, an appellation trail and walking tour of Sonoma Valley wine regions, a gift shop, and picnicking opportunities. Add to this the air outside the gallery, which carries a faint but definite, odd, and wonderful aroma of Necco wafers and cedar, and you've got every reason you'd ever need to add Imagery to your vacation itinerary.

The Best of the Rest Mayo Family Vineyards (13101 Arnold Drive and Highway 12, Glen Ellen, www.mayofamilywinery.com, 707.938.9401, daily 10:30am–6:30pm) is a family-owned and -operated winery that emphasizes single-vineyard wines. Being here is like hanging out in someone's quiet family room and backyard.

Chateau St. Jean's formal garden.

Kenwood

Chateau St. Jean

www.chateaustjean.com
8555 Sonoma Highway, Kenwood
800.543.7572
Daily 10am–5pm

Jay Gatsby would feel right at home in the extraordinary beauty of Chateau St. Jean—and so will you. The ornamental, European-style flower gardens are laid out formally, with beds and paths arranged to form a pattern; their proliferation and sheer variety combine to create gentle aesthetic surprises. The overall effect is one of disarming charm—well groomed without a trace of stuffiness.

Stately paths intersect a heady mix of green and flowering shrubs, hedges, vines, trees, roses, and savory groundcovers that cushion and surround your every step. On one side are lawns, on another a bridge and pond, on yet another a quiet grove of evergreens. Picnic tables are scattered about. It's second to none.

The large tasting room is filled with lovely things to admire and purchase—and equally lovely things to drink and eat, from fancy sandwiches and salads to pâtés, sausages, and cheeses. The reserve tasting room is in an impressive space that feels like a library—masculine and opulent, with wood paneling, a large fireplace, and plenty of panache. You can sample your reserve selections beneath market umbrellas at tables on the patio. Expect to linger over the winery's renowned sauvignon blanc, chardonnay, and cab blends—and expect to wish for a quick return.

St. Francis Winery and Vineyards

www.stfranciswine.com
100 Pythian Road at Highway 12, Santa Rosa
800.543.7713
Daily 10am–5pm

When St. Francis outgrew its former location, just down the road, it opted for large, totally pleasant Mediterranean-style digs. The winery was named in honor of St. Francis of Assisi. In keeping with this spirit, the well-manicured landscape includes a statue of the patron saint of all animals and a tower housing a bell imported from Assisi.

The tasting room has a nice display of lovely ceramics and a few other items, but the main event here is the wine. Behind the tasting room is a large patio area bordered by lawn, vineyards, and scenic mountains. It's a serene location for enjoying a glass of wine or one of the reserve food and wine tastings that are offered all day, every day. Tastings don't require a reservation and could easily serve as a light lunch. Count on being served such delectable combinations as chardonnay with Bellwether Farms' Carmody cheese and quince preserves; zinfandel with four-onion tart; and alicante bouchet (a grape not typically made into a single-varietal wine, this one is produced from vines planted in 1890) with a chocolate, apricot, and walnut brownie.

The winery is a perfect place to host a private event. St. Francis's special events include an annual Blessing of the Animals, a monthly estate vineyard tour, frequent cooking demonstrations, and guest chef dinners.

The Best of the Rest Kenwood is a gregarious hamlet at the northern end of Sonoma Valley. Populated by great wineries, it's a must-see. While you are here, stop at the unassuming **Kenwood Vineyards** (9592 Sonoma Highway, Kenwood, www.kenwoodvineyards.com, 707.833.5891, daily 10am–4:30pm). Kenwood Vineyards is known for its Artist Series cabs, an annual limited-production wine with a label designed by an esteemed contemporary artist. This is the place to go for label collectors—you'll find a box of labels on the tasting bar.

The Best Appellation Event If there is a prettier locale or a better time of year to host a winery open-house event, it's hard to imagine when you're in the midst of sipping wine, nibbling on delicious fare, and taking in the full landscape at the annual **Heart of Sonoma Valley Barrel Tasting Weekend** (www.heartofsonomavalley.com, 866.794.WINE).

Traditionally held at the end of March, the barrel-tasting weekend is a festive frolic through the wineries of Glen Ellen and Kenwood. Almost two dozen wineries and tasting rooms throw open their doors, pop open some barrels, and plunge in a wine thief to fill the glasses of the merry attendees. As in other events of this nature, one of the best parts is having access to wines and wineries that are otherwise unavailable for visiting and tasting— places such as **Moon Mountain Winery** and **Kaz**.

By the time it's over, you can be satisfied knowing you've done more than spent the day in paradise—you've also done a good deed: a portion of the event proceeds is donated to local children's interests.

St. Francis captured in sculpture.

Sonoma, East

Bartholomew Park Winery
www.bartholomewparkwinery.com
1000 Vineyard Lane, Sonoma
707.935.9511
Daily 11am–4:30pm

Bartholomew Park Winery has something for everyone. First comes the pastoral setting in the foothills, which begs to be hiked. And hiked it should be, with three miles of marked trails just waiting for wine-loving adventurers.

If al fresco dining is more your thing, consider that Bartholomew Park has one of the best picnic spots in the Sonoma Valley. Lawn below and shade trees above join to make your Valley-gazing picture perfect. Just in case you don't happen to have lunch at the ready, you can purchase a small assortment of local goods inside the tasting room.

You'll also find more history here than at just about any other spot in Sonoma Valley. The residence you pass on your way into the winery grounds is Haraszthy House, built in the 1860s. It belonged to the colorful Count Agoston Haraszthy, founder of California's first commercial winery.

Inside the unassuming adobe-style building that houses the tasting room is a museum that documents some of Haraszthy's adventures, as well as the building's checkered past (it was once used as a jail). The comprehensive historical perspective on Sonoma Valley as a grape-growing and wine-making region includes photographs, antique winemaking equipment, historical maps, an antique horse carriage, and topography models.

To get to the museum, you'll pass through the tasting room, which samples Bartholomew Park's single-vineyard wines; they're produced by the same talented folks who bring you *Gundlach Bundschu* wines. There's also an aroma sensory bar to explore and a "wall of growers" to peruse. This is a one-stop winery that should not be missed.

Buena Vista Winery

www.buenavistawinery.com
18000 Old Winery Road, Sonoma
707.938.1266
Daily 10am–5pm

From its start, the wine industry has wielded a relentless power, luring everyone from sketchy characters to the most respected and levelheaded of folks. Many have come to search for happiness and good fortune. Some quests have met with great success; others have had less luck but have nonetheless made an impact.

One character who remains larger than life in both his failures and his drive is Agoston Haraszthy. A Hungarian who moved to America and became active in politics and business, the peripatetic Haraszthy then decided to move to Sonoma Valley and grow grapes. The first commercial vintner in California, he built Buena Vista's two stone cellars, each housing three caves, which were intended to be divided between Champagne and still wine. With Charles Krug hired as his winemaker, Haraszthy planned to give Europeans some competition by planting old-world varietals in the late 1850s.

But nearly as quickly as he had arrived in Northern California and begun his winery, he left. Legend has it that his colorful past included allegations of embezzlement; while that may or may not be true, he did move to Nicaragua in the early 1860s under the guise of seeking his fortune in rum. It was there that he is reported to have died while attempting to cross a crocodile-infested river. Now, *he's* the guy you'd want to show you around the winery.

Haraszthy's original vision is still clear at Buena Vista. The winery is set back at the end of the road, hidden behind giant eucalyptus, rambling manzanita, and unruly blackberry brambles. Its wild state makes it easy to imagine what it was like when Haraszthy first discovered the site. Now you'll find the winery to be handsome and charismatic with much of its history intact, from the oak casks and puncheons visible in the wine cellar to the old Champagne cellar that is currently used as the tasting room.

The selection offered for tasting includes current releases, reserve wines, and rare older wines not available anywhere else. Upstairs in the tasting room is an open space decorated with wall panels that offer a compelling glimpse into the history of Buena Vista and Haraszthy's adventures.

Given the peaceful and distant location, it's no surprise that the grounds have been filled with picnic tables arranged along the length of the property. In summer, find a cool, idyllic spot in the shade, and in winter, set yourself up next to a small brook that makes soothing sounds. Just watch out for crocodiles.

Castle Vineyards and Winery

www.castlevineyards.com
1105 Castle Road, Sonoma
707.996.1582
Sat–Sun by appointment only

Tucked away on a quiet country road, Castle gives a whole new meaning to the concept of "garage wine." Visitors who seek out this small producer will find that the tasting room is open when the garage door is up. Buck the dog greets you when you—literally—drive into the winery. Around the yard are tractors, trucks, and grape bins; the toys and bikes scattered beside them confirm that Castle is a homegrown business.

The wines here are made with grapes from twenty-six vineyards throughout Sonoma Valley and Carneros that are managed by Castle owner and winemaker Vic McWilliams. Most of the wines are cool-climate varietals, including pinot noir and merlot, with a couple of heat-loving grapes thrown in, like zinfandel from Sonoma Valley and cinsault from Lodi. Nearly all the small-production wines (most are produced annually in fewer than 200 case lots, with the largest hitting 775 cases) are made available for tasting, including a Port made from syrah that is really yummy.

Sleep among the Vines Just a few minutes from the Sonoma plaza, **Castle Vineyards** (1105 Castle Road, Sonoma, www.castlevineyards.com, 707.996.1582) offers a one-bedroom cottage to visitors who want to enjoy the winery life. Cute and private, it's a great alternative to staying in a hotel.

Gundlach Bundschu Winery

www.gunbun.com

2000 Denmark Street, Vineburg

707.938.5277

Daily 11am–4:30pm

Gundlach Bundschu Winery is America's oldest continuously owned winery, residing on the same land from which founder Jacob Gundlach first harvested grapes in 1858. Luminous oak trees and unruly vines in uneven rows line the driveway that sweeps up to the winery, intensifying the winery's historic image.

From this first impression, you might expect a solemn enterprise run by serious people working hard to preserve their heritage. Forget it. What you get instead is a winery run by a rambunctious, unpretentious family, the Bundschus, who seem to get serious only when it comes to making wine. In fact, through the years, "GunBun" has had the dubious distinction of involvement in several grand pranks. A longstanding friendly rivalry between the Bundschu and Benziger families led to rumors of a Benziger vehicle being "borrowed" by someone in the Bundschu family. Another time, Jim Bundschu, of the fifth generation to run the winery, was one of the major players in the hijacking of a Napa-bound bus carrying Richard Branson, of Virgin fame; the bus was led to a Sonoma soirée.

Day-to-day goings-on at the winery are a lot more sedate, but that fun-loving way of life prevails. The Bundschus have filled the grounds with tables for picnicking, built an outdoor stage for an annual Shakespeare festival, dug a cave to be toured, and created a short hiking path to the top of the hill that houses the cave.

The wine-tasting bar, a small area within the winery, has walls crowded with photographs, ribbons, and other memorabilia that capture the winery's colorful history. Beyond the tasting room, you can see the bottling machine, case stacks, tanks, and forklifts. Loud music from the cellar adds to the lively energy of the room.

All of GunBun's wines are produced from grapes grown on the estate, with the exception of two wines. The winery pours all its wines for tasting, offering a unique range of varietals, from gewürztraminer and kleinberger to gamay beaujolais and tempranillo, along with its proprietary blends, Red Bearitage, Polar Bearitage, and Sonoma Red.

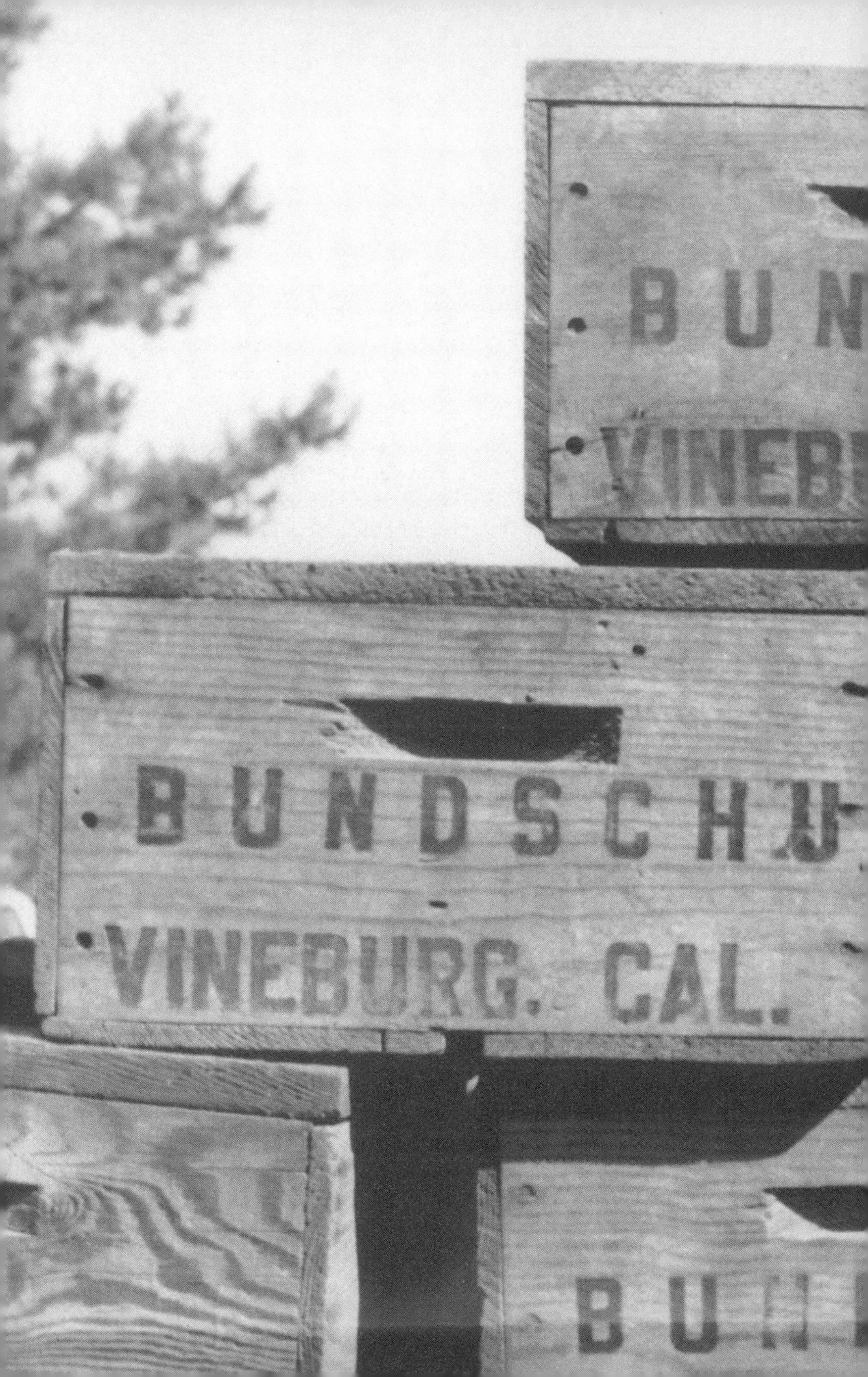
BUNDSCHU
VINEBURG. CAL.

Lunchtime The eastern side of the town of Sonoma has lots of wineries, but the places to eat are all back on the town plaza. **Sonoma Saveurs** (487 First Street West, Sonoma, 707.996.7007) is an unceremonious—and fabulous— French bistro with a menu heavy on foie gras and grilled and rotisserie- cooked meat and poultry. The well-rounded local wine list is color-coded for easy pairing with the menu.

Ravenswood

www.ravenswood-wine.com
18701 Gehricke Road, Sonoma
707.933.2332
Daily 10am–5pm

For zinfandel lovers, a visit to Ravenswood inspires great reverence. It all started in 1976, when Joel Peterson crushed his first zinfandel grapes. Through the years his passion, along with the winery's devoted staff and avid fans, has helped build Ravenswood into an industry phenomenon. Today there is a cult-like following for the winery and the grape.

Peterson's love for his product shines through in the range of wines he produces, from his Vintners Blend wines to the zinfandels made from some of the county's oldest vines. You might expect that a winery that has made such a profound impact on the industry would have a visitor center that is big and boastful. Not true at Ravenswood. In fact, the visitor center is simply a humble stone building set back among lavender, rosemary, native oaks, and olive trees.

Inside, the focus is entirely on the wines served at the tasting bar. Zinfandel, the backbone of the winery, is produced in three tiers. On any particular day, two or more zins are included in the regular five-wine flight, and that many or more in the single-vineyard wine flight. Both flights also include the other wines that Ravenswood crafts, including cabernet, petite sirah, chardonnay, merlot, a proprietary Rhône blend, and one of the various limited-production wines available only at the winery, such as a late-harvest gewürztraminer.

Ravenswood has endeared itself to its customers with its laid-back, anything-goes vibe and has inspired such devotion that a few fans have been known to have the logo tattooed on their bodies! While your first visit probably won't prompt that, you might be inclined to don one of the buttons that the winery hands out, printed with its motto: "No Wimpy Wines."

Sebastiani Vineyards and Winery

www.sebastiani.com
389 Fourth Street, Sonoma
707.933.3230
Daily 10am–5pm

In the 1970s, when the first gas crisis forced a change in travel patterns, lots of Bay Area folks began to take shorter jaunts, making Sonoma a prime destination. It was during that time that many of these travelers became familiar with Sebastiani. They liked it for plenty of good reasons: it provided a tour of the winery (which at the time primarily consisted of August Sebastiani's bird aviary and a room filled with wood carvings attached to redwood tanks) and also offered wine samples in the small, dark tasting room.

As time went on, both visitorship and visitors' wine knowledge increased. Sebastiani upgraded the tours to include information about the winemaking process (the first update was a then very modern slide show!). Gradually, the winery expanded, and little by little the entire property was renovated, including the tasting room and touring area. Today Sebastiani's tasting room is filled to the rafters with such beguiling pottery, linens, wine accessories, jewelry, bird cages, books, and food products that it's almost easy to miss the marble-and-wood tasting bar that takes up the entire back wall.

Before you head there, though, take the self-guided tour. A bit of Sebastiani's history can be viewed in the barrel room, which includes a collection of the wood carvings that played so prominent a role in the winery's early tours. In Samuele's Room (the original tasting room, named for Samuele Sebastiani, the winery's founder), take a look at the stained-glass windows. Then venture to the Radius Room, where some of Samuele's original equipment is stored.

Outside the historic 1913 stone building is a majestic colonnade that is echoed by the line of elm trees on the property's northern edge. Commandeer one of the picnic tables under those trees. It's a great spot to take a break.

Where it all began at Hanzell.

Sonoma, West

Hanzell Vineyards
www.hanzell.com
1859 Lomita Avenue, Sonoma
707.996.3860
By appointment only

On its own eastern-facing hillside in the Sonoma Valley, Hanzell sits quietly, aging as gracefully as the wines that emerge from its cellars. Founded in 1957 by Ambassador J. D. Zellerbach (of the Zellerbach paper company family) and his wife, Hana, Hanzell produces wines grown, vinified, and bottled on the estate.

In addition to its wines of exceptional character, Hanzell boasts a wine-making team that has more than one hundred combined years of work here. The member with the longest tenure is Bob Sessions, who began as winemaker more than thirty years ago; eventually he became general manager and is now a semiretired consultant for the winery. His wife, Jean Arnold Sessions, is Hanzell's dynamic manager, and his son Ben, who has spent more than a dozen harvests at the winery, leads marketing and sales.

Daniel Docher, the current winemaker, has worked with Bob for seven years, while vineyard manager José Ramos has been with the winery for more than two decades.

This tremendous continuity provides a consistent style that, in turn, creates faithful Hanzell clients. And it's no accident: the winery has been under the same ownership since 1975, when the deBrye family, from Australia, purchased it with the intent to maintain the Zellerbachs' enduring high standards and sound values. So today Hanzell continues to use original old-world farming techniques on its forty-two acres of pinot noir and chardonnay vineyards, respectively the second and third oldest vineyards of their kind in the United States. In the winery, traditional Burgundian techniques are used to produce wines meant to age in the bottle for a few years after release.

A visit to the property will include a tour of the winery's new cave, where aging of the twenty-seven-hundred annual case production is achieved. The tour will also take you around the winery itself, which was the first to use stainless-steel tanks for fermentation, and will offer a tasting of both the chardonnay and pinot noir. The wines are truly remarkable. They have finesse and the potential to age like a great Burgundian wine, but they are pure California. Buy them today, but drink them tomorrow.

The idea of endurance carries through to the property's architecture. The winery is a beautifully crafted building with a steeply pitched roof, stone foundation, redwood walls, and slate floors. Handcrafted details—like the way the doors slide open and shut—are evocative of the era in which it was built. Hanzell is also home to one of the wine country's best interpretations of a Burgundian house, with a structure that is both dignified and functional.

But this bow to timelessness doesn't stop with the architecture or even with the wine; rather, it's in the very air. Seek out the signed guest book, a tradition first instituted by Zellerbach in 1961, to find pages filled with names of local winemakers and San Francisco socialites. It's easy to imagine those early visitors: men and women driving up to the winery in fancy convertibles, standing on the porch smartly dressed in hats and gloves, oohing and ahhing over the view, which on a clear day extends all the way to the City. You may find yourself wondering what, besides the superficial alterations, has really changed. And you may find yourself realizing that in truth, some things—like quality, beauty, and refinement—never do.

Moon Mountain Winery

www.moonmountainvineyard.com
1700 Moon Mountain Drive, Sonoma
707.996.5870
By appointment only

The approach to Moon Mountain Winery takes you past a vista so remote and cratered that it feels as though you've actually landed on the moon. This odd lunarscape is the legacy of the 1996 wildfire, which swept across the Sonoma side of the Mayacamas range, destroying vineyards as it went but—rather strangely—leaving nearby vineyards untouched. Just across the road, for example, *Martini's* venerable Monte Rosso Vineyard was blessedly spared the wrath of these fires.

If the approach to Moon Mountain is rugged and intimidating, the winery itself is just the opposite. A series of round structures that both fit into the mountain setting and stand out as unique architectural statements make up the tasting room and yurt-like tank room. A neatly arranged cave where the winery's esteemed cabernet sauvignon, cabernet franc, and zinfandel are aged is attached to the tank room by a wisteria-draped pergola that curves along the contour of the hill.

Inside, the tasting room is spare but well thought out, with picture windows that peer south into the Sonoma Valley. The winery's attention to detail is even carried over to its whimsical bathroom tiles, which picture various phases of wine tasting, from opening the bottle to savoring a sip. Tours are geared toward wine education, so come prepared to learn.

Right: Moon Mountain's hidden winery.

Mendocino County Appellations

Mendocino County, consisting of ten appellations, is as diverse as Sonoma County. Some Mendocino appellations rest against the cool coastline, and others swelter in the hottest part of the county. With this wide range of climes comes the opportunity to grow everything from top-notch gewürztraminer to powerful cabernet. Despite the long history of Mendocino's wine industry, the area has remained rustic, a stark contrast to the sophisticated wines that emerge from within its borders.

ANDERSON VALLEY

The flavor of Anderson Valley is much more Mendocino coast than wine country glam. The dozen or so wineries that pop up along Highway 128, the main thoroughfare, blend into the scenery. The vineyards rise to meet the gentle rolling hills of the valley floor. Known for its cool climate, Anderson Valley grows superb pinot noir, gewürztraminer, and riesling grapes, all of which are used by the area's acclaimed winemakers. (Some of Napa's and Sonoma's most prestigious wineries also source fruit from this region.) The area has also gained recognition for producing world-class sparkling wines.

Esterlina Vineyards & Winery

www.esterlinavineyards.com
1200 Holmes Ranch Road, Philo
707.895.2920
By appointment only

If you're not afraid to get your car dirty—and a little driving adventure only whets your thirst for luscious wine—Esterlina is the place for you. Your pilgrimage to this mountaintop gem takes you two miles up a rugged country dirt road that sees lots more quail than cars. It's a dusty, steep climb—and boy, is it ever worth it.

Esterlina commands majestic views of the fertile stretch of Anderson Valley. But this is a winery with far more than scenery to brag about. Its low-yield hillside vineyards, planted above the fog line, produce truly noteworthy grapes that, along with its Sonoma County fruit, the winery has been selling to top producers for years.

But it's the Esterlina wines that really sing, especially its dry riesling and pinot. So although this tiny facility produces only five thousand cases annually and seats only two people in its minuscule tasting room (outfitted with notably comfortable stools), you will want to do some serious tasting here.

Be sure to pack a picnic before you come so that you can linger for a while under the trees in the shady picnic area—or step up to the terraced patio, where the world is literally at your feet.

Handley Cellars

www.handleycellars.com
3151 Highway 128, Philo
707.895.3876 or 800.733.3151
Daily 11am–5pm (summer until 6pm)

On one end of a peaceful, flowered lawn, an old water tower nobly presides over a nearby redwood visitor building. Beside it, a trellised, vine-strewn patio courtyard is made vibrant with eclectic folk art sculptures and wind chimes. It's a pleasant place to taste wine, eat a picnic lunch, and take a break.

On one hand, Handley Cellars seems worlds away from anything. But on the other, the world is very much part of its tasting room/gallery, which—reflecting the Handley family's multigenerational interest in international folk art—displays and sells folk art and jewelry from every corner of the planet, from New Guinea to Mexico. (As an aside, the family owns the Trader Vic restaurants as well as two retail art shops in San Francisco. But their global interests go well past art collection; they've gone as far as to help villages around the world improve irrigation systems and water supplies.)

In keeping with these cultural traditions, winemaker-owner Milla Handley is known to honor Boontling, a regional dialect used in these parts between 1890 and 1940. It's said Boontling got its start in the hop fields when a man wanted to disguise his derogatory gossip about a young woman. Whether the tale is true or not, Handley has named one of its proprietary blends Brightlighter—a Boontling term referring to city people who live in areas with electric lights.

Handley also sponsors an annual event, held the third week of July, called Expressions of Anderson Valley. In addition to introducing new releases, the event is known for food and wine pairings, barrel tastings, and the talents of local artists and musicians. Perhaps this event is the winery's expression of affection and admiration for its own community culture.

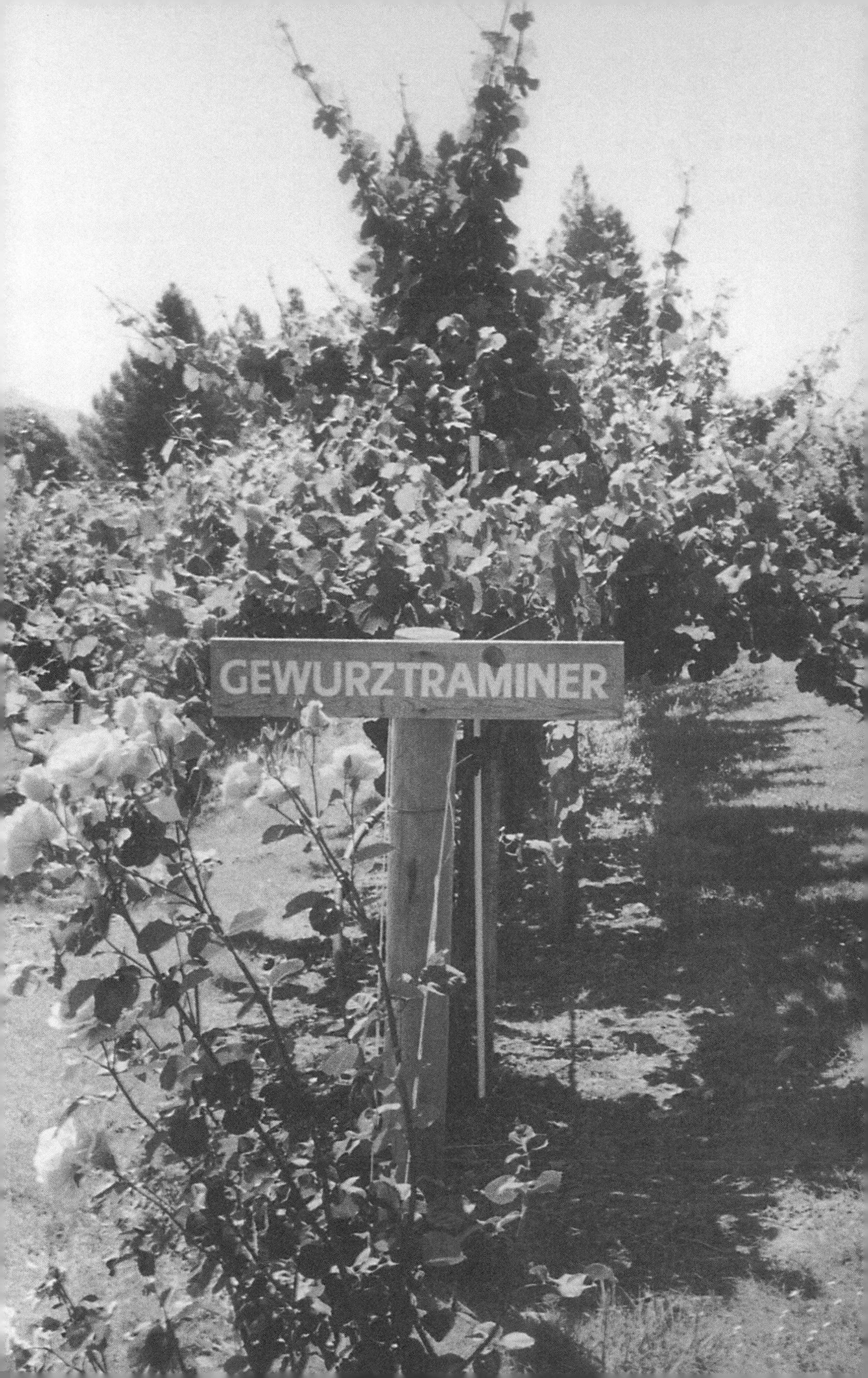
GEWURZTRAMINER

Husch Vineyards

www.huschvineyards.com
4400 Highway 128, Philo
800.554.8724
Daily 10am–5pm

It looks like Hansel and Gretel should have found their way to this winery's adorable tasting room. Started in 1971, Husch was the Anderson Valley's first winery—and it's still the cutest tasting room around: a tiny wood-shingled cottage with a rose-arbored doorway and vine-covered picnic tables, nicely spaced for maximum privacy.

But dinky as it is, the tasting room is lined with cases of wine instead of the usual bric-a-brac, making for a nice change of pace. The grapes used for each vintage are all from family-owned vineyards in the Anderson and Ukiah valleys; two-thirds of the total production is devoted to chardonnay and sauvignon blanc, including Renegade, Husch's signature wine—an original-tasting wild-yeast-fermented sauvignon blanc.

Lazy Creek Vineyards

www.lazycreekvineyards.com
4741 Highway 176, Philo
707.895.3623
By appointment only

It's easy to see what lured Mary Beth and Josh Chandler (he's the son of renowned landscape architect Jack Chandler, and a landscape architect in his own right) to this spot of earth: Lazy Creek is where most people would want to live. Getting here is half the fun, since you have to drive way down a rugged, heavily forested road. You know you've arrived when you see a flower-filled garden blooming amid a sea of vineyards, and an old truck so endearingly rusted it seems like it sprang from the soil.

For a minute everything is totally silent except for the gentle call of birds—until Pokey the dog starts barking. Let him lead you down a gravel path past the family house to the winery. In warm-weather months, tastings are held at an outdoor bar. In fact, the winery is composed of three small shacks behind the Chandlers' home, between which children's toys and winemaking paraphernalia are scattered about.

This is clearly a hard-working place where real people live. And it's got a reputation to uphold: it's the second bonded winery in the Valley, with vines more than three decades old. Today it produces just over two thousand cases annually, half devoted to pinot, the other half divided between chard and gewürztraminer.

To help you enjoy their little piece of heaven, the Chandlers also indulge visitors with some serious hospitality. Their reserved catered lunches are a cross between country-chic dining and a treasure hunt. You're sent out to the vineyard with a map and a glass of wine, and after a leisurely fifteen-minute walk past horses and cows and over easy rolling hills, you arrive at the bucolic picnic spot: a table under a shady bay tree in the middle of the vineyard. Since yet another of Josh's former incarnations was as a chef at Auberge du Soleil, working under the renowned Masa Kobayashi, you know this will be a memorable experience.

Sleep among the Vines Lazy Creek Vineyards (4741 Highway 176, Philo, www.lazycreekvineyards.com, 707.895.3623) in the Anderson Valley rents out its two-room Plum Cottage, breakfast included. You'll feel like you've found your way back to the home you've always wished you had.

Navarro

www.navarrowine.com
5601 Highway 128, Philo
707.895.3686 or 800.537.9463
Summer daily 10am–6pm, winter daily 10am–5pm

One of the more popular destinations in the Anderson Valley, Navarro is known for moderately priced, excellent wines; it is perhaps best known for its gewürztraminer (which always sells out quickly). We are particularly enamored of its rosé, a perfect blend of grenache and syrah—it's like summer in a glass.

In fact, Navarro wines are not sold in retail venues at all. But you can taste the wines at many restaurants and, once you know what you love, make this a purchase destination rather than a place to linger. For although there's a nice-size deck with picnic tables; the requisite views of vineyards and hills; a decent supply of local cheese, fruits, vegetables, and crackers; grape juice for the little ones; and a cute chandelier made from an antique bottle dryer, this slightly cramped tasting room is only pleasantly ordinary. Fortunately, the wines it sells are anything but that—they're truly terrific.

Lunchtime Anderson Valley is fairly small, with only a few choices for lunch. **Libby's** (Highway 128, Philo, 707.895.2646) Mexican fare is always excellent, and the **Anderson Valley Brewing Company** (17700 Highway 253, Boonville, www.avbc.com, 707.895.BEER) offers terrific pub grub and fantastic beer—a great palate cleanser between tastes of wine.

Roederer Estate Winery
www.roedererestate.net
4501 Highway 128, Philo
707.895.2288
Daily 11am–5pm

Roederer's long, narrow, light, and airy tasting room is punctuated by large picture windows overlooking manicured gardens and the Anderson Valley. The walls of the room are hung with late-nineteenth-century illustrations of the Louis Roederer winery and vineyards in France. The prints offer fascinating lessons in history (they were created pre-phylloxera and before trellising), architecture (the Rheims Cathedral is in the background), and winemaking itself (the series shows the production process scene by scene).

Standing at the bar, it's easy to ignore the slightly worn, overly formal, fancy-grandma furniture behind you—the very antithesis of the sophisticated, sexy sparklers you're about to sample. Served in delicate crystal flutes (which are also for sale) etched with the Roederer logo, the flight of hypnotically bubbly wines tends toward an intelligent balance of complexity, flavor, and styling. The flight also includes tastings of pinot. Be warned: although the fee is minimal, the portions are quite small. Special releases and library tastings are also available for sale. The excellent artistically designed lighting (artificial as well as natural) at the bar adds a subtle but important visual enhancement to all tastings, showcasing both the color in the glass and the gently persistent rise of tiny bubble after tiny bubble.

Neighbors to Watch A stone's throw south of Anderson Valley is the Yorkville Highlands. A tiny appellation that is home to only a few wineries, the area is slightly elevated above Anderson Valley, which means it's a touch warmer and friendlier for growing Bordeaux-style grapes. In the tiny town of Yorkville, population twenty-five, **Yorkville Cellars** (25701 Highway 128, Yorkville, www.yorkvillecellars.com, 707.894.9177, daily 11am–5pm) does just that quite handsomely and organically. Or stop by **Meyer Family Cellars** (19750 Highway 128, Yorkville, www.mfcellars.com, 707.895.2341, call for hours), where Matt, son of **Silver Oak** founder Justin Meyer, opened shop to produce Meyer Family Port and syrah.

REDWOOD VALLEY

One of the oldest wine-growing regions in the state, Redwood Valley was established in the 1850s, largely by Italian immigrants. Those early residents planted zinfandel and petite sirah, which are still the signature varietals of the area today. The Redwood Valley is so remote and backwoodsy that it has remained a sleepy region unbothered by crowds, despite the growing attention to its wines. The wines produced here, a percentage of which come from organically farmed vineyards, are luscious and full-bodied.

Fife Redhead Vineyards
www.fifevineyards.com
3621 Ricetti Lane off Road A, Redwood Valley
707.485.0323
Daily 10am–5pm

A visit to Fife Redhead Vineyards is for the intrepid traveler only. Since the winery sits atop one of the hills that form the sides of the Redwood Valley, getting there requires a trip up a long, narrow winding mountain road. Just when you think you've run out of road, you arrive. A short dirt driveway cuts through a vineyard filled with big gnarled, head-trained vines—old vines so thick, muscular, and sturdy they're almost scary.

The tasting-room entrance is reached through a carport; from here you can look down into the depths of Lake Mendocino, blue and shimmering. The small, square tasting room itself is an ode to unpretentiousness: linoleum flooring, a large faux-brick fireplace, and a pine table in the center of the room quickly signal that you're standing in a converted dining room. The bar seems like it's seen its share of family get-togethers and parties, making it a comfortable place to try the zinfandels on which owner Dennis Fife has built his reputation. There's no denying that there's something quite divine about standing arm's distance from the vines that yielded the grapes for the wine you're drinking.

Frey Vineyards

www.freywine.com
14000 Tomki Road, Redwood Valley
707.485.5177
By appointment only

When you visit Frey Vineyards, it's easy to imagine what Northern California was like in the 1970s. The country's first certified organic winery, Frey has retained its original mellow vibe: a homesteading type of place, animated by kids, dogs, foreign student apprentices, and members of the huge, extended Frey family (of the twelve Frey children, all but one work for the winery and all but two live on the ranch with their families and significant others).

The vast grounds are filled with hand-hewn redwood structures, including the winery itself, made from redwood salvaged from a defunct Ukiah winery. Visitors are welcomed for tastings in a camp-like courtyard setting surrounded by homemade benches and tables. The tasting bar itself is crafted of large planks of wood set on top of barrels.

But the folksy setting belies the winery's sophisticated operations and the Frey family's in-depth knowledge about growing grapes using organic and biodynamic methods. While only ninety of the family's almost seven hundred acres are in production, this seems like a lot given that the Freys originally planted grapes as a political protest: at the time, a proposed water construction project would have impacted their land, so in hopes of increasing their property value and warding off such construction, the Freys planted grapes.

The water project never came to fruition. But when John Frey, the oldest son, returned home after studying French-intensive farming in nearby Covelo, he took a stab at serious winemaking. His efforts were well rewarded. Today Frey Vineyards is a thriving business with a dedicated following of health-conscious folks who want organically grown or biodynamically farmed, sulfite-free wine.

Frey Vineyards is without question out of the way (and the road leading to it is not cleared in winter), but if you're willing to make the drive, you're rewarded with a hefty discount on any wines you purchase. Choose among varietals including petite sirah, syrah, zinfandel, chardonnay, and sauvignon blanc, or try Frey's proprietary blends, Natural Red and Natural White—a steal at less than ten dollars a bottle.

Lunchtime Redwood Valley may be an up-and-coming wine region, but that's where its contributions to gastronomy end. Sadly, the selection in nearby Ukiah isn't much better. Your best bet when you're in the neighborhood is to go to the **Bluebird Café** (13340 South Highway 101, Hopland, 707.744.1633) in Hopland. The Bluebird is diner food at its best; its large selection of burgers and sandwiches will fill you up and ready you for an afternoon of wine tasting.

Gabrielli Winery
10950 West Road, Redwood Valley
707.485.1221
By appointment only

With Gabrielli's woodsy-cabin feel, it's easy to imagine sitting in one of the front-porch Adirondack chairs for many happy hours, contemplating your view of the nearby mountains. And you should. Keep in mind that the tasting room is small and minimal, so your best bet is to grab a glass and do your sipping outside.

Silversmith Vineyards
www.silversmithvineyards.com
3700 A Road J, Redwood Valley
707.485.1196
Sat–Sun 11am–5pm

Nestled into the base of the foothills, Silversmith Vineyards has a simple but nice tasting room. Stop by to sample the wines made from grapes grown on the estate, and take the time to chat with the owners, fifth-generation Mendocino farmers who are usually behind the folding table that serves as a bar. You'll experience first-hand the kind of friendliness that permeates this quiet region.

The Best of the Rest The stretch of land from Hopland to Redwood Valley is gradually gaining recognition as a hot spot for growing high-quality grapes and for wines that are full of character yet still reasonably priced. There are a few places that make a good stopover once you're in the neighborhood. ····· In Ukiah, **Parducci** (501 Parducci Road, Ukiah, www.parducci.com, 888.362.9463, daily 10am–5pm) looks like it could be an Italian restaurant straight out of Brooklyn. Its rambling tasting room is crowded with tchotchkes, but the wines are definitely great reflections of what the area can produce. ····· The same can be said of the wines made at the quiet, kind of pretty **Jepson** (10400 Highway 101, Hopland, www.jepsonwine.com, 707.468.8936, daily 10am–5pm), as well as those at the austerely designed **Jeriko Estate Winery** (12141 Hewlitt at Sturtevant Road, Hopland, www.jerikoestate.com, 707.744.1140, daily 10am–5pm). Owned by Dan Fetzer, Jeriko makes some terrific wine, including a rollicking sangiovese.

The Best Appellation Event Bring Dad or leave him at home—but either way, make the trip to the Father's Day weekend extravaganza **A Taste of Redwood Valley** (www.atasteofredwoodvalley.com, 707.485.0323 or 800.760.3739, Father's Day weekend), one of the few events where you can sample and purchase **Cole Bailey** wine. A small-production cab that hails from the local hillsides, it's a high-quality wine at a surprisingly low price—one that reflects how relatively undiscovered this region still is.

Another good reason to attend this roving event is that many of the wineries that throw open their doors for it aren't usually accessible to the public. A one-time ticket price gets you a logo glass to help in your tasting efforts, as well as food to nosh on at each winery, barrel samples, live music, and the chance to meet the winemakers. If you can't make it in June, check out the **Redwood Valley Holiday Sale** (see A Taste of Redwood Valley) in mid-November, when it's bring-your-own-glass for tasting and the wines are on sale for holiday stocking up—and, if you're smart, for holiday stocking stuffing.

SANEL VALLEY

The Sanel Valley lies in southern Mendocino County. It surrounds the town of Hopland, in an area that was once a prolific hop-growing region, and then ventures south through a narrow canyon along the Russian River; ultimately, it reaches Sonoma County. Most vineyards in this area are planted in the plains, which are strongly influenced by the Russian River. Sauvignon blanc, chardonnay, cab, and merlot prevail here and are noted for their ripe fruit flavors and lean tannins.

Fetzer Vineyards at Valley Oaks Ranch

www.fetzer.com
13601 Eastside Road, Hopland
800.846.8637
Daily 9am–5pm

Getting to Fetzer Vineyards means driving slowly between two sensuous rows of half-painted, well-groomed trees. It's a little like driving through the French countryside only to wind up in a remote American village of another century.

In reality, Fetzer is only one mile off Highway 101, and the "village" is a mid-1800s farmstead that serves as home to the cheery tasting room, café, and lodgings that make up Fetzer's Valley Oaks Ranch. While wine may be the commodity Fetzer is best known for, the most compelling reason to visit Fetzer is the absolutely splendid world-class gardens.

A main garden is filled to bursting with native plants, lavender, and herbs—rosemary, thyme, savory, and the like—as well as voluptuous roses, sweet geraniums, and a myriad of other colorful blooms. Entering it through vine-covered arches is the stuff of dreams; you're practically guaranteed to feel more peaceful and tranquil—and intoxicated by nature— after a few deep breaths. Next to the main garden is an organic vegetable garden where the seasons proudly display their wares: tomatoes, squash, pumpkins, amaranth, and corn all grow in neat rows. Unlike at most prized gardens, visitors to Fetzer are encouraged to sip wine while wandering and to pick, smell, and taste anything bearing a "Please Taste" sign. It's a sensory experience few wineries can offer. There are other gardens, borders, and trellises as well, each showcasing a specific type of planting.

Right: A garden path at Fetzer.

If you haven't had enough to sip while cruising through the gardens, you'll want to quench your thirst in the tasting room, where nearly all the estate wines are offered, or in the reserve tasting room, where the reserve wines may be sampled. Or pull up a chair in the simple café adjacent to the tasting room and have lunch, choosing from a wide-ranging menu that reflects the garden's seasonal offerings. The café is also open for breakfast and coffee drinks. Country-style merchandise, from large wicker baskets to earthy ceramics, will beg you to buy them.

Fetzer has always been a leader in combining food and wine, and today this practice thrives via the special events that are held throughout the year. Award-winning chef and wine country culinary authority John Ash leads several classes each year, ranging from grilling fish to cooking mushrooms. Other guest chefs include Emeril Lagasse, who makes his own label of Fetzer wine.

Lunchtime The tiny town of Hopland is so small, it's not surprising that there are only a few eateries. What is surprising is how good each one is. **Phoenix Bread Company** (13325 South Highway 101, Hopland, www.phoenixbreadcompany.com, 707.744.1944) rises to the top of the lunch list, offering a really tasty *fougasse* and scrumptious turnovers, both ideal for a picnic lunch.

The Best of the Rest The number of wineries in and around Hopland is limited, which is why the best way to use your time is to make Hopland your home base for visiting Sanel and Redwood valleys. On your way through, consider stopping just south of town at **Milano Winery** (14594 Highway 101, Hopland, 707.744.1396, daily 10am–5pm), a former hop kiln built in 1947 that has a natural appeal. It's worth a look, a taste, and maybe even a purchase.

GLASSES
to
GRAPES

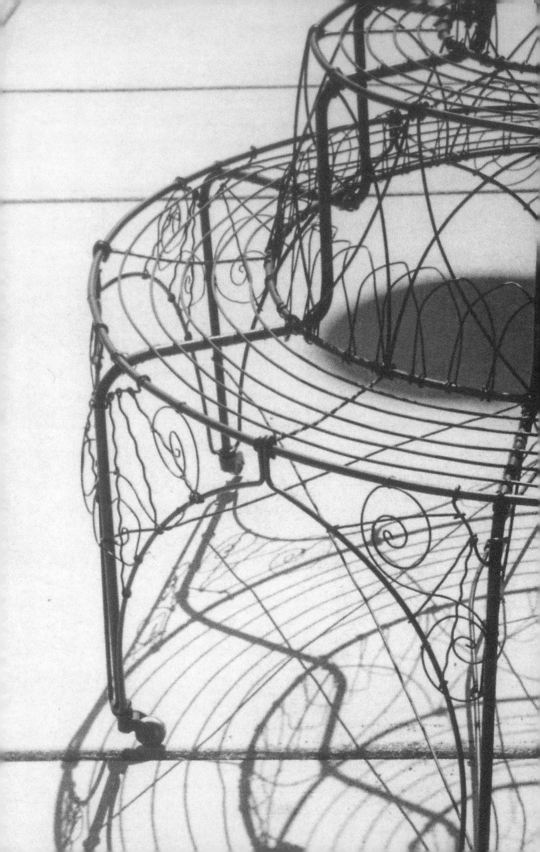

ACCESSORIES

It's no surprise that the wine country is also wine accessory country. Who can resist the allure of lovely shops (both inside winery tasting rooms and out) dedicated to the art of wine service? You can surely expect to find whatever oenophilic accoutrements you may need or lust for, from the practical to the decadent.

While a crystal decanter will not magically transform an indifferent wine into a Grand Cru, it's also true that the curve of a glass, the shape of a decanter, the pleasure of a cleanly removed cork all have a positive effect on the flavor—and certainly the presentation—of wine. So shop. Remember: if you buy it here, it's more than just an accessory, it's a memory.

NAPA COUNTY

Dean & Deluca

www.deananddeluca.com
607 St. Helena Highway, St. Helena
707.967.9980
Mon–Sat 7:30am–7pm, Sun 9am–7pm

> Visitors from the East Coast may be tempted to drive right by Dean & Deluca, thinking it's nothing more than a New York knock-off. Make no such mistake. Half the store is devoted to a phenomenal selection of beautifully presented wines (with personal sales service to match) and all the sophisticated wine toys, glasses, decanters, and other accessories you'll ever need to serve them. It's the best of both coasts—don't miss it.

Mostly French

www.mostlyfrench.com
1227 C Lincoln Avenue, Calistoga
707.942.1552
Sun–Thur 11am–5pm, Fri–Sat 10am–6pm

> Mostly French is the store extraordinaire for wine-loving Francophiles. With its interesting selection of antique winemaking equipment and its dazzling contemporary wine accessories, it makes it easy to add a touch of France to your life. Antique pruning knives make you want to take to the fields. Large woven grape-harvesting baskets incite *A Year in Provence* fantasies. A wine press the size of a toy inspires you to make just enough wine for your family. *Trop?* Set your sights on more practical items, such as colorful ceramic carafes from Provence and corkscrews from Laguiole. *Vive la France!*

Mumm Cuvée Napa

www.mummnapavalley.com
8445 Silverado Trail, Rutherford
707.967.7740
Daily 10am–5pm

> Bubbly lovers, gift-givers, and shoppers, unite! Then head straight for Mumm Cuvée Napa. Mumm carries the widest selection of Champagne and sparkling-wine accessories assembled in the wine country. There are ice buckets of every size, shape, and material. Shelves are lined with dozens

of styles of glasses, from ornate crystal to simple glass flutes. There are even plastic flutes to add a touch of elegance to a picnic. This is the place to fuel those Champagne wishes.

Napa Valley Grapevine Wreath Company

www.grapevinewreath.com
8901 Conn Creek Road, Rutherford
707.963.9983 or 877.776.NAPA
Thur–Mon 10:30am–5:30pm

If you wish you could just pluck a grapevine from the fields and take it home with you, how about the next best thing? Grapevine Wreath Company, a quaint little country store near the Silverado Trail, specializes in decorative and useful items crafted out of grapevines. There are wreaths, plant stands, bottle carriers, cheese baskets, magazine stands, and a huge selection of baskets in every shape and size. Handmade, handsome, and often even handy, these make sweet keepsakes of your trip to the wine country.

China, Farewell Bridal registries ain't what they used to be. Today's brides—and **grooms**—want wine! And at **Domaine Carneros** (1240 Duhig Road at Highway 12, Napa, www.domainecarneros.com, 707.257.0101, daily 10am–6pm), happy couples can register for it by selecting both still and sparkling wines, plus the glasses that marry best to each. Who knows—maybe this trend will bring down the divorce rate.

Spice Islands Campus Store and Marketplace

Culinary Institute of America at Greystone
www.ciaprochef.edu
2555 Main Street, St. Helena
707.967.2309
Daily 10am–6pm

If you want to spit like the pros, take a class at the CIA's Rudd Center. If you want to spit into the bucket of the pros, buy it at the CIA's Spice Islands Campus Store and Marketplace. Along with official Rudd Center spit buckets, the CIA store has a comprehensive selection of wine books, glasses, wine racks, corkscrews, decanters, glasses, and glass tags. It also sells a mix of accessories that includes thermometers, wine bags, and label removers. Shop for gifts, shop for yourself, just shop. This store has it all.

SONOMA COUNTY

Sign of the Bear Kitchenware

435 First Street West, Sonoma

707.996.3722

Daily 10am–6pm

> Sign of the Bear Kitchenware is packed to the rafters with everything you
> need and everything you want for the kitchen. It sells a nifty selection of
> indispensable wine accessories, like glasses, corkscrews, and decanters.
> There are also all the peripheral goods that make drinking wine an occa-
> sion to remember: clever cocktail napkins, handsome trays, adorable olive
> bowls, eccentric chip bowls, Provençal-inspired tablecloths, and sublime
> carafes. Make the time to shop in this store—and don't worry, it gift wraps
> and ships!

Sonoma Wine Hardware

www.winehardware.com

536 Broadway, Sonoma

707.939.1694

Daily 10am–6pm

> Owned by the Wine Appreciation Guild, this no-nonsense store is a wine
> gadgeteer's dream. From expandable wine racks to huge cellars disguised
> as armoires; from glassware to games; from boda bags to blending kits;
> from classic Laguiole corkscrews to state-of-the-art cellar software; from
> foil cutters to cooler wraps; from books to CDs and more, Sonoma Wine
> Hardware carries everything the wine collector could ever need or want.
>
> Shopping here is not about having a stylish experience—it resembles an
> upscale storage facility—but it *does* make a convincing case for function
> over form.

EDUCATION

Sure, studying quantum physics is a blast, and boning
up on your high school French has its merits. But
what could be better than pursuing greater wine
knowledge? While some argue that you further your
oenological education with every sip of wine, others
believe that formal training is a better approach.

Fortunately, the California wine country has enough educational opportunities to satisfy everyone's personal philosophy. From serious novices to erudite professionals and from classroom lectures to hands-on seminars, there's something here for everyone.

NAPA COUNTY

Copia: The American Center for Wine, Food & the Arts

www.copia.org
500 First Street, Napa
707.259.1600 or 888.51.COPIA
Wed–Mon 10am–5pm

Copia offers a comprehensive selection of wine-education activities, from classic tastings to classroom seminars. Time spent here is guaranteed to help you improve your ability to identify, describe, evaluate, and enjoy the juice of the grape. Depending on which course you attend, you may learn to pair wine with food; cultivate your historical understanding of wine and winemaking; learn to preserve and cellar; explore the connections between wine and poetry; unveil the secrets of *terroir*; or master a variety of other wine-related subjects, from barrel making to etiquette.

For the more serious wine student, Copia is also the only West Coast location where one can study for and take London's esteemed Wine and Spirit Education Trust exam. Copia also offers winemaking classes through the University of Davis extension program.

Napa Valley College

www.napavalley.edu
2277 Napa-Vallejo Highway, Napa
707.253.3005

Napa Valley College is geared toward the very serious wine enthusiast or the career-minded individual. A full-scale community college and a product of its environment, it offers a two-year Associate of Science Degree in viticulture, winemaking, and wine marketing and sales, and also has a fully equipped winery and vineyard.

But wait—that's not all. Every semester the college schedule is chockablock with nighttime classes that are less serious and more fun. You can enroll in Home Winemaking, Wines of the World, Wines of California, Cultural Appreciation of Wine, and Sensory Evaluation of Wines. While most of the classes last a full semester, others are only six weeks long. So what are you waiting for? A mind—and a wine education—is a terrible thing to waste. (Note to singles: These classes have been known to result in more than a few marriages between fellow wine lovers!)

The Rudd Center.

Rudd Center

Culinary Institute of America at Greystone
www.ciaprochef.com
2555 Main Street, St. Helena
800.888.7850

There is no better place to master the fundamentals of wine, gain certification as a wine professional, or just hone your wine senses than the Rudd Center at the Culinary Institute of America at Greystone. Originally built as Napa Valley's first wine co-op, Greystone is steeped in wine history and offers a spectacular setting in which to learn about all things oenological.

Completed in 2003 and located in what was the still house, the Rudd Center puts vineyards at your fingertips and wineries at every turn. It's an ideal environment in which to immerse yourself in the glory of the grape. The instructor list alone is impressive, with Karen MacNeil as chair of the center and Jeff Morgan of *SoloRosa*, Judd Wallenbach of *Humanitas*, and Peter Granoff among the faculty. You can learn to identify *terroir* in a glass of wine, understand the great wine regions of Europe, explore the business of wine, and so much more. Programs range from two-day intensive classes to weeklong courses; wine professionals may become certified through the professional wine studies program.

A Paid Education Every harvest, dozens of seasonal wine-related jobs are made available to the uninitiated. They range from sugar sampler (a straightforward task of plucking grapes off the vine, measuring the brix, labeling the grapes, and bringing them back to the winemaker) to grape sorter (perfect for perfectionists who want to make sure not a single piece of MOG—material other than grapes—goes through the crusher with the grapes). If you have a lust to learn the intricacies of winemaking via a hands-on experience, check the want ads of the **Napa Valley Register** (www.napanews.com) for individual winery job listings. Or sign up at any of the several temporary employment agencies in Napa and Sonoma counties that place seasonal employees, such as Nelson (866.939.4343) and Alkar (707.224.5468).

Upper Valley Campus
www.napacommunityed.org
1088 College Avenue, St. Helena
707.967.2900

Upper Valley Campus—the St. Helena campus of Napa Valley College—has a truncated wine program that is geared toward the wine lover who wants to explore a specific topic. Ronn Weigand, a noted wine writer and teacher, leads one-evening classes that focus on a specific wine. In the past, he's explored syrahs from around the world and cabernet sauvignons from California. If you'd rather get your hands dirty than sit and listen, Pat Watkins, another well-known winemaking teacher, offers both home winemaking and beer-brewing classes for the beginner.

SONOMA COUNTY

Affairs of the Vine
www.affairsofthevine.com
696 Elliott Lane, Sebastopol
707.874.1975

Affairs of the Vine's approach to wine education is tongue-in-cheek: its one-day intensive course, designed to give you hands-on experience in growing grapes and making wine, is called Wine Boot Camp. Affairs of the

Vine owner Barbara "Major" Drady gathers the "troops" for a full day that begins in the vineyard. Participants get to experience seasonal activities, from pruning and shoot positioning to harvesting. When the work is done, the troops are led through a workshop that covers such broad topics as aromatic identification, demystifying wine descriptions, and wine and food pairings. Then it's on to lunch in a vineyard before returning to work in the cellar. This time the work is more like play: this is where you blend your own wine and do a tasting. At the end of the day, you'll all have dinner at one of the participating wineries. If you want to learn as much about wine as you can in as short a time as possible, enlist at once in Wine Boot Camp. That's an order!

Homemade Hooch Home winemaking has a long history in the wine country, beginning with immigrants from the old country who were accustomed to making their own house wine, and continuing on to Prohibition-era bootleggers who fermented grapes in bathtubs. Today, home winemakers are mostly die-hard wine lovers who want to try their hand at something they know they enjoy. It's surprisingly easy to make a batch of wine (although making a **good** batch is somewhat more difficult), and it doesn't require an excessive amount of supplies or equipment. To procure what you need, visit the two full-size stores in the Napa-Sonoma area that carry everything for the home winemaker. **Napa Valley Fermentation Supplies** (575 Third Street, [inside the Fairgrounds], Napa, www.napafermentation.com, 707.255.6372, Mon–Fri 9am–5pm, Sat 10am– 5pm) has been the home winemaker's resource for years. Owner Pat Watkins, a well-respected brewing and winemaking instructor in the Valley, is usually on hand to provide assistance and advice. In Santa Rosa, the **Beverage People** (840 Piner Road #14, Santa Rosa, www.thebeveragepeople.com, 707.544.2525, Tues–Fri 10am–5:30pm, Sat 10am–5pm) are tucked away in the back of a warehouse complex, not a bad place to sell their barrels, books, corks, capsules, barrel thieves, presses, bottles, demijohns, bungs, labels, and flasks. During harvest, they also have a binder filled with classified ads offering grapes. A staff of brewers and winemakers offer guidance and support year round.

Ramekins

www.ramekins.com
450 West Spain Street, Sonoma
707.933.0450

Ramekins was founded by Suzanne Brangham, a true epicure who has made as much of an impact on Sonoma Valley's culinary landscape as the Sebastianis, Vellas, or Vivianis by creating a place of worship for wine and food lovers. Housed in a rammed-earth building, Ramekins has become the culinary center of the Valley. Its wide range of cooking classes includes wine and cheese pairings and cooking-with-wine demonstrations. Wine-related field trips are for anyone who dreams about oysters and Champagne at the ocean's edge. Ramekins also sponsors winemaker dinners that match local chefs to local wineries. It's like a new kind of reality show: foodies and winies battle it out to see what comes first, the wine or the food. Not surprisingly, everybody always wins.

Relish Culinary School

www.relishculinary.com
Various locations around Healdsburg
707.431.9999

The epicurean love child of two passionate cooks, Teresa Brooks and Donna del Rey, Relish is a culinary school with a twist: it has no home. Instead, Relish holds classes throughout the county. An exploration of Sonoma County appellations through a wine tasting and discussion might be held at the stylish Hotel Healdsburg. A class on blending zinfandel—along with a cooking demonstration—might take place in Bella Vineyards' cave. Or a Sonoma-style tapas class, taught by culinary personality Michele Anna Jordan, might set up shop at the very hip Roshambo Winery. Whichever class you choose, you can be certain that the wine will be luscious, the food delicious, and the experience unforgettable.

Serious about Wine? Play Games WineSmarts (www.smartsco.com) lets you put to use all that wine knowledge that's as dusty as bottles in the cellar. A cross between Trivial Pursuit and flash cards, WineSmarts is a straightforward question-and-answer game. One hundred colorful cards in four categories—grapes, regions, vocabulary, and wild card—contain brain-teasers such as "True or false: Meritage is a famous Bordeaux wine chateau." And "What is the approximate per capita wine consumption in the U.S. per year? a) 2 gallons; b) 6 gallons; c) 12 gallons; d) 15 gallons." (Answers: false, and 2 gallons.) To quote the WineSmarts tagline, "It'll go straight to your head." **Winerd** (www.winerdgame.com), a board game with synthetic corks as playing pieces, tests the other half of your brain with its sensory-evaluation component. The game begins with all players evaluating three wines. You then advance across the board by correctly answering questions about wine. If you land on a "Blind Taste" square, you're required to blind taste one of the wines. Get it right, go forward. Get it wrong, better sip again. Want your wine served in a game-show format? Play the **World Wine Challenge** (www.trincherofamilywines.com), an interactive Wheel of Fortune-like game, produced by Trinchero Family Estates, that takes you around the world to test your wine IQ. A stop in France may have you scrambling to list all of the Bordeaux varietals, not just the classic five. Another spin may land you in Portugal, where you'll be quizzed about the varietal wines of Port producers.

EVENTS

Wine country events come in all shapes and sizes throughout the year, from the homespun Valley of the Moon Vintage Festival to the world-renowned Napa Valley Wine Auction, from silent to live auctions, and from focused explorations of single varietals to comprehensive regional tastings.

Whether you're looking for a single reason to make the wine country your destination or just an event to enhance a weekend's visit, special events allow you to dine, drink, dance, bid, hike, make wine, cook, rub elbows with stars, or simply people watch. No matter what your tastes, there is a wine country event for every palate, every wallet, and every sensibility.

NAPA COUNTY

Copia's Wine Weekend
www.copia.org
500 First Street, Napa
707.259.1600 or 888.51.COPIA
Autumn

Interested in tasting wine with the legendary Hugh Johnson? How about learning the origins of viniculture with scholar Patrick McGovern? Want to explore a single Napa region in depth, with a wine tasting to boot? You can do all this and more at Copia's Wine Weekend. Still young, this four-day "weekend" tribute to wine is a joint effort between Copia and the Napa Valley Vintners. It includes focused wine lectures, tastings, and industry discussions, as well as a festive awards dinner that honors industry leaders.

The heart of the event, Taste Napa, is an indoor-outdoor, walk-around wine and food tasting and is your chance to experience Napa Valley in one afternoon. More than half the Valley's wineries line up alongside local food producers, offering tastes from wineries that might otherwise be unavailable for visits. Wineries from up and down the Valley, from *Chateau Montelena* in Calistoga to *Bouchaine* in Carneros, are there generously pouring their best.

You are guaranteed to leave with a new—or renewed—appreciation for Napa Valley's extraordinary and diverse wines.

Think Local You didn't hear this from us, but here's the buzz: in the interest of creating good community relations, the Napa Valley Vintners organizes an annual event that brings together vintners and local dwellers. Vineyards throughout the Valley are made accessible to anyone who wants to stop in and chat with the winery principal. To learn about **Afternoon in the Vineyards** and other events, periodically check out the Napa Valley Vintners website (www.napavintners.com) for what's going on. Don't get too carried away acting like a local—before you know it, you may be buying land and planting your own grapes.

Hands Across the Valley

Niebaum-Coppola Estate Winery
1991 St. Helena Highway, Rutherford
707.968.1100
Early September

> When Francis and Eleanor Coppola throw a fundraiser, vintners pull out their most delicious juice, women pull out their most glamorous ensembles, and men pull out their wallets. As a result, Hands across the Valley, an annual fundraiser in its second decade, has raised over one million dollars for Napa County's safety-net food programs since its inception.
>
> Every year in late summer, the beautiful and the generous convene at the formidable Niebaum-Coppola Estate Winery to sip the nectar of more than two dozen of the Valley's best wineries, taste the offerings of local restaurants, and bid on a multitude of must-have items—from cases of wine to celebrity memorabilia. Sports stars, actors, and comedians join the real stars of Napa Valley, the vintners, to mill about the courtyard and fountain until Francis and the guest host take the stage to host a pizza-tossing contest and auction off a few items. Dancing to the strains of an energetic band is the perfect cap to what is always a pleasurable event that works, as its motto says, "Towards a Community without Hunger."

Home Winemakers Classic

www.homewine.com
St. Supéry
8440 St. Helena Highway, Rutherford
707.944.8626
Mid-July

> *Great Legs of Napa Valley. Leap of Faith. Funnyfarm Wines. Scavenger Red.* These are just a few of the wines you'll discover at the Home Winemakers Classic, where today's garage wine becomes tomorrow's cult wine.
>
> Since its inception in 1982, the Home Winemakers Classic has been a fundraiser for the Dry Creek–Lokoya Fire Department, whose firehouse sits up on Mount Veeder, protecting the Mayacamas Mountains. The fire department's participation adds a little extra something you won't find at any other event: firemen hauling ice, showing off their trucks, and offering rides home to those who have forgotten not to drink and drive. But unless you have a thing for men in uniforms, the real attraction here is the walk-around tasting of the wines crafted by home winemakers.

All the wines poured are homemade, and none are available for sale any-where—although with every sip you'll wonder why not, since they're so delicious. And to add to your pleasure, the wine names and labels are as good as the wines. In fact, this is wine marketing at its cheekiest, an effort led by the *Atlas Peak Consortium*, the proud vintners of *Screaming Ego Cabernet Sauvignon, Scarlet Harlot*—"a Grenache of easy virtue"—and *Otto Loss Pig Weinglut Sin Von Del* (say it fast and you'll understand).

Giving Atlas Peak Consortium a run for its money is the equally sassy *Valley Girls*. It has given such names as *Bad Hair Cuvée* to its wine, with winemaker notes that state, "It's like . . . red!"

Unpretentious, with a strong sense of community, this event may poke fun at the industry, but the wines are anything but silly. Most of the seventy-plus winemakers enter their wines into a competition, and the auction has been a great success in raising funds for the fire department. Silent bids are taken on lots of wines provided by the Valley's commercial wineries as well as the home winemakers' wines. Another good thing about this event is that it takes place late in the afternoon. So if you don't snack too heavily, you can load up your loot and head straight out to dinner at one of the mid-Valley restaurants, such as Rutherford Grill or La Toque. All around, this is a relaxed event that brings out your playful side. One guest who accidentally happened upon the Classic by following traffic on the highway appraised the event by remarking, "Just seeing all the smiling faces is worth it."

Napa Valley Wine Auction
Napa Valley Vintners Association
www.napavintners.com
707.963.3388
First full weekend in June

If you come to the wine country only once and attend only one event, the Napa Valley Wine Auction is where you want to be. Its glamorous parties, black-tie events, and red-carpet descent to the Friday-night gala give it an Academy Awards–like air of excitement. A four-day extravaganza, it offers a glimpse into the very best of Napa Valley.

Although it is accused by some of being overelaborate and ostentatious, defenders point out that this sparkly pageantry—from the awesome artwork it inspires to the abundance of delicious food and flowing fine wine—is all in the name of charity. The defenders have our vote: nearly

100 percent of the proceeds is donated to local charities. As long as worthy people and organizations benefit from the kindness of strangers, every extravagant dollar spent by the Napa Valley Wine Auction is worth its weight in gold.

It begins on Thursday with a bang: the sound of wooden bidding plaques hitting the cement floor during the opening barrel auction. Inside the barrel room, the participating wineries—as many as two hundred—offer samples directly from barrels of their best juice. If you like it, you can buy it; bidding boards are set up around the room, where you can sign up to bid on cases of the sampled wines, everything from *Araujo* to *Zahtila*. Typically held at the hosting winery's property, the barrel auction is more than frantic buying—you can also wander around outdoors, sipping white wines and sampling food from local artisans, restaurants, and caterers.

That night and the following day, you may choose from a selection of private winery events. They range from the casual to the formal, simple to elaborate, informational to downright entertaining. Some of the country's best chefs do the cooking, including such culinary luminaries as Thomas Keller and Piero Selvaggio. No matter which event you attend, you're certain to taste the best wines available, including library and reserve wines.

By Friday night, even the heartiest gourmands may begin to feel overfed—but the party's just begun. The Gala is held on the lawn at the chic Meadowood resort, where guests literally walk down a red carpet to a Champagne reception. Major names from the cooking world are behind the stove, like Wolfgang Puck, Alice Waters, and Sirio Maccioni, while Napa Valley's finest chefs line up to help plate the Gala dinner under a big outdoor tent. Dancing, desserts, and after-dinner digestifs do their best to follow.

Saturday dawns in what feels like another era—or, at least, another mood. Women and men alike don their best straw hats, pressed linens, and Italian sandals and head back to Meadowood for the main event: the live auction. Before settling in at a table, there is (once again) ample chance to sample the signature dishes of the Valley's restaurants at the chef-manned booths. The live auction itself is a rambunctious, lively affair, enhanced by the scores of wines available for sampling. Each table is set with several bottles of both reds and whites, and volunteers circulate throughout the day with baskets of bottles that are free for the taking. A walk around the perimeter of the tent is great for people watching—and is another chance to spot celebrities as well as respected vintners and other local characters.

When the last gavel is lowered, it's time for dinner on the great lawn. This last meal is a casual, family-style feast, served at tables lined up on the meadow under a constellation of strung paper lanterns. There's an unbelievable assortment of delectable wines, from *Paoletti* to *Quintessa*, *Chappellet* to *Juslyn*, and *Corison* to *Long Meadow Ranch*. Of course, every good thing must come to an end—and this one ends with swaying to the music under sparkling skies.

Be the Belle of the Ball Want to experience the excitement of one of the wine country's best events without buying a ticket? Consider volunteering. You'll get to attend some of the most fabulous galas, and although you may not be dressed to the nines like the guests, you might walk away with a commemorative shirt, apron, or hat—for free. Two organizations that always use volunteers for events are **Napa Valley Vintners** (www.napavintners.com) and the **Sonoma Valley Harvest Wine Auction** (www.sonomavalleywine.com).

Schramsberg Sparkling Wine Symposium
Schramsberg Vineyards and Culinary Institute of America at Greystone
www.schramsberg.com
1400 Schramsberg Road, Calistoga; 2555 Main Street, St. Helena
800.877.3623
Late summer

Imagine this: A cool marine layer blankets the Napa Valley, and only a thin strip of light over the eastern hills promises that the sun will break through soon. If it's August, you're on your way to pick chardonnay grapes in the Carneros region; if it's September, you'll be taking a small blade to clusters of pinot noir, the other prominent grape used for making sparkling wine.

Welcome to the world of the Schramsberg Sparkling Wine Symposium, your hands-on introduction to all things sparkling, hosted by Schramsberg Vineyards and the Culinary Institute of America. Nirvana for sparkling-wine lovers, this three-day tribute to the world of bubbly will teach you everything there is to know about sparkling wines. Your adventure begins the night before the early-morning grape harvest, with dinner in the vineyards of the venerable Schramsberg, one of the Valley's most scenic and exclusive spots. There you will dine on delicious fare paired with sparkling wine from Schramsberg's cellar. (It's like a sneak peek at what the symposium holds in store.)

The first day is devoted entirely to the vineyard and winery. After picking grapes, you return to Schramsberg, where owner Hugh Davies leads you to the cellar to taste more than two dozen samples of grape juice and wine at different stages of the winemaking process. The rest of the day is spent watching the inner workings of a winery during harvest, including tours of the caves and extensive tastings of sparkling wines. Later, after you've developed an appreciation for the labor-intensive chore of making sparkling wine, you'll have the chance to get your hands a little dirty when you disgorge, dosage, and label your very own bottle of sparkling wine to take home.

The second and third days of the event are held at the Culinary Institute of America. Wine and food authorities Karen MacNeil and Holly Peterson Mondavi also serve as event hosts and play prominent roles in the classroom portion of the symposium. Karen takes you on a comprehensive tour of the sparkling-wine universe, with a focus on Champagne. You'll taste dozens of Champagnes to explore different styles, sugar levels, and classifications, including vintage, nonvintage, and prestige. The following day, Holly guides you through an in-depth food and wine pairing as she demonstrates the compatibility of each Schramsberg sparkling wine with various recipes. If there is a better way to spend three days, we can't imagine what it would be!

SONOMA COUNTY

Sonoma Salute to the Arts

www.salutetothearts.com

707.938.1133

July

The enchanting town of Sonoma is the backdrop for Sonoma Salute to the Arts, which raises funds for the local artistic community. Here you'll find art, wine, and food for days . . . actually for a whole weekend. While Friday night officially starts the festivities with a themed kickoff party, the main attraction of this event is the two days of wine and food tastings that take place in Sonoma's historic plaza on Saturday and Sunday. Saturday morning's hike into the hills is free and sporting, but less energetic folks, including families with children, can browse the terrific displays of paintings, pottery, and wine country garden sculpture in the plaza or frolic in its many playgrounds.

Three stages offer live music and performances, including a cooking demo that dominates one corner of the plaza. Tables bountiful with offerings from Sonoma wineries and restaurants are set up throughout the plaza, providing as much a feast for the palate as for the eyes.

Sonoma County Showcase

Sonoma County Wineries Association

www.sonomawine.com

707.586.3795

July

Set up as multi-day event with a barrel auction on Friday night followed by a sit-down dinner, the highlight of the Sonoma County Showcase is Saturday's Taste of Sonoma food and wine extravaganza.

Taste of Sonoma is set under a huge tent, in which you walk around tasting dishes prepared by local artisanal food producers as well as by chefs from Sonoma, Napa, and more distant reaches of the Bay Area. Every step you take lands you in front of fantastic food and great wines. A bite of foie gras here, a sip of sparkling wine there . . . some ribs here, some syrah there . . . an oyster here, a taste of chardonnay there.

If you can get beyond the food and wine, you'll realize that you're really getting to experience all the appellations of Sonoma. You can taste zins from Dry Creek, chard and pinot from Russian River Valley, and really great cabs from Alexander Valley. And all along, you're getting up close and personal with the winemakers who are there to talk about what's being poured.

With multiple activities taking place throughout the day, Taste of Sonoma has something for everyone, from the silent auction (offering everything from wine to vacations) to beer tasting, cooking demonstrations by renowned Bay Area chefs and cookbook authors, and food and wine pairing seminars hosted by chefs of local wineries. It is a great event that really does leave you with a true taste of Sonoma.

And the Lot Goes to . . . Wine's mass appeal, coupled with its nearly alchemical ability to appreciate in value, makes it the ideal commodity for fundraising. As a result, auctions proliferate in the wine country, a circumstance as beneficial to local communities as it is fortunate for visitors.

Both live and silent auctions are the centerpieces of a wide range of events. At silent auctions, available items range from a single bottle of wine to a vertical of coveted wines from a small producer. Live auctions tend to include lots composed of multiple bottles of wine, or invitations to events, such as a private winery dinner with a winery principal, with a menu featuring rare library wines.

Winning bids at silent auctions can be as low as twenty-five dollars for a magnum of wine to thousands of dollars for an extremely rare collection, while winning bids at live auctions can start at one hundred dollars for a single bottle of wine and reach six-figure heights for lots so elaborate they'll make your head spin.

The complexity of the auction—whether it's a single event or several days of activities—determines ticket prices. Attendance prices range from as low as fifty dollars for a single event at the Sonoma County Showcase to more than one thousand dollars for all the events at the Napa Valley Wine Auction.

As for attire, whatever the event, straw hats prevail during the day. While they're more for function than for style (the California sun can be intimidating), there are always a few spectacular hats that provoke a touch of envy among those with a love for the milliner's art. Women are most often decked out in sundresses or the like during daytime events, while men sport short-sleeved shirts with pressed shorts or linen slacks. For evening, the formality of the event dictates dress. Unless black tie is stipulated, cocktail dresses for women and slacks and a jacket for men are usually worn.

Sonoma Valley Harvest Wine Auction
Sonoma Valley Vintners and Growers Alliance
www.sonomavalleywine.com
707.935.0803
Labor Day weekend

Between the two valleys—Napa and Sonoma—there is always bit of a rivalry when it comes to auctions. Sonoma's Labor Day weekend wine auction has long had a reputation for being the wild one, the more fun one, the one where you let down your hair—and, if truth be told, aspects of this are true. But don't let its reputation fool you; the Sonoma Valley Harvest Wine Auction is sophisticated enough to please even the most demanding and genteel wine snob. Even more important, it's elegantly effective in raising funds for worthy causes in Sonoma Valley.

A celebrity golf tournament with a shotgun start begins the five days of merriment with an actual bang. From there, wine lovers select from a full menu of activities—and best of all, you can pick and choose by buying tickets to individual events. Saturday is the busiest day. Those with a serious interest in wine can seek an educational experience—such as spending the day in a vineyard and being immersed in harvest activities, or joining Bon Appetit's wine and spirits editor, Anthony Dias Blue, as he guides guests through focused wine tastings.

At lunchtime, revelers saunter into a rousing picnic that includes an auction, lavish meal, live music, and the chance to mingle with growers and vintners. The hardiest of guests then take off to get ready for private dinners held at various wineries. This is your chance to visit your favorite Sonoma Valley winery to chat and break bread with the owner. For many people, it's the best part of the whole weekend.

But you won't want to stay out too late, because on Sunday the fun begins at the live auction. In some respects, the Sunday auction feels like a party thrown by and for the local wine community—it's very fraternal. The sometimes-rambunctious vintners take the stage to introduce their lots, dressing in outrageous costumes and performing skits that are in keeping with the year's theme. While their antics may seem silly to some of the Prada-clad crowd, it's undeniable that they succeed in raising the bids: in the first decade of the event, more than three million dollars has been raised for education and youth organizations.

The Sunday auction is held at the Sonoma Mission Inn under a tent (though big, it's relatively intimate compared to Napa's) where you bid, sip wine, and snack. David Reynolds, the enthusiastic auctioneer, hawks lots that include fantasy trips, verticals of rare older wines, and even puppies, all sold to the highest bidder. It's like a backyard party with food stations and volunteers delivering wine—but instead of making small talk, you're expected to raise your paddle. When the last lot is sold, yet another bountiful spread is set out and the crowd relaxes again by eating, drinking, and feeling satisfied that they've contributed to a good deed.

Valley of the Moon Vintage Festival
www.sonomavinfest.com
707.996.2109
Last weekend in September

If sophistication and polish are what you seek in an event, the Valley of the Moon Vintage Festival is not for you. What you'll find instead during this weekend harvest celebration that has been held every year in Sonoma since 1897, is homespun winsomeness and wholesome fun.

Friday night's kickoff gala is held at the town's historic mission and barracks, where you'll find wines from over fifty Sonoma Valley wineries. The remainder of the events—including a contest for inventing new uses for wine barrels, a poster and art exhibit, a grape-stomping competition, a water fight among firemen, a wine and food tasting, and musical and stage performances—all take place in the town plaza. It's small, but there's a good selection of activities to satisfy all ages.

In fact, this is one of the wine country's most family-friendly events, especially on Sunday, when the annual parade takes place. The parade participants are all local—you'll see the high school marching band, the town's oldest fire truck, Native Sons of the Golden West carrying a flag the size of a city block, the peewee football team and its cheerleaders, and Popo the Clown riding around on her scooter. Locals decked out in mid-1800s period costumes celebrate the town's early history by riding on horseback and in carriages. They're flanked by a Wells Fargo stagecoach that follows the Bundschu family, who were predominantly responsible for starting the Vintage Festival.

Throughout the parade, the announcer (who is obviously well connected to the community) offers a running commentary and banters with the parade participants as they pass by ("Hey, Joe, glad you made it. Is the missus feeling better?"). It's small-town charm at its best.

Wine Making 101

Hope-Merrill and Hope-Bosworth Bed & Breakfast Inns, Geyserville

www.hope-inns.com

800.825.4233

A two-weekend event: one weekend in September and one in May

> There's no better way to learn about winemaking than by making your own wine—and Wine Making 101 is a great place to start. This learning-and-leisure educational event is sponsored annually at the Hope-Merrill and Hope-Bosworth inns. Held over the course of two weekends, one in summer and another in spring, it allows wine lovers and wine-maker wannabes to learn, hands-on, how the seasons impact the art of winemaking. You'll enjoy picking and pressing during the first weekend as part of the full experience of turning grapes into wine, and you will return home after the second session with two cases of your own self-labeled, self-made nectar. You can toast your talented self at the weekends' country breakfasts, wine and food receptions, gourmet picnics, outdoor dinners, and private winery tours and tastings.

MENDOCINO COUNTY

Anderson Valley Pinot Noir Festival

Anderson Valley Winegrowers Association

www.avwines.com

707.895.WINE

Third weekend in May

> The beauty of a focused, single-varietal wine tasting is that it offers an opportunity to compare wines side by side. By the time it's over, you're more expert in determining exactly what your likes (and dislikes) are regarding a particular wine and/or producer.
>
> The Anderson Valley Pinot Noir Festival offers this type of supreme comparison-tasting opportunity; it also offers much, much more, beginning with its location in the comely Anderson Valley.
>
> Your adventure begins with the drive to Anderson Valley. If you come by way of the ocean side, you'll wind your way through several miles of a twisty, two-lane highway, lined with redwoods and rambling foliage. Coming up from the Bay Area takes you over the greenest rolling hills, peppered with wildflowers and salted with grazing sheep.

Once you finally arrive, you're rewarded by the festival's venue: a large tent set on a field bordered by vineyards at *Pacific Echo Winery*. The tent houses as many as thirty producers, including *Copain, Elke, Williams-Selyem, Handley, Christine Woods, Lazy Creek, Navarro*, and *Esterlina*. All have vineyards in the area; some have wineries; and a few purchase grapes from growers for their Anderson Valley–appellation wines. Each winery brings several wines to taste, each representing different vintages, vineyards, and winemaking styles.

Although the AV Pinot Noir Festival is quite small by comparison to other events, plan on spending several hours. You won't want to miss the lunch, designed to pair well with any of the wines. Since the crowd is small and manageable, there's a laid-back feeling that makes you want to linger. In fact, why not make a weekend of it, and stay the night in Boonville or Philo? You'll have plenty of time to visit other wineries, and you won't have to tackle Highway 128's hairpin turns after a day of indulging. Be sure to bring cash or a checkbook, since credit cards are not welcome at the festival.

Greenwood Ridge California Wine Tasting Championships

www.greenwoodridge.com
24555 Greenwood Road, Philo
707.895.2002
Last weekend in July

Only the hardy should consider this event. Not because the Wine Tasting Championships are difficult—although they are challenging—but because the location is remote and is reached only by driving up a very long gravel and dirt road. That said, it's a great opportunity to test your wine knowledge and tasting skills.

The competition is divided into four categories: single amateur, single professional, doubles amateur, and doubles professional. It is held at *Greenwood Ridge's* winery, at the top of a magnificent ridge surrounded by Anderson Valley vineyards. The atmosphere is a little dry, with a rather intense focus on competition. While there is food for sale, the only wine poured is during the competition; this is a good thing, since if you're serious about your performance, you wouldn't want to spoil your palate or get a little tipsy. But that doesn't mean you can't make your own party—you can certainly make the day more festive by bringing along friends and a big picnic.

When it's time to compete, contestants take their places at banquet tables inside the winery's cleared-out barrel room. On the tables are baskets of bread, pitchers of water, spit buckets, and one Riedel all-purpose glass per person. The tasting is blind, with eight or more wines poured during each round. The first few require only identification of the varietal. Extra points are awarded during the last few wines for identifying the vintage, region, and winery.

The competitive field is diverse. Amateurs face fellow wine lovers who have a range of tasting skills and experience. Pros go up against wine buyers, retailers, writers, and sommeliers, with equal representation by men and women of a wide age range. The mood of the room is jovial yet serious (but neither snobby nor staid). Wines are poured one at a time; there's a five-minute period in which to evaluate the wine and make a determination before the next wine is poured. After all the wines have been poured and the sheets collected, the wines are revealed. Contestants who reach a certain score are propelled into the next round, and the final highest scorers are awarded such prizes as a stay in one of the area's renowned inns. If you're knowledgeable about wine—and thrive on competition—this is the event for you.

Winesong
www.winesong.org
700 River Drive, Fort Bragg
707.961.4688
First weekend in September following Labor Day

There's no doubt that what makes this fresh-air event so special is its venue: Winesong is held in the Fort Bragg Botanical Gardens, on the northern coastline of Mendocino County. It's a long haul from almost anywhere, but it's well worth the drive, as its faithful following attests.

The wine and food tasting areas are set up throughout the gardens, alongside wonderful musicians (hence the word *song* in the festival name). As you walk through the meandering paths and trails, it seems almost magical to come upon these gustatory and musical oases set among the flora and fauna. Although it is well attended, it never feels crowded.

You will definitely want to be punctual for Winesong—everyone shows up on time or even slightly early. The crowd is completely diverse: every age, style, and attitude is represented, from babies in backpacks slugging back their bottles to older children sipping root beer to serious wine enthusiasts.

The dress code is decidedly casual—jeans and hiking boots or sneakers aren't only acceptable, they're sensible. You might want to wear layers, since the event's proximity to the ocean can mean sudden weather shifts from chilly and foggy to sunny and warm.

This wine tasting and auction offer some of the best wines from Napa, Sonoma, and Mendocino, including such wineries as *McNab* and *Parducci* from Redwood Valley/Ukiah; *Caymus* and *Joseph Phelps* from Napa Valley; *Jordan* from Alexander Valley; *Ravenswood* from Sonoma Valley; and some seventy or so others. The tasting lasts for three hours and is followed by the live auction, which is a bit more formal. Bay Area culinary personality Narsai David hosts Winesong, auctioning such intriguing lots as rare-wine collections, winery lunches and dinners, and romantic getaways on the Mendocino coast. All proceeds benefit the Mendocino Coast Hospital Foundation.

With over two million dollars raised for the hospital since Winesong began in the early '80s, one board member—who works among the three-hundred-plus volunteers, some of whom start as early as 5am to make the event happen—didn't mince words when asked what she likes best about it: "I like the money." It may seem a little too frank, but really, that is what these charity events are about: pulling people together to support the community. It certainly doesn't hurt to taste a few delicious wines along the way.

Wine Country Hospitality Because most wineries have beautiful facilities for entertaining and partying, they often host special events. Nearly every vintner throws some kind of shindig at least once a year, whether it's a casual crush party in the back of the winery or a formal gala in the caves. If you want to visit a winery for more than just the average tasting, consider attending a harvest party at **Clos Pegase**, a holiday chocolate and wine tasting at **Franciscan**, an outdoor movie at **Sterling**, or winemaking fantasy camp at **Greenwood Ridge**. To keep up with who's hosting what event at which winery, subscribe to www.localwineevents.com or check the site when you plan your next visit to the wine country. From the frivolous to the formal, you won't want to miss the next big thing.

LIBRARIES
and
MUSEUMS

When you're visiting the wine country, it's easy to overemphasize the importance of experience: every sip you take, every bottle you buy, every conversation with a winemaker you have brings you that much closer to achieving a well-rounded wine education.

But sometimes there's simply no substitute for book learning, and that's where libraries and museums come into play. These are repositories of invaluable information—some of it historical, some oenological, some viticultural. Libraries and museums offer knowledge free of salesmanship, data unskewed by marketing, and insight loosed from industry. In other words, they offer the purest kind of experience—that of educating your palate by expanding your understanding.

NAPA COUNTY

Copia: The American Center for Wine, Food & the Arts

www.copia.org
500 First Street, Napa
707.259.1600 or 888.51.COPIA
Wed–Mon 10am–5pm

If you've ever wished there were a Smithsonian museum dedicated exclusively to the fine arts of wining and dining, Copia is a dream come true. Equal parts museum, educational institution, cultural center, and organic garden–gift shop–cooking school–film house–concert venue–wine bar–restaurant and more, the nonprofit Copia has a mission to "investigate and celebrate the culture of the collective table through wine, food and the arts." It brings the best of the best together under one wavy roof, and elevates all things gustatory.

Putting aside its myriad attractions to concentrate only on what Copia offers the oenophile is not easy, but for wine lovers pressed for time, it's worth the effort to focus. The museum usually has one exhibit with a wine bent, such as a corkscrew collection, antique ceramic wine vessels, or colorful examples of early wine and grape advertisements. At least one program is offered to the wine enthusiast on a daily basis, ranging from a discussion about a specific wine varietal to a hot topic that's causing an industry stir.

It's always worthwhile to stop, smell, swirl, and sip at Copia's tasting bar. Called the Wine Spectator Tasting Table, it's named for and sponsored by the eponymous magazine. Be sure to take advantage of the Tasting Table's "Winery of the Week" program. Held daily in the afternoon, it offers a complimentary tasting of the wines made by that week's showcased vintner. On Saturdays it's manned by the winemakers and winery proprietors themselves. You'll find the Tasting Table in Copia's luminous central hall, amid art galleries, food and gift shops, and two restaurants (the sophisticated Julia's Kitchen and the casual American Market Café).

Napa Valley Museum

www.napavalleymuseum.org
55 Presidents Circle, Yountville
707.944.0500
Wed–Mon 10am–5pm

The Napa Valley Museum is a small gem. It's perfectly sized, making museum fatigue impossible; it has something for everyone, from fossils to modern art; and it's interactive. It's the perfect place to spend part of a day that is otherwise pretty well devoted to nature, wine, and food.

The museum's permanent exhibits are simultaneously educational and beguiling. First, get a sense of the history of the people and the land through a series of fascinating dioramas. One is about the creation of the Valley; another's chockablock with historical artifacts reflecting the lives of Wappo Native Americans; yet another details the rancho days of the 1840s; and on and on.

Viticulture and wine are well represented in the state-of-the-art exhibit "California Wine: The Science of an Art," which integrates science, agriculture, geology, history, physiology, and wine technology using a multimedia communications program. You can test your knowledge of wine terms, wine and food combos, even your winemaking skills. From root systems to bottling and aging, this exhibit will teach you everything you've always wanted to know about winemaking—and will permanently deepen your appreciation of wine and the art of producing it.

As if all this isn't enough, a rotating art exhibit is always as good as any you'd find at a bigger museum, keeping it on par with the rest of the museum's offerings.

Napa Valley Wine Library

St. Helena Public Library
www.napawinelibrary.org
1492 Library Lane, St. Helena
707.963.5145
Mon and Wed 12–9pm, Tues, Thur, and Fri 10am–6pm,
Sat 10am–4pm, Sun 1–5pm

The Napa Valley Wine Library is both a place and an organization. A forty-plus-year-old entity that collects, stores, and shares important information about Napa Valley's wine industry, it's based in a large room in the St. Helena Public Library.

The Wine Library is filled to bursting with a collection of wine literature, records, and very cool photo archives. An extensive selection of wine-related books runs the gamut from fiction to biographies, textbooks, rare books, cookbooks, and guidebooks. Old plastic school binders hold photos of and fact sheets on all the Napa Valley wineries circa the early 1980s—a must-see for entertainment value alone, but also a superb record of the growth and development of the Valley.

As an organization, the Napa Valley Wine Library offers wine-related classes taught by industry veterans and newcomers alike, such as Ric Forman of *Forman Vineyards*, Nils Venge of *Saddleback Cellars*, James Hall of *Patz & Hall*, Tom Rinaldi of *Provenance*, and Scott Rich of *Talisman*. Classes and field trips are held a few times throughout the year. A one-day seminar is offered every August, which is followed by a single-varietal wine tasting featuring over one hundred Napa Valley wineries.

SONOMA COUNTY

Healdsburg Museum
www.healdsburgmuseum.org
221 Matheson Street, Healdsburg
707.431.3325
Tues–Sun 11am–4pm

The only thing more charming than a small country town is a community venue that reveals the spirit of the town. The Healdsburg Museum is such a place. Housed in the Carnegie Library—a beloved local landmark only a few blocks off the main town square—the museum is compact yet provides a comprehensive overview of the region's history. Photographs, tools, and other objects from the region's early start in agriculture (specifically grape growing and winemaking) are included in the collections. A short visit makes a mighty impression.

Sonoma County Wine Library

www.sonoma.lib.ca.us/wine.html

139 Piper Street at Center Street, Healdsburg

707.433.3772 ext. 5

Mon and Wed 9:30am–9pm, Tues, Thur, and Fri 9:30am–6pm

Harbor a secret lust for the *American Wine Society Journal?* Wish you had saved your back issues of *California Farmer* and *Fruit Winemaking Quarterly?* Afraid a subscription to *WineX Magazine* might be delivered in a suspiciously plain brown wrapper? Relax. The Sonoma County Wine Library has all your oenological journal and periodical needs covered— and offers reference services, online database searches, wine-related art and photography, marketing and technical reports, even consulting services. It's an all-wine-all-the-time kind of place that's a true Mecca for wine geeks and winegrowers, wine intellectuals and wine writers, wine historians and wine marketers, wine collectors and wine obsessers. Even plain old winos would have to love this place.

PICNIC PROVISIONS

Picnics were practically invented for the wine country. The countryside is scenic, the weather temperate, the earth and pressed grapes fresh and aromatic. Romance perfumes the air, making picnicking here a sensual delight.

Many wineries, particularly in Sonoma and Mendocino, offer a spot for enjoying a packed meal. Napa Valley is slightly more limited in its winery picnic locales, but there are dozens of parks throughout the county (including at least one in the center of every town). And, of course, there's always the time-honored tradition of just stopping on the road and settling down to eat beneath a shady tree. Just purchase some provisions from one or more of our favorite places, pack a blanket, and you're on your way to a perfect day.

NAPA COUNTY

Dean & Deluca

www.deananddeluca.com
607 St. Helena Highway, St. Helena
707.967.9980
Mon–Sat 7:30am–7pm, Sun 9am–7pm

Dean & Deluca is a picnicker's heaven. Start at the cheese counter—it's the absolute best in the Valley, laden with countless domestic, imported, fresh, and aged types. The bread counter is equally impressive, stocked with sourdough, sweet French, olive, walnut, and just about every other type of bread that exists—and in every shape known to bakers and sandwich lovers, from rolls to baguettes to batards and more.

An entire case in the back of the store is devoted to premade sandwiches and prepared foods—everything from fresh salads to grilled chicken to succulent pork tenderloin. There are all the usual picnic accompaniments like chips, pretzels, soft drinks, beer, water, cookies, and pastries—and then there's wine, wine, wine, and lots of it. Should you need any tabletop accessories, you'll find those here, too, from fancy baskets to utilitarian (or super-fancy) corkscrews. Why settle for plastic forks when you can dine in style?

Genova Delicatessen

1550 Trancas Way, Napa
707.253.8686
Mon–Sat 9am–6:30pm, Sun 9am–5pm

The wine selection at Genova is small and primarily limited to Italian wines, but with such phenomenal picnic provisions all around, who cares? This is an old-fashioned kind of deli—the sort that makes a sandwich one of life's greatest joys. Piled high between your choice of roll or bread is a terrific choice of meats, from paper-thin slices of Tuscan salami to house-roasted turkey breast. If you aren't in the mood for a sandwich (it could happen), make a lunch out of the countless other options, such as hot polenta with meat sauce, roasted chicken, or an entire antipasti platter of cured meats, olives, roasted eggplant, and zucchini frittata. Once you've picked your main dish, tackle the bountiful refrigerator case filled with salads. And, of course, there's always the requisite array of chips, sodas, and sweets to round out your menu.

Palisades Market

1506 Lincoln Avenue, Calistoga
707.942.9549
Daily 7:30am–7pm

> The small wine selection at Palisades is thoughtful and well rounded, from splits of France's *Vieux Telegraphe Châteauneuf-du-Pape* to full-size bottles of California's *Gott Zinfandel*—the eponymous wine of Palisades' part-owner Joel Gott. One way or another, you'll find the perfect wine to accompany the gourmet picnic you'll assemble from the market's offerings. Creative sandwiches, wraps, and specialty entrées (anything from tamales to macaroni and cheese) are all prepared in-house and are all extremely delicious. A tempting array of baked goods includes the signature Ding-Dong, a must for chocolate lovers. If a snack is all you crave, there's a fantastic selection of cheeses, locally baked breads, chips, condiments, and crackers. One corner of the store is filled with beautiful tableware and picnic baskets for those who really know how to live well.

SONOMA COUNTY

Sonoma Market

www.sonoma-glenellenmkt.com
500 West Napa Street, Sonoma
707.996.3411
Daily 6am–9pm

> You can get lost in the sprawl of Sonoma Market—and once you realize what's here, you kind of wish you would. In addition to its fabulous wine selection, there is a "bar" that caters to every food and food group you can imagine. You'll find an olive bar on the way to the sandwich and panini bar, right next to the sushi bar, just past the tacos and burritos bar, next to the giant salad bar, which is just by the hot bar serving every imaginable thing from chicken to cioppino. Cheeses go on for days. Artisan Bakers and Basque Boulangerie are the two bakeries (each less than one mile away) that restock Sonoma Market during the day, ensuring the freshest bread for the freshest deli meats sold right across the aisle. There's a butcher, a fishmonger with an accompanying chowder bar, bushels of fresh fruit and veggies, and, because you need strength for these things, a coffee bar serving plain and fancy coffee drinks. And just so you can keep your store-hopping to a minimum, stock up on facial care and nutrition products, pretty housewares, and cookbooks while you're here.

Traverso's

www.traversos.com
106 B Street, Santa Rosa
707.542.2530 or 877.456.7616
Mon–Sat 9:30am–5:30pm

While it's true that on a visit to Sonoma County you'll want to concentrate your attention on local wines, it's also true that when in Rome, do as the Romans do: drink Italian wine. If you're so inclined, run, don't walk, to Traverso's, a bright and busy wineshop–cum–deli extraordinaire. Here you'll find not only the best assortment of Italian wines in Sonoma and Napa counties, but also the most appealing, fresh, succulent, house-made Italian specialties and packaged fancy foods. Check out the lasagna, ravioli, salamis, cured meats, cheeses, breads, salads . . . you can get hungry just thinking about it. Traverso's has been in business since 1922, so you know it's doing something right. Get ready to picnic *dolce vita* style.

SERVICES

~~~~~~~~~~~~~~~~

Because hospitality is the name of the game in the
wine country, it extends far beyond the tasting bar.
Want someone to drive you around? Get in the
back seat. Want to safeguard your wine in a cool,
humid place? Hand it over. Don't want to carry
your wine back home with you on the plane? Ship it.
Throughout the three-county area, you'll find everything you need to meet your most sybaritic needs.

SHIPPING

It's painfully easy to overbuy wine here, and even easier to see why: you're at the mothership winery; you've tasted something irresistible; and you're not sure you'll find it at home. So what's the big deal? Why don't you buy a bottle or two—at each winery? But then by the end of a visit you've accumulated a substantial number of bottles, and just the idea of carrying them through the airport and onboard the plane gives you a backache.

Relax. You have options.

There are several businesses that will ship that wine right to your doorstep. Most wine-shipping companies will ship to all but one or two states, due to interstate shipping laws for alcohol. However, if you live in a nonreciprocal state (a state that requires wine to be shipped to a licensed recipient), you may have to pay a surcharge to cover the red tape. Other than that, shipping wine is easy. Just deliver your wine and the shipping company will do the rest, packing it securely and shipping it at whatever speed you want. It might even arrive home before you do.

NAPA COUNTY

Buffalo's Shipping Post
2471 Solano Avenue, Napa
707.226.7942
Mon–Fri 8am–6pm, Sat 9am–5pm, Sun 12–5pm
> Buffalo's Shipping Post is conveniently located on the frontage road next to Highway 29 and will ship to every state except New Hampshire and Kentucky.

Cartons & Crates
253 Walnut Street, Napa
707.224.7447
Mon–Fri 8am–5pm, Sat 10am–3pm
> Cartons & Crates ships wine to every state except Utah. It also sells wooden wine boxes and a wide assortment of packing materials. This is also the place to transport home the fragile handmade pottery you couldn't resist buying and don't even want to consider carrying on the plane.

SONOMA COUNTY

Fitch Mountain Packing
424 Center Street #A, Healdsburg
707.433.1247
Mon–Fri 9:30am–5pm, Sat 10am–2pm

> Utah and Kentucky are the only states to which Fitch Mountain will not ship, except to a licensed recipient. If you live anywhere else, you're in luck—your package will be delivered directly to your door.

STORAGE

If wine bottles are spilling out of your kitchen cabinets and you've already thrown away half your shoe collection to make closet space for wine, it's time to think about renting a wine locker. Wine storage lockers range from plywood cubbyholes to state-of-the-art facilities built expressly to protect, preserve, and store bottled wine. Plain or fancy, all are temperature- and humidity-controlled so that your wine stays perfectly safe and you can start shoe shopping again.

The services offered by many wine storage places can be pretty much all-encompassing. Most offer private lockers, inventory tracking, consolidation, receipt of delivery from wine clubs, wine pick-up from wineries and retailers, in-house trading, and seven-day-a-week access. Additionally, most storage services will ship wine to you when you decide you want a bottle or two. What could be better? You know your wine will be safe and well kept—and at a cost that's minor compared to replacing a badly stored and spoiled bottle.

NAPA COUNTY

55 Degrees
www.fiftyfivedegrees.com
1210 Church Street, St. Helena
707.963.5513
Mon–Fri 8am–5pm, Sat 8am–12pm

> On a shady side street in St. Helena, 55 Degrees is so attractive you might confuse it with a winery. Its stone façade, meant to convey the image of a cave, is a reminder that this is a good place to safely store and age your wine and grow your collection into an investment.

Napa Valley Wine Storage

www.napavalleywinestorage.com
1135 Golden Gate Drive, Napa
707.265.9990
Daily 6:30am–8pm

> Being part of a larger self-storage building is an advantage of Napa Valley Wine Storage in that it provides greater accessibility. The relatively new facility offers a backup system to safeguard against any energy outages. It's on the southern outskirts of Napa, making it a convenient stop on your way in or out of town.

Napa Wine Lockers

www.napawinelockers.com
736 California Boulevard, Napa
707.257.2903
Tues and Thur 2–6pm, Wed and Fri 9am–1pm, Sat 9:30am–12pm

> Napa Wine Lockers has tripled in size since it opened in 1998, proving that more people want to store their collections properly. It's on a quiet street just a few blocks away from Highway 29, and its clients include a long list of wine professionals.

SONOMA COUNTY

All Ways Cool

www.allwayscool.com
3351 Industrial Drive #1, Santa Rosa
707.545.7450
Mon–Fri 8:30am–5:30pm, Sat 10am–2pm

> All Ways Cool might sound a little like a high school yearbook inscription, but it's a very grown-up business. In addition to its storage facilities, the company works in tandem with Bottle Barn (see page 67) to offer customers regular notification of good wine deals. Each month a Sonoma County winery is featured on the website, further broadening your exposure to wine and its makers.

TRANSPORTATION

For most wine country visitors, schedules and finances dictate that the best way to see most of the area is to drive their own cars. There are a few exceptions to this rule. An airport shuttle takes the hassle out of finding your way from the airport to your destination town. Or, when you want to take in the view, freely imbibe, and not worry about the road, private limousines and winery shuttles are good options. And for those evenings when driving back from dinner after a lovely meal—and even lovelier wine—is risky, a taxi is always a reliable mode of transportation, and it's only a phone call away. From a single ride to a chauffeured trip, and from simply practical to utterly extravagant, several companies offer services to get you out of the driver's seat.

NAPA COUNTY

Antique Tours Limousine Service
www.antiquetours.net
707.226.9227

> If panache is what you crave in a car, Antique Tours Limousine Service can offer you the best. Its flamboyant fleet of 1947 Packard custom convertibles and its 1948 hardtop are not your ordinary limos; these are all about style and flair. Even the drivers look the part, with their natty hats and rakish clothing.

Black Tie Taxi
1755 Industrial Avenue, Napa
707.259.1000

> Black Tie Taxi is available to shuttle you from hotel to restaurant, winery to winery, B&B to airport, and every place in between. Whether for a short jaunt or an all-day rental, Black Tie Taxi uses towncars for service in the Napa Valley.

California Wine Tours/Evans Transportation
www.californiawinetours.com
4075 Solano Ave, Napa
800.294.6386

California Wine Tours offers regularly scheduled shuttle buses from Napa to San Francisco and Oakland airports. In both Napa and Sonoma counties, it also offers a wide range of charter vehicles, from sedans to full-size buses. This is a reliable, full-service transportation company that's been around a long time and is well known in the community. Service is available every day, and reservations are recommended.

SONOMA COUNTY

California Wine Tours
www.californiawinetours.com
22455 Broadway, Sonoma
800.294.6386

See California Wine Tours in Napa, above.

Sonoma Airporter
www.sonomaairporter.com
18346 Sonoma Highway, Sonoma
707.938.4246 or 800.611.4246

The Sonoma Airporter provides door-to-door service to San Francisco Airport from anywhere in Sonoma Valley. Service is available every day, and reservations are required.

Sonoma County Airport Express
www.airportexpressinc.com
2255 Airport Boulevard, Santa Rosa
707.837.8700 or 800.327.2024

Sonoma County Airport Express is the main mode of transportation to and from Oakland and San Francisco airports for most of Sonoma County. Unlike the Sonoma Airporter (see above), it does not service Sonoma Valley. Full-size buses pick up and drop off at several convenient locations, including the Santa Rosa airport. Service is available every day, and reservations are recommended.

Sugar Cubes, Apples, and Wine Sometimes the old-fashioned art of winemaking seems to cry out for an equally classic counterpart—like, say, a horse-drawn carriage ride through miles of vineyards. **Flying Horse Carriage Company** (www.flyinghorse.org, 707.849.8989) offers morning and afternoon buggy rides through the Alexander Valley, complete with snacks and cold refreshments. The three-hour adventure includes tastings at up to five wineries and one wine cave tour, and is guaranteed to slow your touring pace to a mellow and leisurely trot.

MENDOCINO COUNTY

Mendo Wine Tours & Limousine Service
www.mendowinetours.com
45020 Albion Street, Mendocino
707.937.6700

Due to the remote nature of Mendocino's wine country destinations, we recommend renting a car at the airport and driving yourself to and from your hotel. But if money is no object, Mendo Wine Tours can pick you up from the airport and drive you to pretty much wherever you'd like—to the Anderson Valley, or even farther north to the coastal towns of Mendocino and Fort Bragg. Mendo also offers private limousine services on an hourly basis.

Planes, Trains, and Automobiles Let's face it, they don't call it wine "country" for nothing. Wide-open spaces, bluer-than-blue skies, and year-round temperate weather define this splendid territory. Nature this inspiring has a positive effect on even the most citified sensibility—you may be startled by the strength of your uncharacteristic urge to get out of the car and try something new.

So go for it. Mount a horse, jump onto a bicycle, row a boat, hop a train, strap yourself into the seat of a helicopter, hook up to a biplane, float in a balloon, get off-road in a jeep, ride downriver in a gondola, or hike the hills. With a bit of research, you may even find the activity you want to try includes—surprise, surprise!—wine tasting. For a list of activities that can satisfy even the most adventurous (yes, there's even skydiving—just watch out for the vines), check **www.napavalley.com** or **www.sonoma.com** for a comprehensive selection of things to do and related transportation options.

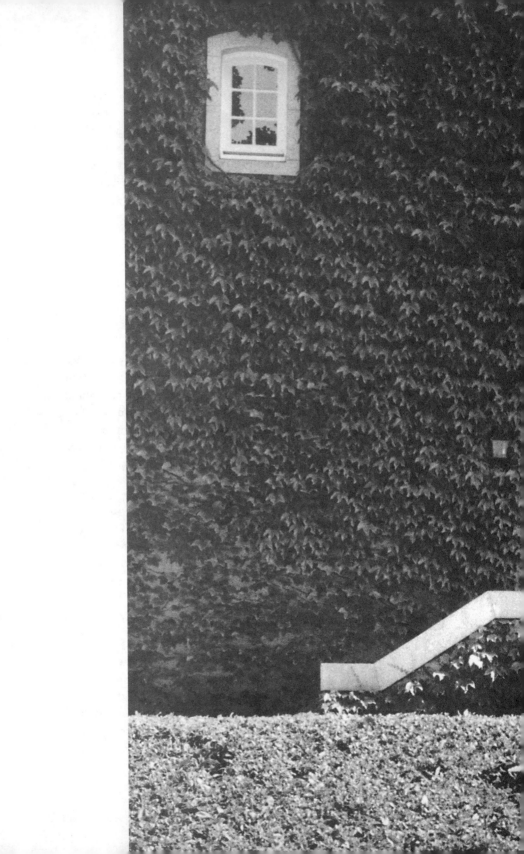

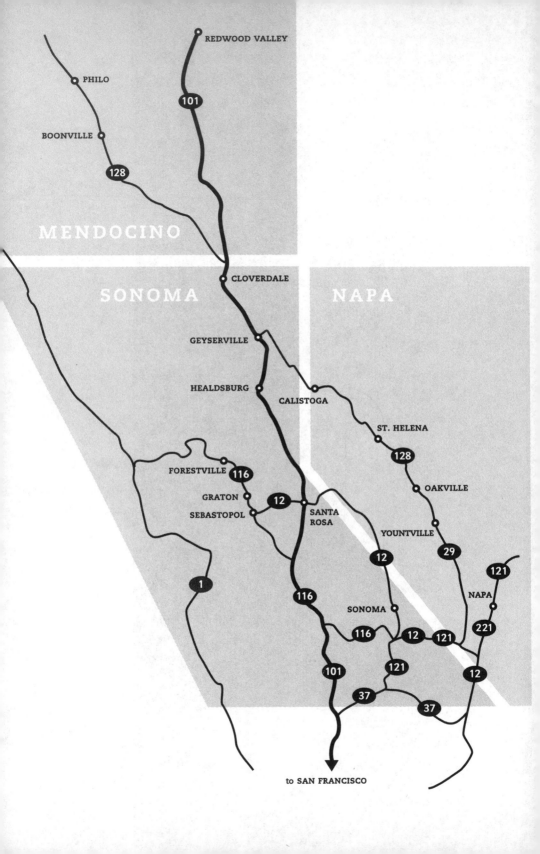

DRIVING
DISTANCES

	approximate distance	approximate time
San Francisco to Sonoma	45 miles	1 hour
Sonoma to Santa Rosa	20 miles	30 minutes
Santa Rosa to Healdsburg	15 miles	15 minutes
Healdsburg to Geyserville	9 miles	10 minutes
Geyserville to Redwood Valley	50 miles	1 hour
San Francisco to Napa	45 miles	1 hour
Napa to Yountville	6 miles	7 minutes
Yountville to Oakville	4 miles	4 minutes
Oakville to St. Helena	6 miles	8 minutes
St. Helena to Calistoga	9 miles	12 minutes
Calistoga to Santa Rosa	17 miles	30 minutes
Calistoga to Healdsburg	20 miles	30 minutes
Calistoga to Geyserville	25 miles	30 minutes
Geyserville to Cloverdale	10 miles	10 minutes
Cloverdale to Boonville	27 miles	45 minutes
Boonville to Philo	5 miles	10 minutes
Napa to Sonoma	15 miles	25 minutes
Sonoma to Santa Rosa	20 miles	30 minutes
Santa Rosa to Sebastopol	7 miles	10 minutes
Sebastopol to Forestville	9 miles	15 minutes
Graton to Santa Rosa	10 miles	15 minutes

INDEX

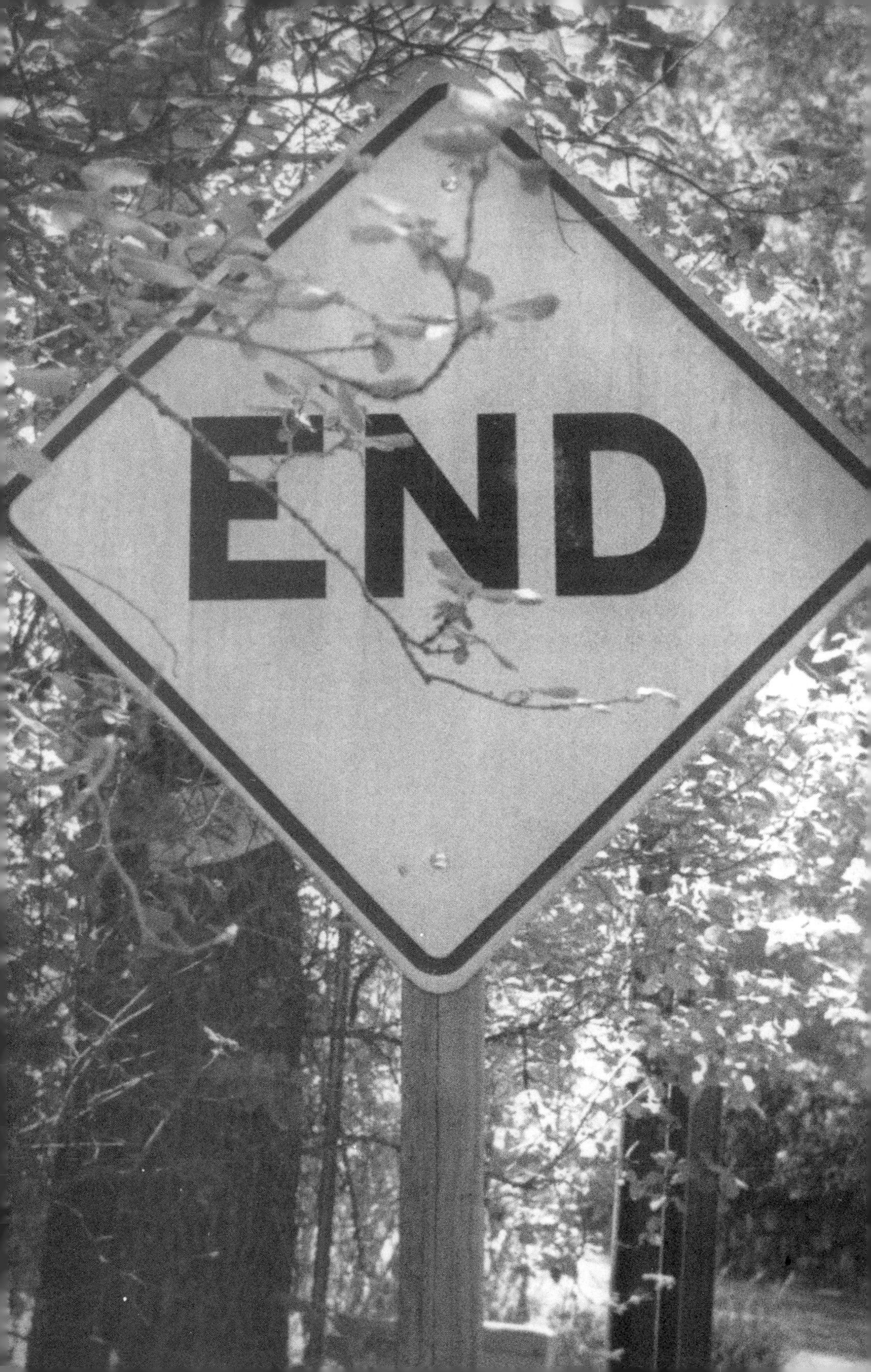
END